Norman D. Stevens
Editor

Postcards in the Library: Invaluable Visual Resources

*Pre-publication
REVIEWS,
COMMENTARIES,
EVALUATIONS . . .*

"**P**ostcards offer innumerable glimpses of what folks believe are visual keys to people, places and things. They are the popular culture pennants which celebrate the ordinary and sometimes even the exceptional and the spectacular. Prurient to moral, exquisite to sardonic, they smooth out communication and defuse the need to be voluble. The media is never so much as the message. One of the first to recognize the significance of postcards, Norman Stevens has become the walking encyclopedia of the subject, the maestro of collecting, the guide to individuals and libraries. Here he has the platform needed to impress upon us all the imperative need to preserve the popular messages. Backed by a group of experts, this is the first manual on the subject which cuts to the major points so necessary to understand if library, if individual, is to join the fraternity of postcard fans. Highly recommended for anyone arrested by the postcard and its place in history."

Bill Katz
*Professor, School of Information
Science and Policy, SUNY/Albany*

"**P**ostcards in the Library: Invaluable Visual Resources* provides the first serious discussion about postcards as a component of library collections. Norman D. Stevens has assembled a fine selection of essays which address why libraries should be collecting postcards and what they should be doing with them. Its articles describe a wide variety of postcard collections in libraries, demonstrate the scholarly potential of postcard collections, offer practical advice about selection, cataloging and preservation of postcards, and provide annotated bibliographies of scholarly works. As a help to librarians with postcard collections and all others interested in these paperboard gems, this is the best available reference guide."

Wayne Martin Mellinger, PhD
Professor of Sociology, Ventura College

"**P**ostcards, like old photographs, are coming to be recognized as valuable artifacts of cultures of the past. From the cliched messages on old postcards, thoughtful scholars read a great deal about culture and people. This study, by far the finest to date, is an extraordinarily important pioneering work in collecting and archiving, covering three areas: descriptions of postcard collections (one collection of a million cards), suggestions of how postcards can enrich general scholarly studies, and advice to librarians on how to collect and preserve postcard collections. Librarians and scholars will be grateful to the twenty authors in this volume for their splendid work in preserving these important ephemera."

Ray B. Browne, PhD
Secretary-Treasurer, Popular Culture Association, Bowling Green, OH

"The subtitle of Norman Stevens' edited collection of essays, *Postcards in the Library: Invaluable Visual Resources,* correctly identifies two crucial issues. Postcards offer cultural historians an invaluable way in which to gauge the values and visions of a culture. Postcard advertisements offer a glimpse of technological developments and shifting consumer tastes; postcard views document a slowly evolving landscape and an increasing urbanization; the often tasteless postcard comics reveal the public's sense of humor and its pronounced racial and ethnic prejudices; the "glamour" cards reflect the vision of American youth and beauty; postcard commemoratives document almost every major and minor event–social and political. In short, for the amateur or professional scholar/historian interested in "seeing" what life was like during the first half of this century, the postcard is indispensable.

Until very recently, however, the great archives of postcards were not to be found in libraries, but in the hands of private collectors. As the essays in Steven's important collection show, that neglect is beginning to end. *Postcards* offers its readers twenty-one articles that describe representative collections of cards held in libraries, the scholarly uses to which postcards have been put, and the organizational schemes in use to categorize and catalogue postcards. In addition, one article deals with preservation options and techniques and the collection concludes with two bibliographic essays: one lists important books on the history and collection of postcards and the other details examples of scholarly research based on postcard evidence.

Because of the incredible numbers of postcards that survive, because most of those cards are in the collections of individuals who are often seeking a "permanent" home for their collections, and because of the research potential that postcards have, libraries and historical societies must pay more attention to the postcard as a cultural and photographic resource. *Postcards* is a perfect guide for the librarian. It ought to be in every historical society and library in the United States."

George Miller
Professor and Chair, Department of English, University of Delaware

The Haworth Press, Inc.

Postcards in the Library:
Invaluable Visual Resources

Postcards in the Library: Invaluable Visual Resources

Norman D. Stevens
Editor

The Haworth Press, Inc.
New York • London

Postcards in the Library: Invaluable Visual Resources has also been published as *Popular Culture in Libraries,* Volume 3, Number 2 1995.

The development, preparation, and publication of this work has been undertaken with great care. However, the publisher, employees, editors, and agents of The Haworth Press and all imprints of The Haworth Press, Inc., including The Haworth Medical Press and Pharmaceutical Products Press, are not responsible for any errors contained herein or for consequences that may ensue from use of materials or information contained in this work. Opinions expressed by the author(s) are not necessarily those of The Haworth Press, Inc.

The Haworth Press, Inc., 10 Alice Street, Binghamton, NY 13904-1580 USA

Library of Congress Cataloging-in-Publication Data

Postcards in the library: invaluable visual resources / Norman D. Stevens, editor.
    p. cm.
    "Also published as Popular culture in libraries, volume 3, number 2, 1995"–T.p. verso.
    Includes bibliographical references (p.).
    ISBN 1-56024-776-2 (alk. paper)
    1. Libraries–United States–Special collections–Postcards. 2. Libraries and pictures–United States. I. Stevens, Norman D.
Z692.P65P67 1995
026'.76956'6–dc20
                                    95-46638
                                        CIP

INDEXING & ABSTRACTING

Contributions to this publication are selectively indexed or abstracted in print, electronic, online, or CD-ROM version(s) of the reference tools and information services listed below. This list is current as of the copyright date of this publication. See the end of this section for additional notes.

- *Children's Literature Abstracts,* International Federation of Library Associations, 5906 Fairlane Drive, Austin, TX 78757-4417

- *CNPIEC Reference Guide: Chinese National Directory of Foreign Periodicals,* P.O. Box 88, Beijing, People's Republic of China

- *Film Literature Index,* Film and Television Documentation Center, Richardson 390 C/1400 Washington Avenue, SUNYA, Albany, NY 12222

- *Human Resources Abstracts (HRA),* Sage Publications, Inc., 2455 Teller Road, Newbury Park, CA 91320

- *IBZ International Bibliography of Periodical Literature,* Zeller Verlag GmbH & Co., P.O.B. 1949, d-49009 Osnabruck, Germany

- *Index to Periodical Articles Related to Law,* University of Texas, 727 East 26th Street, Austin, TX 78705

- *Informed Librarian, The,* Infosources Publishing, 140 Norma Road, Teaneck, NJ 07666

- *INTERNET ACCESS (& additional networks) Bulletin Board for Libraries ("BUBL"), coverage of information resources on INTERNET, JANET, and other networks.*
  - JANET X.29: UK.AC.BATH.BUBL or 00006012101300
  - TELNET: BUBL.BATH.AC.UK or 138.38.32.45 login 'bubl'
  - Gopher: BUBL.BATH.AC.UK (138.32.32.45). Port 7070
  - World Wide Web: http: / / www.bubl.bath.ac.uk./BUBL/ home.html
  - NISSWAIS: telnetniss.ac.uk (for the NISS gateway)
  The Andersonian Library, Curran Building, 101 St. James Road, Glasgow G4 ONS, Scotland

(continued)

- *Konyvtari Figyelo-Library Review,* National Szechenyi Library, Centre for Library and Information Science, H-1827 Budapest, Hungary

- *Library & Information Science Abstracts (LISA),* Bowker-Saur Limited, Maypole House, Maypole Road, East Grinstead, West Sussex RH19 1HH, England

- *Newsletter of Library and Information Services,* China Sci-Tech Book Review, Library of Academia Sinica, 8 Kexueyuan Nanlu, Zhongguancun, Beijing 100080, People's Republic of China

- *Sociological Abstracts (SA),* Sociological Abstracts, Inc., P.O. Box 22206, San Diego, CA 92192-0206

SPECIAL BIBLIOGRAPHIC NOTES
related to special journal issues (separates)
and indexing/abstracting

☐ indexing/abstracting services in this list will also cover material in any "separate" that is co-published simultaneously with Haworth's special thematic journal issue or DocuSerial. Indexing/abstracting usually covers material at the article/chapter level.

☐ monographic co-editions are intended for either non-subscribers or libraries which intend to purchase a second copy for their circulating collections.

☐ monographic co-editions are reported to all jobbers/wholesalers/approval plans. The source journal is listed as the "series" to assist the prevention of duplicate purchasing in the same manner utilized for books-in-series.

☐ to facilitate user/access services all indexing/abstracting services are encouraged to utilize the co-indexing entry note indicated at the bottom of the first page of each article/chapter/contribution.

☐ this is intended to assist a library user of any reference tool (whether print, electronic, online, or CD-ROM) to locate the monographic version if the library has purchased this version but not a subscription to the source journal.

☐ individual articles/chapters in any Haworth publication are also available through the Haworth Document Delivery Services (HDDS).

Postcards in the Library: Invaluable Visual Resources

CONTENTS

ABOUT THE EDITOR

Norman D. Stevens, PhD, has held various administrative posts in major academic institutions, including Howard University, Rutgers University, and the University of Connecticut where he served as Director of University Libraries from 1988 until his retirement in 1994. Dr. Stevens has written extensively on many aspects of library administration, history, humor, networking, and related subjects. His book *A Guide to Collecting Librariana* (Scarecrow Press, 1986) was based on his own extensive collection of library ephemera, including over 25,000 library postcards.

About the Contributors

Barbara L. Anderson, who began collecting postcards as a child, has been actively collecting postcards and doing research on postcards for the last few years. She has had numerous articles about postcards published in a variety of magazines. She is currently continuing her research on the postcards of Mount Vernon with the hopes of producing an extensive checklist and accompanying text.

Donald R. Brown, the founder of the Institute of American Deltiology, is a graduate of Ursinus College, the University of Illinois (MA in History), and the University of Wisconsin at Madison (MLS). His professional career was spent at the Detroit Public Library, Western Michigan University, and, from 1970 until he retired in 1991, the Pennsylvania State Library. A deltiologist since 1943, he is keenly interested in studying, and demonstrating, the value of postcards as documents of our society.

John K. Crellin, the John Clinch Professor of the History of Medicine at the Memorial University of Newfoundland, points out that "Postcards serve as an invaluable resource to raise questions about the place of patients in health care and, of course, much more."

Elena S. Danielson, after 16 years, has just begun to get a sense of the riches, such as the postcard collections, of the Hoover Institution Archives at Stanford University where she is Associate Archivist. In 1992 she worked with colleagues in Moscow to install a joint Russian-Hoover exhibition in the Russian parliament building, and has planned special exhibits at the Hoover Institution Archives for such distinguished visitors as Mikhail Gorbachev and Margaret Thatcher.

Lois R. Densky-Wolff received an MA in Librarianship from the University of Denver in 1968. Archivist at the Special Collections

Department of the University Libraries at the University of Medicine and Dentistry of New Jersey since 1960, she previously was archivist of The Joint Free Public Library of Morristown and Morris Township. A member of the Garden State Post Card Club, she has been developing postcard collections in libraries for many years.

Meredith Eliassen works with the Marguerite Archer Collection of Historic Children's Books in the J. Paul Leonard Library at San Francisco State University. She earned her BA in Broadcasting from San Francisco State University and her MS from the Graduate School of Library and Information Science at Simmons College in Boston. She is the author of *A Guide for Emmy Award-Winning Programs, 1974-1986* (1991) that was written for the Northern California Chapter of the National Academy of Television Arts and Sciences.

Richard H. Engeman has been the Photographs and Graphics Librarian in the Special Collections and Preservation Division at the University of Washington since 1984. A graduate of Reed College, he has an MLS from the University of Oregon and anticipates receiving an MA in History from the University of Washington in 1996. He previously held positions in the libraries of the Oregon Historical Society, the San Francisco Maritime Museum, and the South Oregon Historical Society.

Katherine Hamilton-Smith has been Curator of the Curt Teich Postcard Archives at the Lake County Museum since 1982. She is a certified archivist who holds a BA in Art History from the University of Nebraska and an MA in Art History from the University of Chicago. She is Chair of the Illinois State Archives Advisory Board and past Chair of the Visual Materials Section of the Society of American Archivists. She is currently involved with the American Association of Museum's 1994/95 National Research Demonstration program to Advance Education in American Museums.

William H. Helfand is a consultant in areas relating to art and medicine for the National Library of Medicine, the Philadelphia Museum of Art, and other institutions. He has published a number of articles and books on the history of pharmacy and on his own collecting interests that include caricatures, postcards, posters, prints, and other ephemera related to medicine and pharmacy.

Jennifer Henderson is a Chicago-based free-lance writer who specializes in deltiological topics. She also collects postcards on a wide variety of topics including, in particular, recipe postcards.

Claudia Hill received her BA from Colgate University and her MA in Art History from the University of Chicago. She is currently the Conservation Editor for the Getty Art History Information Program's *Art and Architect Thesaurus*. As a result of her contribution to this volume, she has a renewed appreciation of the value of postcards for historical research in art.

Martha McPhail is Special Collections/Catalog Librarian at San Diego State University. She is currently working on a book *Baja California in Postcards* that is based on the holdings of the John R. and Jane Adams postcard collection at San Diego State University.

Mary K. Mannix, who has been Library Director of the Howard County Historical Society (Ellicott City, MD) since 1989, is also a reference librarian at the Lilienfeld Library of the Johns Hopkins University School of Hygiene and Public Health. She has an MA in American History, with a certificate in Museum Studies, from the University of Delaware and an MLS from the University of Maryland. She previously held positions with the Maryland Historical Society and the Baltimore City Commission for Historical and Architectural Preservation. The project described in her paper was originally developed in a course, taught by Dr. Marilyn Pettit, on Computers in Archival Administration at the University of Maryland.

Jan Merrrill-Oldham is the Malloy-Rabinowitz Preservation Librarian in the Harvard University Library and the Harvard College Library. In 1980 she completed a National Endowment for the Humanities fellowship in preservation and conservation at the Yale University Library. Since then she has been active in the field of preservation through her work in writing, lecturing, developing conference programs, and working in various capacities with associations and organizations engaged in long-range preservation planning and policy development.

Timothy D. Murray is Head of the Special Collections Department at the University of Delaware Library. His interest in poetry postcards developed from his work with the literary ephemera that is an essential component of contemporary literature collections.

Jack Robertson has been Fine Arts Librarian at the Fiske Kimball Fine Arts Library at the University of Virginia since 1987. With academic training, and research experience, in art and architectural history, his interest in historic picture postcards rests on the conviction that ephemeral files of printed and illustrative matter are frequently treasure troves for research inquiries. He is committed to combining the research value of pictorial archives and vertical files with new technological innovations such as HTML and the World-WideWeb to create powerful archiving and accessing mechanisms.

Loriene Roy is Associate Professor and Minority Liaison Officer in the Graduate School of Library and Information Science at the University of Texas. She teaches such graduate courses as Public Libraries, Bibliographic Instruction, Information Resources in the Humanities, and Library Services to Native American Populations. She has a collection of over 1,000 postcards of public libraries and also collects cards relating to library education and the Anishinabe/Ojibway culture.

Richard Saunders, a librarian in the Special Collections Department at Montana State University, works with the premier collection, which includes postcards and other ephemeral materials, on the Yellowstone region. A certified archivist, he has a BS and an MS (Western American History) from Utah State University and an MLIS from Brigham Young State University. Prior to joining the staff of the Montana State University Library in 1992, he worked as a manuscripts cataloger in the Special Collections Department at the University of Utah and earlier as a project archivist at the Utah State Historical Society.

Alison M. Scott has been Head Librarian of the Popular Culture Library at Bowling Green State University since September 1993.

She has pursued graduate work in American studies, library science, and religion at the University of Chicago and Boston University. Her professional experience includes special collections work at the University of Chicago, Columbia University, and Smith College. She has published articles on such diverse people as Eugene Field, Sherlock Holmes, and Virginia Woolf.

Norman D. Stevens is now Director of University Libraries Emeritus at the University of Connecticut where he served in various administrative positions from 1968 to early 1994. His library postcard collection, which he began in 1960, now numbers about 25,000 cards and is part of a larger collection of librariana that is described in his *A Guide to Collecting Librariana (1986).* That collection will eventually be transferred to the Centre Canadien d'Architecture/Canadian Centre for Architecture in Montréal. He is also an avid collector of other popular culture materials including postcards depicting books and reading. Dr. Stevens is a regular reviewer for *Popular Culture in Libraries* and, from 1982 to 1994, wrote the column "Our Profession" for the *Wilson Library Bulletin* in which he reviewed new material for professional librarians.

Chris Wolff is co-owner and proprietor of the Old Book Shop, a used, out-of-print, and antiquarian book shop in Morristown, NJ. He has been dealing in postcards for over twenty years and, since 1974, has served as Editor of *Hilites,* the newsletter of the Garden State Post Card Club.

INTRODUCTION

Welcome to the World of Postcards

Norman D. Stevens

Since their introduction as a means of postal communication in the late nineteenth century, postcards have undergone many transformations. Over the past one hundred years, their popularity has waxed and waned. Although other means of communication for the conveyance of brief messages, including most recently electronic mail, have largely replaced postcards, they are still being published in great quantities. New computer and printing technologies make it easy, and inexpensive, to produce high quality color postcards in relatively small quantities. The day of the real-photo postcard as it once existed may be long gone but today, for example, it is possible to create such a card by buying a pre-glued postcard back to which you can attach a picture that you have taken yourself. Advertisers, artists, craftspeople, hotels and motels, restaurants, and individuals continue to have postcards published to convey their image whether or not the cards themselves are ever used to transmit a written message that is actually mailed to another person. In the pre-World War I Golden Age of postcards, postcard collecting was a major craze. As the popularity of postcards declined after that period, interest in collecting postcards also declined although it never died out altogether. In recent years there has

[Haworth co-indexing entry note]: "Welcome to the World of Postcards." Stevens, Norman D. Co-published simultaneously in *Popular Culture in Libraries* (The Haworth Press, Inc.) Vol. 3, No. 2, 1995, pp. 1-4; and: *Postcards in the Library: Invaluable Visual Resources* (ed: Norman D. Stevens) The Haworth Press, Inc., 1995, pp. 1-4. Single or multiple copies of this article are available from The Haworth Document Delivery Service [1-800-342-9678, 9:00 a.m. - 5:00 p.m. (EST)].

been a steady growth of interest in used postcards of all kinds, but especially in those from the dawn of the postcard era, largely on the part of individual collectors who recognize the extent to which those cards provide important visual information about so many elements of society in a way that no other objects do.

As common objects from the world of popular culture, postcards, like so many other kinds of popular culture materials, have been largely ignored by libraries. As ephemeral items intended to be used and discarded, postcards are clearly not the kind of "important" or "permanent" publications that libraries like to collect. As single items issued in enormous quantities, postcards present challenges that libraries are not necessarily prepared, or willing, to deal with. Many libraries that have postcard collections seem to have acquired them almost by accident as part of some other collection that they regarded as an important acquisition. The reasons given by librarians for not collecting postcards are legion. There are no ready sources of supply; there is no established means of national bibliographic control; there are no cataloging standards; there are no reviewing media and few, if any, library-oriented reference guides to aid in the selection process; used postcard dealers are not, for the most part, members of the book trade; the time and effort involved in the acquisition, organization, and servicing of great quantities of inexpensive single items is too costly; individual postcards, which is the way that librarians are apt to look at postcards, have little, or no, intellectual value. Above all, perhaps, is the fact that in many libraries existing postcard collections have not been utilized extensively by serious researchers. Those are the primary reasons that librarians can find for rationalizing their failure to collect postcards even when such material might otherwise fall well within the range of their established collection development policy. Intellectual snobbery, I suspect, is really the crux of the matter. Librarians, like many other academicians, tend to regard postcards, and other artifacts of popular culture, as trivial and insignificant.

Since, as librarians, we depend so heavily on the literature of "Our Profession" for guidance, the almost total lack of any serious discussion about postcards in that literature may well be, in fact, another primary reason why libraries have neglected postcards. Nobody has told us why we should collect them, or what we should do with them if we do acquire them. Bill Katz's landmark 1981 article "Postcards Are Popular, But Not in Your Library" (*Collection Management* 3:25-50 (#2)) is one of the few articles in the library literature that deals with postcards as a component of library collections. Based on a survey of ninety-six American academic, public, art museum, and other special libraries, he concluded that only a very few libraries had any serious interest in postcards. While his basic purpose was to encourage libraries to take a more active interest in collecting postcards, that article appears to have had little impact especially if judged by the continuing lack of attention to postcards in the library literature.

Postcards, individually and collectively, contain a great deal of information that can be of real value to students and researchers. An individual postcard, which may now be a unique item, may contain the only visual image of a building, monument, person, place, or other object at a specific period of time. A collection of postcards may represent the best set of images available of the architecture of one type of building, an historic event, or a city or town. Postcards offer a window into the world as it was viewed by the society of its time. The messages written on postcards may reveal a great deal about individual and/or societal attitudes and ideas. Above all, because they were produced as items for mass consumption and often not with an apparent conscious literary or social purpose, postcards are a true reflection of the society in which they were produced. Those are some of the compelling reasons why libraries should take a far more active and serious interest in establishing and maintaining postcard collections and in encouraging use of those collections.

A survey similar to Katz's conducted today might well produce very similar results. There does not appear to have been a substantial increase in the number of libraries with major postcard collections in the past fifteen years. Such a survey, however, would not necessarily offer a complete and accurate picture. An increasing number of libraries do actively collect postcards. The Loyola Marymount University Library in Los Angeles, for example, now has a general postcard collection that may number as many as a million items. Other libraries, like the Montana State University Library that has a collection of postcards depicting Yellowstone National Park, have begun to build postcard collections in specific areas that complement a specialized collecting interest. The Curt Teich Postcard Archives and the Institute of American Deltiology represent major collections devoted exclusively to postcards.

This special volume, like Katz's article, promotes the idea that there are valid reasons for libraries to collect postcards in three ways. First, it offers a number of articles that describe, in more detail than Katz's survey did, the postcard collections in a variety of libraries of different kinds and sizes. Second, it offers several articles, and a selective bibliography of other articles or books, that indicate the very real ways in which the effective use of postcard collections can result in, or contribute to, substantive scholarly publications. Finally it offers, both directly and indirectly, advice and suggestions on myriad issues, like preservation, that libraries face in dealing with these ephemeral fragments of popular culture.

It is, unfortunately, abundantly clear that, in most cases, existing postcard collections are a vastly underutilized scholarly resource. We are fortunate that few libraries have the time, or the inclination, to weed collections once they have been acquired. We are especially fortunate that many librarians, who understand the potential value of postcards as the basis for serious research, have continued to establish and develop postcard collections in anticipation of their eventual discovery by scholars. We are equally fortunate that scholars like Albers and James, Mellinger, Schor, and others have undertaken major research projects using postcards that demonstrate the ways in which postcards can be used in research, and that have begun to establish a standard methodology for the analysis of postcards.

Postcards, especially given the wealth of information that an individual card may contain, represent an ideal visual resource for incorporation into the digital technological projects that so many libraries are now experimenting with. Until, however, existing postcard collections are more heavily used by researchers, those collections are likely to be overlooked when such digitizing projects are planned. Many postcard collections may continue to languish in libraries, but hopefully not be discarded, until scholars in the twenty-first century recognize the enormous potential that those fragments of the past have for studying so many aspects of society in the late nineteenth and twentieth centuries. This volume is the first extended discussion of the role of postcard collections in libraries and of the value of postcards as research materials. These contributions offer the first extended discussion of the role of postcard collections in libraries and of the value of postcards as research materials. I, and the other contributors, trust that it will not be the last such discussion. Instead, we hope, that it will at last initiate an acceptance of postcards not only as a subject deserving of greater regular attention in the literature of "Our Profession" but as a vital element of more and more library collections.

TWO PRIMARY POSTCARD COLLECTIONS

The Curt Teich Postcard Archives: Dedicated to the Postcard as a Document Type

Katherine Hamilton-Smith

COLLECTIONS

The core collection in the Curt Teich Postcard Archives, acquired in 1982 in "raw" form by the Lake County Museum in Wauconda, Illinois is the industrial archives of the Curt Teich Company of Chicago which operated from 1898 through 1978 as the world's largest volume printer of view and advertising postcards. The company's archives was created through a policy of saving examples of every image they printed. Company records and the original production materials for each postcard image were also saved. Chromolithographic materials in the core collection, numbering approximately 360,000 individual images, depict the United States, Canada, and some other foreign countries in those first eight de-

[Haworth co-indexing entry note]: "The Curt Teich Postcard Archives: Dedicated to the Postcard as a Document Type." Hamilton-Smith, Katherine. Co-published simultaneously in *Popular Culture in Libraries* (The Haworth Press, Inc.) Vol. 3, No. 2, 1995, pp. 5-16; and: *Postcards in the Library: Invaluable Visual Resources* (ed: Norman D. Stevens) The Haworth Press, Inc., 1995, pp. 5-16. Single or multiple copies of this article are available from The Haworth Document Delivery Service [1-800-342-9678, 9:00 a.m. - 5:00 p.m. (EST)].

cades of the twentieth century. The overwhelmingly predominant format in this core collection is postcards and postcard folders. The company also printed brochures, souvenir booklets, letterhead, business cards, and advertising coasters and blotters. These materials, which constitute about two percent of the holdings, make up a small, though important, portion of the collection.

The main, and complementary portions, of the Teich Archives core collection are the postcard files that consist of one to several copies of each card printed by the Teich Company, which are filed in boxes and organized chronologically, and 600 postcard albums compiled by the Teich Company during all their years of operation that include one copy of each postcard printed, arranged chronologically.

In addition to postcards, the collection includes approximately 100,000 working "job" files, that date from 1926 to 1960. Each file is unique and varies in size and content, but they tend to contain the following types of materials: Curt Teich forms that tracked production steps and orders; correspondence with clients; photographic prints and negatives; letters and paper documents; artist's drawings, renderings, and other layout materials; and a wide variety of physical remnants (fragments of wallpaper, linoleum, textile swatches, pieces of tile, carpet, etc.) used to clarify design elements or colors in the finished postcards. Other materials and formats in the job files include handcolored proofs, tissue and plastic overlays, Rubylith® sheets, postcard folders, and extensively retouched photographs. All of these materials provide invaluable insights into the design and production steps and processes employed in printing postcards, detail interactions with clients, and shed light on the evolution of printing technology in the mid-twentieth century.

Since 1991, the Archives has engaged in an active program of collecting postcards and postcard albums to add to the core industrial collection. This program has resulted in the acquisition of fifteen albums, dating from 1899 to 1960, and approximately 25,000 postcards. The purpose of developing a collection of postcard albums is to document how people have systematized personal collections of postcards since the turn of the century. Even the small group of albums amassed by the Archives so far show a startling variety of individual personalities and interests. Distinctive items in the collection are as follows:

- The Tobias and McInnis Family albums (two albums), dating from circa 1905 through the 1920s, were given to the Teich Archives by the Chicago Public Library's Department of Special Collections. The albums, which are examples of typical albums of the period, hold about 200 postcards each. The cards are mostly views of towns, cities, and resort locations throughout North America and Europe, but also include holiday, political, and comic subjects.

- The Minnie Canin album is from the same period as the McInnis and Tobias Family albums, but is so atypical of that period as to be an aberrant example. Compiled about 1919 in Russia by Minnie Canin, a young woman who later immigrated to the United States, this album includes only 9 view postcards out of 207. The other postcards are portraits of authors, composers, and philosophers such as Gogol, Gluck, and Schopenhauer; allegorical, political, mythological, and religious subjects; and reproductions of sculpture and painting. The cards are in four languages: English, French, Russian, and Yiddish. At the time this album was collected by the Archives, a brief oral history was taken from Minnie who is now in her nineties. Born in the late 1890s, Minnie was well read and well educated in her youth; she loved literature and the arts. She is Jewish and lived her early life in a ghetto at the time of the pogroms in Russia. In her late teens, she fled to America and taught herself English. She travelled a great deal in the middle eastern countries and the Far East, but lived most of her adult life in New York City and Philadelphia. Minnie Canin's album provides an insight into her varied and stimulating life and, as such, is a very personal testament.
- Another album, dating from 1899 to about 1904 contains 117 rare "Gruss aus" (the German for "Greetings from") postcards, considered the early precursors of American view postcards. This album also contains an example of a rare Victorian-period "cross writing," postcard where text is written in several layers in several directions, and often in more than one ink color, in order to get the most use out of a small writing space.
- Three albums of military subjects were recently acquired from the Fort Sheridan Museum. Two were compiled during World War I and include photographic postcards of life at Camp Custer and Camp Grant in the United States as well as views of European locations. The third album was put together by a G.I. serving with the army in the Pacific theatre of operation during World War II. It includes views of New Guinea, the Philippine Islands, Australia, and other locations in the Pacific.
- A recent addition to the Teich Archives' album collection, which dates to the turn of the century, includes over 800 postcards, examples of Victorian-period cut scrap, and advertising cards and circulars for products ranging from coffee and flour to stoves and thread. Many images in this album, which exhibit evidence of stereotypes of

their day, will be of interest to historians studying women's history and African-American history.

Albums of postcards are increasingly rare. Albums are often partially, or completely, disassembled because the postcards within them are more valuable to dealers and collectors as individual items than they are in album format. As *Ancestry* genealogist Karen Frisch-Ripley explains in her 1991 book *Unlocking the Secrets of Old Photographs,* "[Postcards] already in old albums should remain intact if for no other reason than that they represent a unified body of images, assembled by the individual who put them there in the first place. The order of photos within may have certain significance in terms of identification which should be given consideration and studied as a potentially valuable clue." Certainly, the Minnie Canin album as well as others in the Teich Archives are excellent examples of this fragile link with the past.

In the summer of 1992, the Teich Archives acquired a collection of military postcards and related materials from the de-commissioned Fort Sheridan Museum on the Fort Sheridan Army Base, north of Chicago. The collection contains over 500 photographic and chromolithographic postcards, the three postcard albums described above, and several postcard booklets mostly from French locations such as Blois, Remy, and Lyon. These materials relate principally to World Wars I and II, and the Spanish Civil War. Significant items within this collection are: a series of Chicago Daily News Postals from World War I; candid and formal views of camp life at several American Army installations; photographic postcards of convalescing soldiers in England during the First and Second World Wars; a variety of related subjects such as the Red Cross and medicine; and personal postcard correspondence between individual servicemen and their families back home.

In 1992 the Windy City Postcard Club of Chicago, one of the oldest collecting clubs in the United States, gave a major collection to the Teich Archives. Since the 1950s, the club had been compiling a complete archive of the production of the V.O. Hammon Company. V.O. Hammon, which operated from offices in Minneapolis and Chicago, printed view and advertising postcards of towns and cities in the Midwest from 1900 to the early 1920s. The collection, which numbers approximately 5,000 postcards, includes views of: Illinois, Missouri, Minnesota, Indiana, Wisconsin, Ohio, and Michigan.

In 1994, the renowned glaciologist Dr. William O. Field of Great Barrington, Massachusetts gave his collection of 7,000 postcards to the Teich Archives. Dr. Field, now in his nineties, had collected postcards since the age of six. His personal collection, as well as that of his father, documents

Europe and America from 1895 to the 1950s. Strengths in the collection include: steamships, railroads and other travel images; pre-World War I politics (especially German and Austrian); English athletes; European cities at the turn of the century; museum reproductions; and views of Canada. One of the albums in this collection documents the European "grand tour" of Dr. Field's parents in 1900-1902.

In 1993, the Teich Archives began collecting artist-created pieces that are intended to be postally used. The most recently acquired example of this "mail art" is the 1987 lithographic postcard folder "Sandwich" by Chicago artist Sally Alatalo. The front and back covers are black and white images of bread slices. Inside are four color lithographic images, of olive loaf luncheon meat, lettuce, tomato slices, and mayonnaise and mustard. This new "mail art" collection adds a fine art component to the Teich Archives that documents another, more contemporary, use of the postcard format to present visual information.

Finally, the Teich Archives is actively collecting smaller groups of postcards from individual donors. The range of topics covered in these smaller collections, which date from 1893 to the present, is as broad as it is possible to imagine. Significant among these smaller collections are: a comprehensive collection of about 2,000 postcards from the 1933-34 Century of Progress Chicago World's Fair; the original set of ten souvenir postals produced for the 1893 Columbian Exposition that are thought to be the first picture postcards in the United States; and 383 cards from the Leonie DeAngelis Hall collection of fashion, genre, holiday, and patriotic subjects another part of which was given by the donor to the New York Public Library in 1992.

INTELLECTUAL CONTROL

The contents of the Teich Archives are computer cataloged by subject, date, and geographic location using a custom program originally written in 1983 in dBase II and now in FoxBase. Views may be located by searching in any of those categories. Boolean searches, for example a search for "all views related to harvesting" in "the province of Saskatchewan," are also possible. A six-year-long project to catalog the core collection, which was completed in January 1991, produced an automated database for 360,000 images. Since the Teich Archives began its acquisition program in 1991, three information fields have been added to the database structure. The new information fields indicate: whether or not a postcard has been used for correspondence; whether or not the message, if any, relates to the image on the front of the postcard; and whether or not the postcard is a photograph or a photomechanical image.

A 1,902 term thesaurus, which controls subject searches in the Teich Archives' database, was devised in 1983 using subject heading lists from the Library of Congress, the Chicago Historical Society, and George Watson Cole's *Postcards, the World in Miniature* (1935). In a decade of working with the collection, the thesaurus has grown like Topsy. Since the completion of the cataloging of the core collection in 1991, subject headings are added to the thesaurus in response to research use of the Archives. Examples of new categories added recently include: two under the major heading of WOMEN–Social Attitudes and Work Force; three under the major heading of HIGHWAYS–Route 66, the Lincoln Highway, and the Dixie Highway; three under the major heading of GENRE–Family, Style/Popular Culture, and People Eating; and one under the major heading of RESIDENCES–Sod Houses. Subject headings are often altered for easier access. New minor headings under the major subject of ADVERTISING, RESTAURANTS & BARS include categorization by ethnic cuisine (e.g., German, Polynesian), as well as Food & Food Preparation. Entire new categories have been added to the thesaurus, including, for example, the major subject heading of TIME with the following minor headings–Days of the Week, Months of the Year, Night Views, Sunrise, Sunset, Spring, Summer, Fall, Winter. Categories are also added as new types of postcards are acquired by the Archives. One new major heading is NOVELTIES with the following minor headings–Leather, Feathers, Die Cut, Mechanical, Embossed, Handmade, Installments, Beads & Glitter, Puzzle, Metal, Silk & Ribbons.

While the current thesaurus remains useful, the intention is to develop additional subject headings for architectural style. Images of buildings in the collection are currently cataloged by use of the building as, for example, INDUSTRY, OIL/Gas Stations, or EDUCATIONAL BUILDING/Primary School. In 1995, a project funded by the Graham Foundation for Advanced Study in the Fine Arts will develop subject headings designed to provide access to the collections by architectural style as, for example, GAS STATIONS/International Style. This will give researchers another important way to use the Teich Archives.

New finding aids for researchers studying the history, and courses, of historic routes are currently being developed. One of the most frequently received research subjects at the Teich Archives is for information about such historic routes as Route 66, the National Road, the Dixie Highway, the transcontinental Lincoln Highway, transcontinental U.S. Route 20, and Route 1 on the East Coast. The intention of this ongoing project is to create finding aids for materials in the Teich Archives representing these highways that will provide better access for research. The Teich Archives holds one of the nation's largest collections of Route 66 materials. Other large collections may be found in state historical societies in Illinois, Missouri, Kansas, Oklahoma, Texas, New Mexico, Arizona, and California as well as the corporate archives of companies such as Texaco, Sears, and JC-Penney, that hold records of their activity in the Route 66 states. The Teich Archives holds materials related to all aspects of activity (e.g., tourism, commerce, town planning) along Route 66 in all eight states through which the highway traveled. It also contains materials of a similarly comprehensive nature for all the major roadways in the United States.

In the summer of 1992 a new cataloging initiative was initiated, to provide better access to the materials in the 100,000 original job files described above. A team of three people is currently working to create an independent catalog of the files' contents. By September 1994, the work file project team had examined approximately 32,000 files from 1926, 1927, the 1930s, and 1941. The final product of this project will be an information database of the materials in the job files. Researchers will be able to access this information by date and material type. A design historian's search in this database might be for "all samples of carpet in the 1940s" or "all examples of linoleum in the 1930s." An architectural historian's search might be for "all examples of vitrolite used on 1930s and 1940s storefronts." Plans call for inputting the information currently being compiled by the project team into a database in late 1995.

Plans to prepare an analog or digital image database of the Teich Archives are currently under consideration. Such a catalog would have the same search capabilities as the current database. It would allow researchers not only at the Archives but in research libraries and institutions across the country to search the collection *visually*.

USE

The Curt Teich Postcard Archives is a department of the Lake County Museum, an operational division of the Lake County Forest Preserve District (see Photograph 1). The Museum and Archives are located 40 miles northwest of Chicago in the Lakewood Forest Preserve, 27277 Forest Preserve Drive, Wauconda, IL 60084. The Museum is open daily except for Christmas, New Years Day, and Thanksgiving. The Teich Archives is open for research by appointment, Monday through Friday. It can be reached by telephone (708-526-8638), FAX (708-526-1545), or electronic mail (teicharc@nslsilus.org.).

FIGURE 1. Home of the Curt Teich Archives

In fiscal year 1992/93, the most recent year for which statistics are available, the Teich Archives received 1,190 requests for research or technical assistance. The Teich Archives, which is listed as a single collection on the national OCLC database, is used by a variety of scholars, institutions, companies, and individuals. It is not necessary to visit the Archives to use its resources. About ninety-five percent of the reference requests received are handled by Archives staff for researchers who may never visit the institution. In fiscal year 1993/94, $24,000 was realized from research use and member support of the Teich Archives. A full reproduction service is available through which prints and transparencies as well as color laser copies may be requested. Fees for these services vary depending on use.

The Archives is used extensively by publishers as a source of visual materials. It contributed material for six volumes in the *People Who Have Helped the World* biography series for children including images for the articles on Betty Friedan, Edward R. Morrow, Norman Bethune, John Muir, Ralph Nader, and Jane Addams. *American Heritage, Metropolitan Home, Mirabella, Chicago Magazine, National Geographic*, and *Vogue* and other periodicals also use the Teich Archives as a resource. A recent American Heritage feature on dirigibles, focusing on the wreck of the dirigibles *Shenandoah* and *Akron*, used images from the Archives.

Museums and other historical agencies use materials for exhibition purposes. The Indiana Historical Society used images of roadside structures and landscapes from the Teich Archives in its exhibition "Ducks, Diners, and Drive-Ins: Indiana's Roadside Architecture." The Minnesota Historical Society used images of towns in that state for a multimedia theatre exhibit in the Society's new Minnesota History Center. "Home Place Minnesota," which opened in May 1993, is a series of stories about people and memory in Minnesota told through first person narrative, sound, music, images, objects, and settings. The Musée de la Civilisation in Québec used the collection for views of car culture and evidence of the influence of the automobile in North America for a 1993 exhibit on that topic. The Illinois Arts Council used images of churches in Illinois for an exhibit entitled "Sacred Space" that toured the state of Illinois from 1990-92. The new National Postal Museum in Washington, D.C. borrowed several postcards for an exhibit on postal history, that opened in late 1993.

Companies use the Teich Archives as a resource for institutional research. The Hershey Chocolate Company requested 1920s views of its Pennsylvania plant for use in a new visitor center. An industrial engineering and research firm in Colorado uses the views of now abandoned industrial sites or gas stations to establish the location of underground storage tanks or other potential toxic waste hazards.

Architects use vintage views of structures which are in restoration and planning work. Venturi, Scott Brown, and Associates, which is famous for the groundbreaking 1972 Yale School of Architecture studio and produced *Learning from Las Vegas*, uses the Teich Archives in their research of American urbanism, and in the preparation of presentations to prospective clients. Architectural preservationists also use the collections. Historic preservation planner Donna DeWeese used images of Covington (LA) in a presentation supporting the National Trust's Main Street Program to city officials. A group of preservation planners in Kansas City, who were trying to save portions of their sprawling General Hospital complex, used images to document the progression of its construction from 1908 through 1918. The Illinois State Historic Preservation Agency used Boolean search capabilities to identify views of Carnegie libraries in Illinois, for a 1993 publication. Many branches of the National Park Service have used the Teich Archives, in conducting architectural and landscape preservation surveys. One example was the use of a series of views of the Jefferson Memorial and Lincoln Memorial to show landscape changes every five years from the date of the construction of the buildings to the present.

Scholars use the Teich Archives in myriad ways. A Smithsonian National Museum of American History (NMAH) post-doctorate fellow used images documenting the changing personification of beauty from 1860 to 1945. Another NMAH fellow sought turn of the century views of Chicago department stores. A historian from the Smithsonian used the Teich Archives in a study of covered bridges. St. Mary's College of Maryland historian Michael Berger used the collection in his study of library book-mobiles and the development of library services. Berger also used the Archives for material for his essay "The Car's Impact on the American Family" in *The Car and the City: The Automobile, the Built Environment, and Daily Urban Life* (1992). Graham Foundation scholar Martin Treu is currently using the Archives for his study on the history of signage. A librarian from the National Gallery of Art's Center for the Advanced Study of the Visual Arts, working for the Samuel H. Kress Foundation, has used the Archives in her five-year study of Kress five-and-dime stores, that will be published in 1995. Purdue University sociologist Roger Finke, and University of Washington professor of sociology and comparative religion Rodney Stark used views of ethnic catholic churches and catholic travelling chapels for their study *The Churching of America, 1776-1990: Winners and Losers in Our Religious Economy* (1992). Landscape historians, such as Dr. Charles Beverage, editor of the Frederick Law Olmstead

Papers, who recently used images of park landscapes created by Olmstead, are also frequent users.

Other types of uses include: local and regional history; video and television production; and theatre and film set design (an especially strong use of the Teich Archives' original photographic and physical remnant materials). Examples of film use of the Teich Archives include: WNET, New York Public Television in research for the "American Masters" series documentary on the life and career of the "King of Swing" Benny Goodman; a documentary for British television (London Channel 4 TV) on America's interest in mobile homes and mobile living, called *Home on Wheels*; a documentary for Dutch Public Television on Route 66; and the film *Changing Our Minds: The Story of Evelyn Hooker*–that described her groundbreaking scientific research into male homosexuality, using methods employed in psychology as the first study of the gay population as a "normal" or non-criminal group.

Lastly, but importantly, individuals seeking personal information are also welcome. For a woman who wanted a view of her grandfather's gas station in a small town in Minnesota in 1915, the Teich Archives located a 1915 postcard printed to celebrate the opening of his new business of the gas station, with her grandfather standing in front of the building.

SUMMARY

In *Historic Preservation* Magazine, Kim Keister called the content of the Teich Archives, "like the nation it portrays . . . vast, complex, populist, and sometimes tacky. Views of small towns capture the commonality of Main Street America (there are over 10,000 towns and cities represented in the Teich Archives). Early views of larger urban centers show assemblies of modest nineteenth century vernacular storefronts. In the 1920s and 1930s cityscapes produced such historicist confections as Chicago's Wrigley Building and such art deco spectacles as New York City's Empire State Building, the Rockefeller Complex, and the Chrysler Building."[1] Author and cultural observer Lena Lencek explains, "For the American metropolis, these [postcard] . . . images have come to be the analogue of snapshots in the family album, chronicling the moods and growth patterns of the urban space."[2] Photographer Walker Evans also pays tribute to the postcard as documentary and emotional artifact:

One can, in effect, re-enter these homely old pictures and situate oneself upon those pavements in downtown Cleveland, Chicago, or Springfield, Massachusetts. One can penetrate these extraordinarily unbeautiful buildings that were, withal, accented with good marble and mahogany and brass.[3]

The postcard was one of the earliest commercial uses of photography and its potential as a visual document for twentieth century cultural studies is vast. Photography's rise in popularity after 1900 mirrored the concurrent growth and exponential changes in the North American built environment, and in the social fabric. Which objects, structures, and documents best symbolize a common experience shared among the greatest number of people? Perhaps a case can be made for the aggressive and comprehensive collection of postcards as *the common document* of the first three quarters of the North American twentieth century. On their familiar surfaces were recorded every aspect of life in the twentieth century; family, community pride, consumerism, industry, the news. Other libraries, archives, and historical institutions collect postcards relative to their individual interpretive scope. The Teich Archives is one of the largest publicly held collections of postcards anywhere, devoted exclusively to the postcard as a document type, that combines the systemic and comprehensive industrial archives of the world's largest volume printer of postcards, with a growing accumulation of postcards from private collections.

NOTES

1. Kim Keister "Wish You Were Here" *Historic Preservation* 44:57-61, 1992 (#2).
2. Lena Lencek "Architecture the Way It Was" *Metropolis*, 1988 (March).
3. Walker Evans "Main Street Looking North from Court House Square: A Portfolio of Postcards from the Trolley Car" *Fortune* 37:102, 1948 (May).

The Institute of American Deltiology: An Emerging Resource

Donald R. Brown

PURPOSE AND FUNCTIONS

The Institute of American Deltiology (IAD), a postcard research center, was incorporated as a non-profit operating foundation on December 28, 1993 in Myerstown, Pennsylvania. Its collections include approximately 400,000 picture postcards supplemented by a library of 2,000 books, booklets, typescript monographs, subscriptions to 60 periodical publications, and approximately 1,200 slides of postcards from the collection. The focus of the IAD is on the picture postcard as a resource for the study and documentation of the American heritage, particularly local history, material culture with an architectural emphasis, and popular culture. The collection priorities for the IAD are:

- Postcards printed and published by North American firms.
- Real photographic postcards from all fifty states and other parts of North America.
- Postcards relating to each of Pennsylvania's 67 counties, regardless of subject or place of publication, with a particular emphasis on postcards from rural areas, small towns, and urban neighborhoods.
- The literature of deltiology, particularly the bulletins and newsletters of various North American postcard collectors' clubs.

The primary purposes of the IAD are:

- To educate the public in the Commonwealth of Pennsylvania, the United States, and North America on the role and significance of the

[Haworth co-indexing entry note]: "The Institute of American Deltiology: An Emerging Resource." Brown, Donald R. Co-published simultaneously in *Popular Culture in Libraries* (The Haworth Press, Inc.) Vol. 3, No. 2, 1995, pp. 17-25; and: *Postcards in the Library: Invaluable Visual Resources* (ed: Norman D. Stevens) The Haworth Press, Inc., 1995, pp. 17-25. Single or multiple copies of this article are available from The Haworth Document Delivery Service [1-800-342-9678, 9:00 a.m. - 5:00 p.m. (EST)].

picture postcard as a document for the study and interpretation of local history.
- To enhance and promote public appreciation of, and participation in,
  the collection and study of picture postcards.
- To establish a research facility, featuring a library and a museum, for
  the collection, study, preservation, application, public display, and
  enjoyment of historically meaningful, and graphically significant,
  picture postcards.

The specific activities by which the IAD seeks to carry out its purposes are:

- Establishing a permanent headquarters in a historically significant
  building, which was formerly a general store, in Myerstown, Pennsylvania (see Photograph 1). The site, which is owned by the founder
  of the IAD, is provided for use by the IAD free of charge. The IAD
  building will eventually house:

  - A library and museum of postcards arranged by subject, geographical
    region, or other appropriate criteria. The library and museum collec-
    tion will be available for public use and viewing at regular hours as
    available staffing, including volunteers, allow. At this time, several
    deltiologists and historians in the area have indicated a willingness to
    assist on a volunteer basis with the staffing of the IAD library and
    museum and the coordination of its activities.

    - Archival facilities for the sorting, filing, cataloging, storage, and
      preservation of significant postcards.

    - Research facilities for the further study of all aspects of deltiology.

- Lending and borrowing of postcards between the IAD and other libraries, museums, historical agencies, publishers, authors, editors,
  and individuals engaged in postcard based research.
- Offering public lectures and visual presentations designed to
  introduce the public to the field of deltiology, and to encourage the
  preservation of postcards as an important component of the historical record.
- Conducting forums and symposia, in cooperation with other experts
  in the field, designed to explore better methods for the preservation,
  study, and use of postcards.
- Fostering scholarly research projects in the field of deltiology both
  alone and in conjunction with libraries, museums, historical agencies, and academic institutions, and making the results of such re-

search available to the public through the publication of articles, books, catalogs, and other miscellaneous publications.

BACKGROUND AND ORIGINS OF THE IAD

The picture postcard emerged during the late nineteenth century from the plain governmental postals that were first introduced in Austria in 1869 as a means of brief and convenient communication. The United States issued its first postals in 1873. Early on, a few of those postal cards were illustrated to advertise businesses and their products and, in 1893, as souvenirs of the World's Columbian Exposition in Chicago. It was during the first decade of the twentieth century that picture postcards, by then privately printed, flowed like an avalanche down the American slopes as a means of recording the appearances of our towns and countryside, our buildings and events, and our families. That avalanche created what has become an extremely useful archive for the study of American history and material culture. It also created the first wave of intense interest in post-card collecting that, after World War I, receded, as the publication, distribution, and use of postcards ebbed. From the 1920s through the 1940s there were, however, a small band of dedicated postcard collectors who kept the hobby alive.

For Donald R. Brown, the founder of the IAD, it was the discovery that postcards were an extension to publications such as *National Geographic,* especially as an alternative to travel during World War II, that led to initial interest in collecting postcards. The local community librarian encouraged his interest in postcards by providing direction to *Hobbies Magazine* with its monthly column "The Picture Post Card" and its listings of sources for the purchase of postcards by mail. By 1946 he had become an active member of the Post Card Collectors' Club of America (PCCA), a pioneer organization for that hobby. Exchanging postcards and information by mail with dozens of collectors on the national roster of the PCCA established a pattern of collection development that continues to the present time. At the time he graduated from high school, his collection numbered 20,000 postcards arranged geographically. The first public display of his collection took place at the Myerstown Community Fair in 1947. Since then postcards from his ever-growing collection have been shared for a wide assortment of popular and research oriented projects.

That teenage collector eventually undertook graduate studies in American History followed by a course of professional education in library science. As his formal learning expanded, so did the size and scope of his

PHOTOGRAPH 1. Headquarters of the Institute of American Deltiology

Note:　The Institute of American Deltiology, 300 West Main Avenue, Myerstown, Lebanon County, PA, 717-866-7747. Building, neo-classical in design in the vernacular. Built 1849 by Thomas Bassler, entrepreneur on the Union Canal and local education leader. Corner space housed General Store, 1850s-1929, 1940s-1950s. Purchased, July 8, 1982 by Donald R. Brown, Myerstown native, for a postcard research center. The Institute of American Deltiology was incorporated here December 28, 1993 by Donald R. Brown. This postcard produced by Nancy Gambler, Lebanon, PA, 1993. Photo taken on May 31, 1993. Background church–Myerstown United Church of Christ.
Reprinted with permission. The Institute of American Deltiology, Myerstown, PA.

postcard collection. Its contents reflected his changing interests and tastes as well as those of the time.

During the 1950s and the 1960s, the hobby of postcard collecting changed as large numbers of people with diverse educational backgrounds and interests took up collecting. By this time the hobby became to be referred to as deltiology and postcard collectors came to be called deltiologists. The term deltiology was coined in November 1944 when Rendell Rhoades, a collector from Blanchester, Ohio, accepted a challenge from Bob Hendricks, then editor of *Post Card Collectors Magazine,* to find fitting names for the hobby that would identify postcard collecting in the same way that terms philately and philatelist identified stamp collecting and stamp collectors. Rhoades contacted Ethel M. Miller, a librarian at Ohio State University, who, in turn, consulted Dr. K. M. Abbott of the Classical Languages Department. They recommended deltiology, derived from the Greek words deltion (a small illustrated tablet or image) and logos (the science or study of knowledge), to designate the hobby and deltiologist to designate the collector.

By the end of the 1960s deltiology had taken on new life. A handful of publications about the history and variety of postcards had appeared especially in England and Europe. In America, catalogs listing pioneer card issues had been published and the first price guides to antique postcards had begun to appear. Local postcard collectors' clubs, many of which were formed in the years immediately after World War II, flourished and now issued bulletins containing the results of deltiological research on artists, postcard photographers, printers and publishers, and unique sets and subjects. There are now over 100 collectors' clubs in North America of which about a dozen publish bulletins containing articles of substance. The IAD, in an effort to preserve the work of those collectors and their clubs, makes an effort to collect complete runs of those bulletins with the intention of eventually indexing their contents.

THE CONTENTS AND ARRANGEMENT
OF THE IAD COLLECTIONS

Donald R. Brown's ever growing personal postcard collections have formed the basis for the collections of the IAD. Those collections continue to grow based, as before, largely on myriad daily contacts and sources that are familiar to any practicing deltiologist. Among those are mail purchases from sources found in the deltiological literature, the generosity of friends and acquaintances, contacts made at public programs and workshops, and regular attendance at postcard shows and paper memorabilia bourses.

During the 1960s, he spent considerable time establishing subject files to complement his original geographical files for the postcards that now comprise the collections of the IAD. As a result the subject files now consist of at least 700 categories, separated by reinforced acid-free labeled dividers, with standardized cross-references to other points in the subject files and, occasionally, to points in the geographic files. There are at least 90,000 postcards in the subject files and approximately ten percent of those cards are duplicated in the geographical files. The geographical files, because of the typical content of postcards, continue to house by far the larger part of the collection. It now contains at least 270,000 postcards of which at least 110,000 are from Pennsylvania.

The Pennsylvania collection is arranged by both subject and location. The subject portion of that collection contains approximately 11,000 cards under such categories as arts and crafts, building types, historical periods, industries, types of libraries, occupations, religious denominations, studio photographers, and transportation. The larger quantity of cards in the geographical portion of that collection are divided, first, into separate segments for lithographic cards and real photographic cards. Within each segment, the postcards are arranged geographically county-by-county and within each county by the name of the place depicted.

Subject headings are assigned to reflect the collection's patterns of use, whether for the general study of popular culture or for academic research, and will continue to evolve on that basis. Broad categories in the subject files currently cover such topics as advertising, architecture, expositions and fairs, postcard printers/publishers, and signed artists/illustrators. Those categories are further subdivided by the specific names of firms or individuals or appropriate modes or topics. The advertising category alone, for example, contains over a hundred sub-headings such as: Advertising–Farming–Equipment; Advertising–Farming–Products; Advertising–Books; Advertising–Periodicals; Advertising–Transportation–Automobiles; and Advertising–Transportation–Buses.

American architecture comprises another main segment of the subject files. At least 12,000 postcards are arranged in those files by chronological period or historical style as well as under the names of individual architects and firms. The documentation that the IAD collections provide for the architecture and history of Chicago is typical of the strength of those collections and the arrangement of those collections are typical of the range of access that is provided. The Chicago School category in the subject files, for example, contains hundreds of postcards filed alphabetically under the names of architects and their firms. There are an additional 11,000 postcards documenting the history of Chicago in the geographical files under Illinois–Chicago. Those, in turn, are filed under dozens of sub-categories such as businesses and products, churches, colleges, industries, libraries, medical facilities, modes of transit, organizations, parks, schools, sports facilities, and transportation facilities. When identifiable, Chicago cards may also be arranged by specific neighborhoods, ethnic groups, activities, and/or events. Postcards produced by most processes are included in one or the other of those files.

For the most part, however, real photographic postcards are grouped together in the geographical files where they are further arranged alphabetically by the name of the photographer when known. Postcards produced by the well known early twentieth century photographer Charles Child, of Chicago, are, for example, filed under Illinois–Real Photos–Photographers–Childs, Charles. Since the archives of the Charles Child studio are housed at the Chicago Historical Society, the IAD devotes little effort to collecting his postcards. That demonstrates the coordinated acquisition and referral policies that have been adopted by the IAD even though they have not yet been fully documented.

The postcards of the IAD are physically maintained and preserved in double-drawer 15″ × 16″ steel units. Over two-thirds of the cards have been placed in clear polyethylene sleeves to protect their surfaces. Only a few of the postcards are currently housed in archival quality Mylar sleeves. Such sleeves are preferred, of course, but cost remains a prohibitive factor that will be addressed only after other priorities relating to improved electrical support and climate control have been funded. Rare and valuable cards, which includes those with a value of more than $50, are stored in climate-controlled bank security locations.

A DREAM COMING TRUE

Midway through Donald R. Brown's library career he conceived the idea of establishing a multi-functional institution dedicated to conserving, exhibiting, and sharing postcards and making them available for research. In 1969 that idea was only a dream. The opening of the Curt Teich Postcard Archives at the Lake County Museum in Wauconda, Illinois in the early 1980s provided the world of American deltiology with its first real dedicated gallery, library, and research facility. The Curt Teich Archives provided a useful model for the founder of the IAD as he contemplated whether a similar facility, based on his collections, would ever be desirable or feasible.

In the interval, every opportunity was taken to share postcards from his growing collections for displays in libraries, at commercial locations, at church and community events, and at postcard club shows throughout the eastern half of the United States. The club shows, in particular, provided an excellent visual forum for demonstrating the multiple dimensions of postcards as documents of communication and the graphic arts as well as of local history, social history, and popular culture.

Postcards often provide the only authentic insights into the daily activities in, and appearances of, urban and rural neighborhoods. This is most true of the images on real photo postcard stock especially when they also contain messages sent to family and friends. Real photo postcards were usually produced in very limited quantities. They portray the activities, attitudes, and tastes of bygone eras and show material culture in the vernacular as few other sources can. The size and strength of the real photo postcard images in the Brown collection had a major influence on the development of the IAD.

Without being aware of the plans for the location of the Curt Teich Archives at the Lake County Museum, the founder of the IAD took an important first step towards the establishment of another postcard research facility in the early 1980s. He purchased a sizable 1849 building in Myerstown in the heart of the Lebanon Valley in eastern Pennsylvania. A ground-floor corner of the three story building had been used for a general merchandise store from 1867 until it closed in 1929. During the next four decades, the building, which was the home of Myerstown's longtime librarian, served as the location for many community activities including the planning of the community's public library in 1936. It was on this site that the IAD was incorporated in December 1993.

The corner commercial space has been restored as closely as possible to its appearance in 1849 although, of course, there is no postcard to depict it as it appeared at that time. Two new wooden counters have been constructed under which there is space for metal files housing approximately 300,000 postcards. Electrical circuits are now being strengthened to provide for the application of electronic technologies that will allow for the cataloging and duplicating of postcards on the premises. In the meantime, postcards from the IAD collection are made available for popular culture and other research projects using the existing geographical and subject files.

The Institute of American Deltiology is located at 300 West Main Street in Myerstown, PA 17067. It is a private non-profit foundation, established in late 1993 by Donald R. Brown, that is open to the public. At this time, appointments to use the collections of the IAD are recommended. Please call 717-866-7747.

APPENDIX

IAD Publications

"Short Historic Survey of the Post Card in the U. S. A." (10 p. typescript) $2.00.

First developed as a handout for the June 1977 Detroit program of the History Section, Reference and Adult Services Division, of the American Library Association, this survey is revised periodically. In addition to providing basic information about the history of American postcards, it addresses the role of postcards in research, their preservation, and their place in archives and libraries.

"Picture Postcards: Yesterday's Heritage, Tomorrow's History" (6 p. typescript) $2.00.

Produced in April 1991, this document outlines the chronological development of picture postcards from the plain governmental postals first authorized in Austria in 1869, and in the United States in 1873, to the present time. Changes in format, chief publishers and printers, and sketches of the key eras in the history of postcards in North America are described and dated.

"The Picture Post Card: Aspects Useful for Genealogy Searchers" (8 p. typescript) $2.00.

This resource handout to accompany a slide program developed for genealogical organizations was produced in August 1994. It includes, along with a brief history of postcards, specific information on the value of postcards in genealogical research including how to date postcards, sources, and useful reference guides.

REPRESENTATIVE LIBRARY
COLLECTIONS

Pacific Northwest
and Other Postcard Treasures
in the University of Washington Libraries

Richard H. Engeman

At the University of Washington, we keep some of our best research materials down in the basement, in the Special Collections and Preservation Division. Here we keep not only the Libraries' rare books and regional histories, but also the paper ephemera, the posters and broadsides, the menus and maps and engravings and photographs and architectural renderings, and the postcards: all materials of great visual interest, but materials whose research value is only beginning to be understood and exploited by academic researchers.

There is no denying that the world relies more and more on visual materials to convey information, and scholars no less than the rest of society find that they not only use images, but that they must now study how they are used, how they can be used, and what they mean. Images,

[Haworth co-indexing entry note]: "Pacific Northwest and Other Postcard Treasures in the University of Washington Libraries." Engeman, Richard H. Co-published simultaneously in *Popular Culture in Libraries* (The Haworth Press, Inc.) Vol. 3, No. 2, 1995, pp. 27-34; and: *Postcards in the Library: Invaluable Visual Resources* (ed: Norman D. Stevens) The Haworth Press, Inc., 1995, pp. 27-34. Single or multiple copies of this article are available from The Haworth Document Delivery Service [1-800-342-9678, 9:00 a.m. - 5:00 p.m. (EST)].

omitted for years from academic journals as mere expensive and frivolous adjuncts to text, have begun to take a rightful place as meaningful evidence, or as a concise paradigm, or even as essential elements of a thesis. All of these visual materials present problems of authenticity, accuracy, interpretation; but the problems parallel those of textual evaluation, and we can expect that the problems will be dealt with as visual materials assume a larger place in the library and research environment.

ORIGIN OF COLLECTION

The University of Washington Libraries' postcard collection originated with a faculty member, Caroline Ober, who taught Spanish at the university from 1897 to 1929 (see Illustration 1). From a very early date, Professor Ober was a notable victim of the postcard craze, and she actively initiated postcard trades with dozens of other collectors around the world. She also used postcards to maintain close ties with many of her former pupils and with her well-traveled family. She made sure that her correspondents both received and sent a wide variety of cards, and many of the recipients eventually gave the cards she sent back to her.

For many years the Ober postcards, which had been separated from her papers in the University Archives, idled away in bundles piled into old liquor boxes in a basement storeroom. Several years ago, however, they emerged from the liquor boxes and were rehabilitated to form the core of the present postcard collection.

Professor Ober's catholic interests resulted not only in cards from such popular places as England and France, but also from Spanish-language nations (Argentina, Cuba, Ecuador) and places to which she traveled (Japan and China); Russia, too, is well-represented. Also abundant are the cards for holidays, political cartoons, advertising items, portraits, generic greetings, and photocards and homemade postcards.

CONTENT, SCOPE, AND SIZE

The original Ober collection is especially strong in cards from the Pacific Northwest, British Columbia, and Alaska. Regional history is a primary collection effort in Special Collections, and so we have built upon this emphasis. Within the region, we have especially sought out images depicting Native Americans, architecture and the built environment, and industries such as logging and agriculture (see Illustration 2).

ILLUSTRATION 1. This postcard announcing an Esperanto conference in Bucharest in 1909 was collected by Caroline Ober who was a professor of romance languages as well as an avid postcard collector.

Reprinted with permission. Special Collections Division, University of Washington Libraries, FM-25, Seattle, WA 98195 (UW Neg. #15116).

ILLUSTRATION 2. The eagle, star, and two flags on this postcard suggest that Buffalo Bill Cody represents all of America and not just the West.

COLONEL WILLIAM F. CODY. (BUFFALO BILL.)

Since Special Collections also houses the book arts collection and has strong holdings relating to the graphic arts, we have also emphasized acquiring cards that use unusual materials (such as wood, metal, leather, fabric, etc.), that demonstrate particular printing processes, or that are graphically appealing or unusual.

We have not made an exact count of the collection but we did do an estimate some years ago; we then continued to add a count of new acquisitions to this figure. Our present estimate, then, is 57,771 cards, perhaps 20% of which relate to the Pacific Northwest.

CURRENT COLLECTING PATTERNS AND SOURCES

A small budget permits the purchase of some cards, usually regional photocards. Most other cards are acquired through donation, sometimes through longtime friends who know our wants and needs. For a number of years, for example, one friend frequented local antique shops and flea markets, where she purchased postcards and gave them to us as an annual present. Her choices were often eclectic, but the sheer quantity brought us many important cards and helped round out the collection's geographical coverage. Many library staff contribute recent postcards, and the Manuscripts and University Archives Division has transferred to us unused cards found in personal and faculty papers.

Regional photo cards are the most common purchase. The limited quantity available, and their high collectibility, mean they are less likely to arrive as donations. Local book and paper ephemera dealers are the usual sources, but some items are found at antique and collectible shops, or at garage sales.

LOCATION, ORGANIZATION, AND ARRANGEMENT

Perhaps 90% of the postcards have been arranged by topic or locality; the categories were locally devised and are rather idiosyncratic, but at present they are workable. There are also a number of postcards which are housed in archival collections, i.e., they are kept together by photographer or collector. These are accessible as a genre through our database of photographic collections.

All regional cards are protected by Mylar sleeves and filed in locked metal file cabinets. All other cards are kept in archival "shoeboxes" in our locked stack area. Mylar sleeves are frequently placed on these cards, too, if they have earned them, such as those with fragile parts (glitter, a small calendar, real photo cards, etc.). Users fill out a registration card to use graphics materials such as postcards, and are given instructions in care and handling, including the use of gloves with unsleeved postcards.

RESEARCH VALUE AND USE

As pieces of paper ephemera, postcards have frequently been dismissed as useful sources of information or as significant research materials. But they do have value, and the value has become increasingly apparent to researchers. Postcards are valuable as individual items for illustrative purposes, and they can be useful in quantity as markers of popular taste and attitudes. Their appeal is often heightened today (despite the obvious likelihood of inauthenticity) because they may provide the only image of a building or scene in color, and the ease of color reproduction, too, is altering our perception of the value of images in conveying information.

Examining postcards of a town or city can quickly establish what features or characteristics of the place were seen as distinctive or valuable. Postcard publishers hoped to issue cards that would appeal both to tourists and to residents, who frequently sent cards to friends and relatives who might never visit the place. Cards depicting public buildings, railroad stations, parks, and busy streets were in effect benchmarks of civic achievement. They enabled both visitors and out-of-towners to see exactly how well the city compared with others.

Library exhibits curated by Special Collections staff frequently use postcards, and one was in fact devoted to them: " 'Hope to be there on Monday': the Postcard and the Western Traveler." In this exhibit, postcard images and messages were used along with tourist brochures and booklets, snapshots, and souvenirs to depict the changing role of tourism in the American West as the automobile became the major mode of travel. Among the themes that became apparent during the development of the exhibit was the American society's fascination with certain aspects of Western scenery. The largest trees, the highest falls, the deepest canyons, the most colorful geothermal pots, the most convoluted and contorted landscapes: the West of the postcard was a phantasmagoria of nature. The exhibit title was derived from a message found on the back of a card, and it is representative of millions of such messages sent in the days when an auto trip in the West was filled with exhilarating uncertainties.

Other Special Collections exhibits have made good use of postcards, such as those we have done on the railroad influence on Pacific Northwest settlement patterns (many railroad-issued cards promoted agricultural and industrial opportunities), the sesquicentennial of the Oregon Trail (a notable series of cards was published by "professional pioneer" Ezra Meeker, who crossed the plains in a covered wagon, and did it again decades later by auto, train, plane, and again by covered wagon!), hotels and hospitality in the Pacific Northwest, and the place of mountains and mountaineering in regional consciousness.

"Yugoslavian Costume: A Tribute to Blanche Payne" was a recent University Libraries exhibit that included many postcards. Payne was a pioneer costume historian and University professor who traveled in what was then Yugoslavia in the 1930s, collecting textile and costume samples, taking photographs, commissioning sketches, and collecting postcards that documented regional costume. The recent destruction of libraries and other cultural repositories in this region has given Payne's collection, including her postcards, an unanticipated value and importance.

The journal *Pacific Northwest Quarterly*, published at the University, carries a regular short feature, "Primary Sources," to bring new or neglected regional historical collections to the attention of researchers, and our postcard collection was the topic in the July 1992 issue. When the feature was submitted, the journal was also seeking illustrations for another article that described a transcontinental auto tour made in 1924. The submission of the postcard feature prompted a visit from the editor, who eventually included the auto tour article in the same issue as the postcard collection description. Among the illustrations used in the auto tour piece are seven postcard views from our collection, as well as two from other sources. Postcards provided, for example, the scene of the spectacular highway loops approaching Lewiston, Idaho, in the canyon of the Snake River; a street scene in the small town of Hood River, Oregon; and the bungalow-style Garden Court Tourist Park in Boise, Idaho.

When a lecturer needed images of vernacular architecture in the West, his successful search of our postcard collection was transformed into slides of postcard views of Main Street scenes, mining structures, and motels. An anthropology graduate student culled the collection for risqué images, for a study of popular attitudes about sex. Another graduate student, in art history, surveyed the numerous postcards that depict Native American women in stereotyped situations, such as poses that suggest the Madonna and child; these again are reflective of popular perceptions. The messages on such cards often provide additional bits of evidence about popular attitudes: "This is quite Western, isn't it? Did you ever see an Indian squaw? We see them here in Seattle in numbers about hop-picking time."

As that quote also suggests, cards raise questions as often as they help answer them. There is surely an explanation for the fact that during the

1910s, for example, Halloween cards frequently carried a romantic message along with (or in place of) one tied to black cats and witches. Other holidays such as St. Patrick's Day also exhibit romantic overtones on postcards. The iconography of postcards, along with other popular published images, is due for some study.

Since so many researchers are unaware of postcards as a distinct visual resource, the Special Collections staff has made an effort to direct them to the postcard collection. We are well known for our collection of historical and regional photographs, and the postcards provide a valuable supplement to that collection in many fields. It has been more difficult to make researchers aware of our resources when their interests are in fields not connected with regional history–fields such as art, sociology, anthropology, geography, area studies, or political science. Exhibits, the Libraries' newsletter for faculty and staff, and classroom presentations by Special Collections staff, have been our principal means of advertising. In the very near future, on-line information–including images–about Special Collections and its holdings promises an even wider audience. The prospect of making postcard images available electronically is enticing. We may eventually find that libraries are the accepted place to preserve, catalog, and authenticate original postcard images, while their electronic surrogates are what is in common use.

Postcards presently hold a small but fascinating place as visual tidbits and pop culture touchstones, and they have value in library collections even for these purposes. But postcards can also be used to seriously address other historical and esthetic issues, especially when researchers can examine and evaluate dozens or hundreds of examples. Library collections are what can make this kind of study possible.

Why Libraries Collect Postcards:
Two Case Studies

Lois R. Densky-Wolff

INTRODUCTION

Documenting and promoting an interest in local history by libraries often entails the creative use of available resources. Collecting postcards for research, exhibition, and publication value is one excellent way to achieve such a goal. Postcards can be acquired at reasonable cost to establish a discrete collection that can broadly document a specific subject or locale. One academic and one local library in New Jersey have developed postcard collections to graphically illustrate, on the one hand, medical history in the state of New Jersey, and, on the other hand, the history and development of Morristown and the surrounding area.

The Special Collections Department at the University of Medicine and Dentistry of New Jersey (UMDNJ) is a history of medicine collection with a special focus on the history of health sciences in New Jersey. The Local History and Genealogy Department at The Joint Free Public Library of Morristown and Morris Township (Morristown-Morris Township Library) specializes in New Jerseyana particularly of the Morristown, Morris Township, and Morris County area. These two libraries are representative libraries that have benefited from collecting, preserving, and using postcards to achieve their collection development goals by augmenting the visual record.

UNIVERSITY OF MEDICINE
AND DENTISTRY OF NEW JERSEY

UMDNJ is New Jersey's university of the health sciences offering academic programs at seven schools on campuses in Newark, Piscataway/

[Haworth co-indexing entry note]: "Why Libraries Collect Postcards: Two Case Studies." Densky-Wolff, Lois R. Co-published simultaneously in *Popular Culture in Libraries* (The Haworth Press, Inc.) Vol. 3, No. 2, 1995, pp. 35-39; and: *Postcards in the Library: Invaluable Visual Resources* (ed: Norman D. Stevens) The Haworth Press, Inc., 1995, pp. 35-39. Single or multiple copies of this article are available from The Haworth Document Delivery Service [1-800-342-9678, 9:00 a.m. - 5:00 p.m. (EST)].

New Brunswick, Stratford, and Camden. The schools of the University are the New Jersey Medical School, New Jersey Dental School, Robert Wood Johnson Medical School, School of Osteopathic Medicine, School of Nursing, Graduate School of Biomedical Sciences, and School of Health Related Professions. The University Libraries System serves faculty, staff, students, and researchers at free-standing campus libraries. The Special Collections Department of UMDNJ is administered by the University Libraries and serves the entire University community but is physically located at the George F. Smith Library of the Health Sciences on the Newark Campus.

The mission statement in the department's collection development policy asserts that it "collects, maintains, preserves, promotes and provides access to materials documenting the history of medicine in general, United States and New Jersey history of medicine in particular, and UMDNJ history. Resources include rare books, books, pamphlets, journals, ephemera, original documents, broadsides, posters, manuscripts, oral histories, trade catalogues, almanacs, illustrations, indexes, photographs, videotapes, audiotapes, slides and postcards."[1]

Special Collections, a relatively young collection,[2] began acquiring photographs in 1986. Departmental staff realized that by developing a topical postcard collection they could acquire photographic images systematically for many New Jersey medical subjects for which original photographs are difficult, if not impossible, to locate. Postcards documenting the history of the health sciences in New Jersey have been actively sought by the Department since 1990.

The collections currently totals 292 postcards representing 138 hospitals, asylums, sanitariums, pharmaceutical companies, pharmaceutical advertising, pharmacies, and miscellaneous medical subjects; ninety-nine distinct New Jersey hospitals are represented. Postcards dating from the golden era of postcard production at the turn of the century through the modern era provide a broad spectrum of images complementing the department's photographic collections. Seventeen postcards are "real photos" contributing particularly unique images of New Jersey medical topics, such as a 1929 view of the defunct Bonnie Burns Tuberculosis Hospital in Berkeley Heights and the Marquier Pharmacy in East Orange in 1906.

"Hospital Postcards: The New Jersey View" was organized as a mini-exhibit at the Smith Library in the fall of 1992 to commemorate the 100th anniversary of the U.S. picture postcard in 1993 by highlighting over thirty-five postcard images from the collection. The exhibit was also regarded as a valuable way to promote and publicize the growing postcard collection. It was later converted into a traveling exhibit and shown at the Health Sciences Library at Stratford, the campus library for the School of Osteopathic Medicine.

The research, and many original exhibit labels from, "Hospital Postcards: The New Jersey View," was used as the basis for a two-part pictorial article published in the state medical journal.[3] The New Jersey physicians responded positively to the article, which was gratifying to the Department since this is an audience it especially wanted to reach.

THE JOINT FREE PUBLIC LIBRARY
OF MORRISTOWN AND MORRIS TOWNSHIP

The Morristown-Morris Township Library is a medium-sized suburban public library located in Morristown, the county seat. The library's primary constituency is the townspeople of Morristown, Morris Township and the surrounding area. Established as a private association library in the nineteenth century, the Morristown-Morris Township Library's collections contain many rare books and manuscripts donated by early association members that form the basis of the Local History and Genealogy Department's collections.

The Local History and Genealogy Department contains a strong collection of books, manuscripts, photographs, maps, newspapers, microforms, oral histories, artwork, and postcards documenting New Jersey with special emphasis on Morristown, Morris Township, and Morris County history and genealogy. The department's geographically-related postcard collection was initiated many years ago by former librarians to augment the visual record contained in the photograph collection.

The postcard collection totals approximately 2,300 postcards of which 170 are "real photo" postcards. The collection is a rich resource that complements and often supplements the library's extensive photograph collection when requested views are not available in the photographic holdings. The postcards date from the "private mailing card" era of 1898 to the modern era, and primarily document buildings and architecture, places, and local events.

The collection provides a fascinating look at Morristown and vicinity in the first quarter of the twentieth century. Standard views include businesses, churches, fire departments, historic and public buildings, hospitals, hotels and taverns, railroad stations, residences, schools, streets, trolleys, and other topics specific to the history of Morristown, such as the Morris Canal and artist-signed postcards by Thomas Nast, Jr. A number of the "real photo" postcards provide examples of the work of early Morristown or Morris County photographers, or bear the imprint of early Morristown stationers. The extent to which the collection documents the locality has led to a broadening of the collecting scope to include more New Jersey postcards.

The Morristown-Morris Township Library postcard collection has been utilized primarily in conjunction with exhibitions. Numerous displays promoting New Jersey and local history, or to promote regional and national events, have used postcards exclusively or to enhance other materials on exhibit.

In 1991, for instance, postcards of Ft. Nonsense, the Ford Mansion, and Jockey Hollow were displayed to commemorate the rededications of Ft. Nonsense by the Morristown National Historical Park. An exhibit on Speedwell Ironworks was installed using postcards to complement a new ironworks exhibit at nearby History Speedwell in 1992. In April 1993 to observe National Library Week, a display on the Morristown-Morris Township Library was developed partially with views from postcards. Commemorating National Preservation Week in May 1993, postcards depicting historic Morristown residences were displayed. Reproduction postcards of the Christmas drawings of Thomas Nast are often used to accompany other holiday displays each winter.

Thomas Nast (1840-1902), a Morristown resident from 1872 until his death, was an illustrator and cartoonist whose work in *Harper's Weekly* brought him wealth and renown. Publications bearing his illustrations are actively collected by the Local History and Genealogy Department. His death preceded the active postcard collection period prior to World War I. The Library does collect Nast reproduction postcards and the original postcards by his son, Thomas Nast, Jr. (1865-1942). He was primarily a graphic artist who in 1905 published a series of "lovely lady" postcards that the Morristown-Morris Township Library has acquired; some of these postcards were used to illustrate an article about Nast Jr.'s life.[4]

A significant example of how the Morristown and Morris Township Library has used its postcard collection to promote its graphic collections is a book published by the Library on local history.[5] While heavily emphasizing the photograph collections, the book included a number of postcard views that illustrated the text. Another instance in which postcards from the collection were used is a local photographer who copied selected Morristown street views, blew up the images, hand tinted the prints, and sold the resulting artwork.

CONCLUSION

Postcard collecting is more than the acquisition of ephemeral material. Postcards provide libraries with the opportunity to acquire views impossible to get anywhere else. This is especially true for "real photo" postcards which depict unique views and are often one of a kind images.

The sheer quantity of postcards produced during the height of the postcard collecting craze between 1900 and World War I means there is "better pictorial documentation represented in postcards of American life and culture than from most other sources."[6]

Most printed postcards were made by professional not amateur photographers, resulting in postcards with excellent production values. These photographers, however, sometimes produced more mundane views since the profitability factor meant each view had to reach the widest audience. "Real photo" postcards made by amateurs often produced the most serendipitous results. While professional photographers might document special town, regional, or national events, the amateurs were more likely to capture that view of grandma's house, or the family sitting on the front porch in all their Edwardian splendor. In a local history collection, these views often are the more valuable to the library because they depict everyday life at a certain moment in time and place in this country's past.

But unique "real photo" postcards are not the only reason for libraries to establish, maintain, and use postcard collections. As demonstrated by the examples of UMDNJ's Special Collections Department and the Morristown and Morris Township Library's Local History and Genealogy Department, libraries benefit by developing another resource that can be utilized by themselves, and their patrons, in ways which enrich both their collections and services.

NOTES

1. *University of Medicine & Dentistry Guide for the Development of Special Collections* [Newark, NJ : UMDNJ], November 1990, p. 4.

2. For a history and complete description of the collection see, B.S. Irwin. "The Legacy of New Jersey Physician Book Collectors," *New Jersey Medicine* Vol. 89, No. 11 (Nov. 1992), pp. 829-832.

3. L.R. Densky-Wolff. "Hospital Postcards: The New Jersey View, Pts. I and II," *New Jersey Medicine*, Vol. 91, Nos. 2 & 3 (Feb. and Mar 1994), pp. 85-89 and 160-165.

4. L.R. Densky. "Thomas Nast, Jr.: A Son's Pursuit of His Father's Art," *Journal of The Thomas Nast Society*, Vol. 3, No. 4 (1989), pp. 3-19.

5. Cam Cavanaugh. *In Lights and Shadows: Morristown in Three Centuries*, Morristown, NJ : The Joint Free Public Library of Morristown and Morris Township, 1986.

6. R. Chris Wolff, postcard dealer and collector, in a conversation with the author.

Postcards
from the Marguerite Archer Collection:
A Treasure Trove for the Study
of Childhood

Meredith Eliassen

INTRODUCTION

The world that children create for themselves is a place where play becomes communication, exploration and learning. Every part of this world taking on special importance. Who we are as children has an impact on what we become as adults. Before the advent of radio, television and computers, and the child as a consumer, children explored the world initially with the aid of a variety of printed visual materials. They learned language through repetition and interaction with family members using hornbooks, primers0, and then, readers. Those formal methods of teaching literacy and communication have been well documented. How children informally interpret and assimilate language has not been as well documented because it enters the private world of children's play. In this article, I will describe how postcards, along with other ephemeral materials, in the Marguerite Archer Collection of Historic Children's Materials are more than souvenirs from faraway times and places, or instruments in familial communication. Postcards can be important in understanding how children learned language, symbolism and communication as they gained access into popular culture of their times.

[Haworth co-indexing entry note]: "Postcards from the Marguerite Archer Collection: A Treasure Trove for the Study of Childhood." Eliassen, Meredith. Co-published simultaneously in *Popular Culture in Libraries* (The Haworth Press, Inc.) Vol. 3, No. 2, 1995, pp. 41-49; and: *Postcards in the Library: Invaluable Visual Resources* (ed: Norman D. Stevens) The Haworth Press, Inc., 1995, pp. 41-49. Single or multiple copies of this article are available from The Haworth Document Delivery Service [1-800-342-9678, 9:00 a.m. - 5:00 p.m. (EST)].

HISTORIC CHILDREN'S MATERIALS AT SAN FRANCISCO STATE UNIVERSITY

The Marguerite Archer Collection of Historic Children's Materials of the J. Paul Leonard Library at San Francisco State University is a special collection of books and artifacts sampling the lives of children living during the nineteenth and twentieth centuries. The Archer Collection serves to support research and teaching activities of the campus and community in the areas of education, communication and other fields in the study of children and children's literature. The collection was donated to the Leonard Library by Mrs. Marguerite Archer in 1982.

Marguerite Archer, an educator, innovator, and collector, taught reading. She was the guest editor for an issue of *School Library Journal* devoted to "individualized reading." As a librarian, she explored ways of meeting children's differing styles of learning, and developed an early elementary media center in Westchester County, New York. Later she became a Professor of English and Library Science at Shippensburg State College in Pennsylvania. She was a founding member of the Assembly on Literature for Adolescents of the first National Council of Teachers of English. Mrs. Archer collected in several areas that were of interest to her, and her collecting patterns could best be described as eclectic.

Originally a collection of approximately 3,500 historical children's books, textbooks, and periodicals, as well as ephemera and realia, including puzzles, toys and educational games, the Archer Collection is a major scholarly resource that illustrates the progressive development and growth of children's literature from the early nineteenth century to 1920's. It includes many original editions of literary classics, as well as early textbooks and related teaching aids. Recently, the parameters of the Archer Collection have been expanded to include all rare and valuable children's materials held by the J. Paul Leonard Library. The Collection also includes Mrs. Archer's papers, the papers of Wilhelmina Harper, Children's Librarian for Redwood City Public Library, and a collection of historic children's books donated by Fairfax Public Library.

In 1991, the Library received an LSCA (Library Services and Construction Act) grant to create access for the Archer Collection via the INVESTIGATOR on-line catalog. As a result of this grant, almost 6,000 volumes are now accessible to students and researchers.

While books in the Archer collection can be found via the on-line catalog, there are many paper objects, card games and toys that do not appear in the library's on-line catalog. Marguerite Archer collected a wide assortment of clippings, illustrations, and bibliographies, and non-book materials that complement the book collection. Some postcards that are part of books and souvenir folders can be found by searching the on-line catalog. However, most of the postcards are available only through checking local finding aids that are available in Archives/Special Collections during regular business hours.

POSTCARDS IN THE MARGUERITE ARCHER COLLECTION OF HISTORIC CHILDREN'S MATERIALS

The collection of postcards in the Archer Collection represents an important component of our collection of artifacts. This sampling of postcards covering a century of various printing and production techniques, documents social aspects of childhood and the family along with the changing landscape of California. Although we have tried to collect materials relating only to children and childhood, many strange and wonderful words and images have found their way into our collection. Postcards are especially difficult to weed, since there are so many aspects of life, society, economics, politics and geography, that impact on children's views of the world as they grow. Postcards, as a public form of communication, were naturally part of a child's world, even if they were not sent directly for the child. A sampling of the different kinds of postcards in the Archer Collection demonstrates how illustrations communicate various themes—we have postcards with images of children and their toys, illustrations from children's books, geographic locations, and promotional and ideological messages. The Archer Collection was originally based upon the items listed in the *Peter Parley to Penrod Bibliography*. One of our major efforts has been to develop as complete a collection of the works listed there as possible. This includes newer substantial versions of these works. As a result of Mrs. Archer's original emphasis, there is already an excellent collection of certain authors and certain illustrators, both historical and current. This includes examples of certain illustrators (Greenaway, Rackham, & Nielsen) as well as examples of types or methods of illustrations (collage, silhouettes, hand-colored plates and engravings). Since literature for children in the nineteenth century concentrated on moral education, conduct of life, and religious education, the Archer Collection has a number of postcards with religious themes. There are also many examples of "Rewards of Merit" and "Birthday Greeting" cards that were given to children from school teachers and Sunday school teachers. Many were printed like postcards but were meant to be given out rather than mailed. Publishers of Sunday school literature produced weekly lesson cards with colorful illustrations on the front and lessons on the verso. Many of the Easter postcards contain religious themes, whereas the Christmas postcards are more secular with family scenes. One interesting religious post-card in the collection, "Religious Sects of Lancaster County (Pennsylvania)," depicts Quaker women walking on the street.

San Francisco State University is known for its curricular emphasis on increasing multicultural awareness. The Archer Collection has a solid core of books about various cultural groups, written in various languages and periods, reflecting different social attitudes. The postcards along with ephemeral materials have greatly strengthened this part of the collection. They serve to document many stereotypical images which have influenced generations of people around the world.

Other materials in the collection represent an interest in our local area. Over half of the postcards in our collection are of San Francisco and California. The San Francisco Bay Area has been the setting of a broad range of children's books and other materials for children. The Bay Area is also the home of a number of current children's authors and illustrators. There were a number of important early postcard companies in California several of which are represented in the Archer Collection.

There is an extensive collection of toy and moveable books in the collection that compare to novelty postcards in design and appeal. We would like to add examples to our collection. Because of their unique format style, those books are very fragile and require special care. Fairy tales, folklore and fables support many areas of the curriculum, including drama, creative writing, art and some multicultural programs. They also support education and storytelling programs. Some of the postcards in our collection have illustrations accompanied by music or nursery rhymes. They demonstrate that art for children can express extraordinary beauty and timeless wisdom. Postcards have become an important part of the Archer Collection both for instructional purposes and as visual aids in exhibits.

HIGHLIGHTS FROM THE ARCHER COLLECTION

Our sampling of postcards, in conjunction with other ephemeral paper artifacts demonstrates the breadth of private communications between children and adults as well as the quality of printing and illustration for children. Postcards, aside from the messages that may appear on the back, contain a substantial amount of information about society at a given time by documenting such things as events, patriotism, commercial advertising, and graphic art. The large scale production of commercial picture post-cards in the United States commenced with souvenirs sold at the World Colombian Exposition in Chicago in 1893. The earliest dated postcard in the Archer Collection is entitled, "Three Black Crows" (1899). The majority of cards in the collection are undated but were produced between 1900 and 1920.

ILLUSTRATORS AND THE ART OF THE POSTCARD

Children loved to get things in the mail that were just for them. One postcard from the collection that illustrates this excitement and the joy of reading is simply called "The new picture book." It shows three children reading in a big cozy wicker chair. Often picture postcards were collected just for their illustrations and were never sent. Like postage stamps and penny collections, they were affordable, available and gave children access to new worlds. Postcards signed by the artist are especially collectable, because some publishers would not print the artist's signature, due to laws requiring royalties for the artists.

One example of a popular English illustrator in the Archer Collection is a group of 25 Caldecott postcards, from original drawings by Randolph Caldecott (1846-1886), that were produced in sets of four cards. All of the Caldecott books in the collection have been well used by children. Caldecott was one of the most important and beloved illustrators of children's books of all time. His style was embraced by Edmund Evans, the most celebrated English engraver and printer of Victorian children's books in color. In our postcard collection there are examples of his illustrations from *The Queen of Hearts*, *An Elegy on the Death of a Mad Dog*, *The House that Jack Built*, *John Gilpin*, *Sing a Song for Six Pence*, and *The Three Jovial Huntsmen*. These postcards all included verses from children's poetry or nursery rhymes with illustrations from the Frederick Warne books.

Another postcard from an English illustrator is "Ride a cock horse," from the book, *English Nursery Rhymes* (English nursery rhymes. Series no. 44. London: A. & C. Black, circa 1915). This card includes a nursery rhyme with music and an enchanting illustration by Dorothy M. Wheeler depicting an elegant lady on a white horse and a little boy with a pony-on-a-stick. Dorothy M. Wheeler studied at the Blackheath School of Art where she developed her skills as a watercolorist, and landscape and figure painter. She soon received commissions from Carlton Studios and *Strand Magazine*, and developed a reputation for illustrating nursery rhymes and children's books, including the earliest of Enid Blyton's stories. Her work was regularly exhibited at the Royal Academy and the Society of Women Artists. Her illustrations from *English Nursery Rhymes* were the first to appear on postcards.

A wonderful example of American illustration is the Roosevelt Bears postcards, circa 1906-08. Our series of illustrated Roosevelt Bears were the creation of Seymour Eaton, who wrote a series of stories in rhymes illustrated by V. Floyd Campbell. These postcards, which were published in two sets, were reproductions of the color plates from the books. The first came from *Teddy B and Teddy G, the Roosevelt Bears: Their Travels and Adventures* (1906); the second was reproduced from *More about Teddy B and Teddy G: The Roosevelt Bears* (1907). We have one postcard from each set along with examples of toys, games, and china with the famous illustrations.

Jean de Brunhoff's popular French illustrations were the inspiration for a series of postcards, "Babar le petit elephant," which are photographs of costumed people. Based upon Babar, the hero of a series of picture books written and drawn by Jean de Brunhoff (1899-1937) and then his son Laurent (1925-), these photo cards are a modern adaptation of an earlier work. The Archer Collection has: "Achête un chapeau: (No. 2), "Fait de la patisserie" (No. 6), "Fait de la peinture" (No. 7), and "A la fête foraine" (No. 10). [Paris: Éditions d'art Yvon, circa 1980-1990].

GREETINGS AND OTHER MESSAGES

There are many postcards in the collection that celebrate special occasions, such as birthdays and holidays. One is a postcard printed in Bavaria which has a stork delivering a baby boy high over the rooftops of the city. You can tell it is a boy because of the black man's hat on the baby's head. Many postcards were designed to send holiday greetings. "Halloween Greetings" [0624–Printed in Saxony] warns "Beware your fate is in your own hands," and has a witch and a caldron brewing. There are a variety of Valentines, New Years, Christmas and Easter greetings in the Archer Collection, many that were printed in Germany dating from 1906 to 1920 judging by the postmarks. We also have earlier forms of cards that serve the same function as the postcards.

The Archer Collection has a few examples of humorous postcards published by the *American Journal Examiner* in 1906 that are referred to as "Magic Postcards." The instructions were to hold the postcards over heat–a gas jet, match, lamp or hot iron and see what happens. Since, in the interest of preservation, we have never attempted to do this, I don't know what the result would be–hopefully not a fire.

African-Americans were often negatively portrayed in visual images, and, perhaps, especially those, like postcards, that have their origins in popular culture. Two such postcards from the Archer Collection are "A sudden rise in wool," which depicts an African-American girl who has been startled, so that her hair is standing on end, and "Three Black Crows," which shows three African-American children playing dressed like savages [copyrighted, 1899 and published by Knaffl & Bro., Knoxville, Tenn].

In the same fashion, Asian-Americans in California were pictured on postcards with phrases like, "Velly smart boy" or comments on the verso such as: "The narrow streets of San Francisco's Chinatown continually echo to the shrill cries of native children, many of whom are gaily costumed. Street games, some Chinese and some American, are played by these youngsters."

Patriotic cards were popular when illustrated cards were still a novelty. Usually published in sets of six, they often depicted some common theme, such as Memorial Day, the Fourth of July, or one of the President's Days. About 1910, Raphael Tuck published several sets of "Decoration Day" cards (No.158) for distribution in the United States. One of these cards in the Archer collection is from a set, distinguished by a red, white and blue border, that uses the theme the "aged veteran."

The Archer Collection has a large selection of shape and linen books, paper dolls and cutouts along with postcards from the Raphael Tuck Company. The Raphael Tuck Company was first established in Germany in 1866, where it was known as the "Art publishers to Queen Alexandra." When the company moved to England, the patent was changed to "Art Publishers to their Majesties the King and Queen." Tuck's postcards came in a variety of novelty categories, such as advertising, seasonal, greetings, souvenir, photo cards, historical, views, embossed, comic, fold-out, shaped–you name it they printed it–but always with vivid colors and a lot of detail. By the turn of the century, Tuck was producing nearly 40,000 different pictorial postcards.

An extraordinary example of a book of postcards that would appeal to children, (which unfortunately is not in the Archer Collection), is the *Queen's Dolls' House* [London: Raphael Tuck & Sons; Souvenir issued by Fleetway Press Ltd., at the British Empire Exhibition in 1924]. This wonderful volume contains 48 postcards mounted in a scrapbook with authoritative descriptions on the address-side of each postcard of the Queen Mary's Dolls' House and all of its contents. The details in the illustrations and text is among the best documentation of this "mother of all doll's houses" that is available primarily because Tuck had an exclusive invitation from the Queen's Doll's House Committee to create "a faithful and permanent record of this wonderful miniature palace and its priceless contents in a manner that will appeal alike to all who have been fortunate enough to inspect it at the British Empire Exhibition and to those less happily situated." Like most Tuck cards, that book offers an image of a world far different from ours.

RESEARCH VALUE AND USE

To this point I have described some of the postcards in the Archer Collection primarily as artifacts. One of the values of postcards as a component of a larger research collection lies in the information they can provide that helps illustrate larger issues. In that respect the postcards in the Archer Collection are valuable in three ways: in presenting and understanding images of children; in understanding creativity and how children used postcards; and the role that the postcard played in familial communications.

IMAGES OF CHILDREN

From an historian's perspective, real photo cards are probably the most intriguing type of card. Postcards with children present a precious window to the history of childhood. Cards which portray children with a doll or teddy bear document not only fashions, but how children interacted with their toys. *Teddy Bears on Paper* includes a section of real photo postcards that document children of all ages with their teddy bears. These images were usually taken by itinerant photographers, or family members, with a child with his or her favorite bear and only a few cards would be produced from the negative. From these early photographic records, researchers can learn about children's clothing and dress, as well as their interaction with their toys.

For researchers interested in children and childhood, the verso of the postcard is often more interesting than the illustration on the front of the postcard, especially after postal regulations were changed to provide a divided back that allowed for a brief message as well as the address to be written on the back. Through those messages researchers can analyze descriptions of illnesses, family moves, vacations, and other happenings all of which were directly and concisely conveyed. As language usage has changed greatly in the twentieth century, postcards can document how communication has changed in the past hundred years.

Postcards are more than souvenirs from faraway times and places, they are instruments of familial communication. They are important in understanding the child's learning process of languages. Siblings, cousins, parents, grandparents, and friends could easily communicate ideas and messages. The child's ultimate process is towards adulthood. Often the first written communication that a child receives is a postcard from a relative, which gives the child a sense of self esteem. This leads to the child beginning to send short messages on postcards (sometimes illustrating the cards themselves or changing the existing illustration to suit their needs). The next step is to enclose the letter in an envelope.

Postcards in the Marguerite Archer Collection of Historic Children's Materials have become an important tool in understanding how children learn language, symbolism and communication in popular culture. Play, communications and learning come to life with the exploration of printed visual materials, as children informally interpret and assimilate language and symbols in their private world of children's play. These treasures can be found in the Special Collections/Archives Department of the J. Paul Leonard Library of San Francisco State University. That department is open to the public Monday through Thursday, from 1 p.m. to 5 p.m., and Friday, from 1 p.m. to 4 p.m. All Special Collections materials are non-circulating. For more information, call 415-338-1856.

REFERENCES

Cope, Dawn and Peter. *Illustrators of Postcards from the Nursery*. London: East West Publications, 1978. (28).

Fox, C. & Lanshoff, H. *The Doll*. New York: Abrams, 1977. (47).

Hammond, S.E.E. *Pasteless paper construction*. The Bruce Milwaukee Publishing Company, c1921. Introduction.

Hillier, Mary. *Teddy Bears: A celebration*. New York: Beaufort Books, 1985.

Laver, James. "Foreword." *The Picture Postcard & Its Origins by Frank Staff*. New York: Frederick A. Praeger. (7).

Mullins, Linda. *Teddy Bears Past & Present: A Collector's Identification Guide*. Cumberland, Maryland: Hobby House Press, Inc., 1986.

Nicholson, Susan Brown. *Teddy Bears on Paper: A carefully researched text and price guide about Teddy Bear graphics on antique paper items*. Dallas: Taylor Publishing Co., 1985.

Schoonmaker, Patricia N. *A Collector's History of the Teddy Bear*. Cumberland, Maryland: Hobby House Press, Inc., 1981.

Willard, F. W. & Wigg, P. *A Handbook of arts and crafts*. Dubuque: William C. Brown Publishers, 1985. (9-15).

California Here We Come:
The Adams Postcard Collection
at San Diego State University

Martha McPhail

THE SETTING

The John R. and Jane Adams Postcard Collection, which is housed in the Special Collections Department of the Malcolm A. Love Library at San Diego State University in San Diego, consists of approximately 200,000 postcards. The scope of the collection is wide-ranging, both geographically and topically, with numerous specimens from major postcard publishers.

Nearly all the postcards were donated to the University Library in 1989/1990 by Dr. and Mrs. Adams. Dr. Adams, one of the University's most distinguished professors of English, and his wife were major benefactors of the University who had long contributed important gifts to the Library, including a substantial Henry James collection. Dr. and Mrs. Adams assembled their postcard collection through persistent searching over a period of sixty years.

The Adams Postcard Collection has a detailed finding aid that includes an index. The cards are housed in 250 acid-free postcard boxes on 66 linear feet of shelving. Many postcards are enclosed in polypropylene sleeves, and all will eventually be enclosed to ensure their preservation. Staff and student assistants have devoted numerous hours to the arranging, describing, and processing of the postcards.

Dr. and Mrs. Adams had arranged their postcards both topically and

[Haworth co-indexing entry note]: "California Here We Come: The Adams Postcard Collection at San Diego State University." McPhail, Martha. Co-published simultaneously in *Popular Culture in Libraries* (The Haworth Press, Inc.) Vol. 3, No. 2, 1995, pp. 51-58; and: *Postcards in the Library: Invaluable Visual Resources* (ed: Norman D. Stevens) The Haworth Press, Inc., 1995, pp. 51-58. Single or multiple copies of this article are available from The Haworth Document Delivery Service [1-800-342-9678, 9:00 a.m. - 5:00 p.m. (EST)].

51

geographically. That scheme has been followed, for the most part, within Special Collections. The major categories include San Diego, California, U.S. views, foreign views, publisher, topical, and card types. Within these categories, further description is provided in the finding aid for contents of each box.

CALIFORNIA

There is a particularly comprehensive collection of postcards representing San Diego and California, as might be expected by the donors' sixty years residence in San Diego. The more than 4,500 postcards of San Diego County, which are housed in fifteen boxes, constitute an especially rich resource for the pictorial history of the region. The earliest cards pre-date the 1915-16 Panama-California Exposition held in Balboa Park. That significant event boosted the production of postcards of San Diego, many of which are preserved in the Adams Collection. As with other U.S. expositions, the 1915 exposition served as a major tourist attraction; many of the thousands of visitors who came to San Diego for this event purchased picture postcards to send to family and friends back home. San Diego was then a small town in the southwestern corner of the country that was geographically remote with an underdeveloped port and industrial base. Agriculture had been the primary reason for pioneers to settle in the San Diego area as its temperate climate allowed citrus and vegetable crops to thrive year-round. Many visitors to the exposition wrote notes on their postcards extolling the climate and the beauty of San Diego. Many local historians attribute the growth of San Diego in the early part of the century to exposition visitors who decided to settle in San Diego as well as the enticing descriptions of San Diego that they sent to the folks back home.

Another exposition held in Balboa Park in 1935-36 produced the same results; population increased from visitors who relocated to San Diego after the fair. Both of these expositions are well-documented by picture postcards, almost all of which are found in the Adams Collection. Nearly half of the cards have personal inscriptions that are a rich source for assessing the impressions made by the fairs and San Diego upon the tourists. Not all of the postcards sent home depicted the exposition grounds, buildings, and events. Views showing hotels, downtown, the harbor, beaches, La Jolla, Julian, San Diego State, and numerous other places, buildings, neighborhoods, activities, and people in San Diego County were also popular.

Postcards published after the 1935-36 fair that depict nearly all aspects of San Diego provide important documentation of the area's rapid growth and development. The establishment of San Diego as one of the nation's principal home ports for the U.S. Navy during World War II brought in thousands of sailors as well as other new residents to work in the emerging aerospace and shipbuilding industries. These industries, ships in the harbor, and sailors in uniform are widely depicted on postcards issued during World War II.

Many of the scenes of San Diego in the Adams Postcard Collection are complemented by 170 archival collections concerning San Diego organizations and people. For example, the Hotel del Coronado, a landmark tourist hotel since it was established in 1888, is one of the most frequently depicted buildings in San Diego postcard history. There are 55 linear feet of records of the Hotel del Coronado in Special Collections. Those records include correspondence, guest registers, programs of events, financial accounts, photographs, and other written documentation of its storied past. Since postcards were not included in the transfer of the Hotel del Coronado's archives, the Adams Collection provides visual documentation of its prominent role in San Diego's tourist history. Another building frequently depicted on postcards is the Old Globe Theater in Balboa Park and the records of this nationally-known theater also are held in Special Collections.

There are fourteen boxes of postcards containing 8,500 images that depict other California cities and natural wonders. Three boxes cover the development of Los Angeles and its suburbs, including Long Beach, Palm Springs, Laguna Beach, etc. The cards of Pasadena include numerous images of the famous Rose Parade, with many hand tinted cards showing floats made of colorful flowers. Santa Barbara, Monterey, San Francisco all are well-represented in the Adams Collection. One group of 110 cards depicts the aftermath of the 1906 San Francisco earthquake. The natural beauty of Yosemite National Park, which always has enticed photographers and artists, is well-represented by many striking black and white photographs or artistic impressions. The string of missions established by Franciscans along the California coast during the late 18th century have been frequently photographed for postcards. Finally, there are numerous postcard depictions of the sites of the California Gold Rush in the Adams Collection.

POSTCARDS OF OTHER STATES

There are fifty-two boxes of postcards from the other states of the union, including approximately 4,000 cards of Massachusetts, 5,500 of New York, and 1,500 of Michigan. Postcards from Florida are, however, among the fewest (510), even though the growth and development of that picturesque state mirrored that of California in many respects. Many historic sites, national parks, and scenic wonders are amply covered in this part of the collection where western America is particularly well represented.

POSTCARDS FROM ABROAD

Other countries are illustrated through 20,000 postcards housed in thirty-three boxes collected during the Adams' summer travels. As an English scholar, Dr. Adams visited Great Britain numerous times. There are 2,600 postcards from England, Scotland, and other parts of Great Britain housed in four boxes. There are also 2,000 postcards of Canada, 1,700 of France, 1,400 of Italy, 2,600 of Germany, 1,700 of Belgium, Holland and Sweden, 1,100 of Switzerland, and 1,800 postcards from Spain, Russia, Portugal, Romania, and Hungary. Postcards from China and Japan are housed in two boxes. One box includes scarce postcards from the South Sea Islands, New Zealand, and Australia. Another contains 575 postcards from the Middle East. There are also numerous images of Central and South America contained in two boxes.

MEXICO

Especially significant, certainly for students and scholars at San Diego State University, are two boxes of 750 postcards from Mexico. Tijuana and Ensenada in Baja California are very well-represented. The population of Baja California, like that of San Diego, was quite light until the 1920's. A small border town of a few thousand people, Tijuana's growth exploded during Prohibition in the United States. Gambling, horseracing, and drinking establishments enticed California tourists, led by Hollywood stars, seeking weekend diversions. The vivid depiction of these pursuits comprise the largest group of cards contained in this part of the Adams Collection. Tourism remains a major industry of Baja California, especially Tijuana, presently a city with over one million population. The ongoing cross-border commerce and tourism are depicted graphically through numerous images of customs and immigration stations.

PUBLISHERS

Dr. and Mrs. Adams arranged many of their postcards by publisher and forty postcard boxes remain arranged in this manner. There are ten boxes with 5,000 cards of Detroit Publishing Company, fifteen boxes with 7,000 Hugh C. Leighton Co. cards, seven boxes with 3,900 Edward H. Mitchell, five boxes with 3,500 specimens of Raphael Tuck and Sons, and two boxes with 850 cards published by Union Oil. Most of the Tuck cards are subarranged by topic, locale, or holiday/special commemoration. Catalogs of postcards produced by these companies also are contained in the Adams Postcard Collection.

POSTCARD TYPES

A category that may require future rearrangement is now designated as "card types." Although most of these cards are distinctive representations of the postcard publishing industry, they do not readily fit into categorization by topic or locale. This category, which comprises 28 boxes, includes one box of postcards used for advertising purposes. Other boxes include: one of 193 postcards that are decorated by ribbons, embroidery, and similar attachments; one of 250 embossed leather postcards; one with 190 postcards with novelty mechanical contraptions; one of stamp and coin cards; and one with miniature photo sets, private mailing hacks, three-dimensional images, and other creative cards. There are also seven boxes containing approximately 400 postcard folders and sets.

One box of cards has been the recent subject of research by a professor emeritus who is interested in the philatelic aspect of postcards. He has been examining the commemorative stamps, cancels, and Red Cross seals on postcards, along with specimens issued by railway post offices.

TOPICAL AND OTHER POSTCARDS

The largest single category of postcards in the Adams Collection is a topical collection of sixty-four boxes representing 50,000 postcards. One large grouping of seven boxes containing 5,000 postcards depicts airplanes, many of which were manufactured in San Diego or elsewhere in Southern California. This group, which richly illustrates one of the great manufacturing achievements of the twentieth century, is particularly meaningful in a city where the Spirit of St. Louis was built. Prominent aviators are also featured in this group, as well as airplane builders, including Claude Ryan, Glenn Curtiss, and Charles Lindbergh. Boats, ships, freighters, tankers, and other means of maritime transportation are depicted in two boxes of postcards; trains, depots, trolleys are well depicted as are automobiles and trucks. Pet lovers will find two boxes of postcards of cats, dogs, horses, birds, and other animals.

Four boxes of postcards illustrate costume and dress over the past century both in the United States and abroad. These cards are particularly interesting to students learning costume design, as the cards depict a variety of hats, coats, capes, dresses, suits and shoes. Along with the library's extensive book collection depicting costumes, these postcards are especially useful to illustrate social life and customs over the past one hundred years. Baseball, football, golf, fishing, bullfighting, rodeo, and other sporting and leisure pursuits are well represented too.

Many colleges are represented by the sports cards, but there is also a separate box with representations of their campuses, fraternities and other campus groups, mottoes and songs. Three boxes contain comic images, many of which would now be considered to be stereotypical humor. This group offers a rich resource for examining stereotypes in popular culture as do another group that depicts native Americans and African-Americans. Many museums have produced postcards to make their collections more widely known. The Adams Collection contains eight boxes of postcards with reproductions of artworks from museums in the United States and other countries. All of the major art postcard publishers, such as Stengel, Sborgi, Hermes, Lapina, Hoesch, Rotograph, Arthur Schurer, E.R. Weiss, and the Continental Art Company, are represented in the collection.

Another significant group of cards focuses upon Hollywood and Broadway stage and screen stars. This includes postcards of now demolished theaters, movie houses, and studios. One box of cards features musicians, composers, performers, music halls, and opera divas. Political figures also are well represented in three postcard boxes of the Adams Collection. Mrs. Adams carefully collected U.S. presidential political campaign cards starting with Grover Cleveland's campaign in 1892. Theodore Roosevelt, Woodrow Wilson, Calvin Coolidge, and the rest of the presidents, and many presidential candidates, through Ronald Reagan are represented in this group. The Adams Collection is an excellent source for locating photographs of minor royalty and politicians not easily located in reference books.

The importance of the two expositions held in San Diego has been noted. Other postcards in the Adams Collection are from expositions and fairs in St. Louis, Denver, Toronto, Paris, Philadelphia, Texas, and New York, and elsewhere from 1898 through 1963. Some cards present patriotic images, and others fruits and flowers, children, and beautiful young women.

Many postcards were designed to send greetings to friends and relatives on specific holidays such as Christmas, New Year's Day, Easter, Thanksgiving, and Halloween. Valentine postcards, which usually contain romantic verse, are especially numerous. Eleven boxes of such postcards are in the collection.

The Adams Collection also contains several hundred oversize and/or uncut postcards that are separately shelved in 23 numbered folders in flat file cabinets. These larger postcards principally depict cities, towns, and natural beauty spots, rather than topics. San Diego and California are particularly well-represented in these attractive postcards. Some postcards from the Adams' travels were assembled into albums. While many have been removed from the albums for preservation purposes, some that remain as assembled are also shelved in the flat files.

ADDITIONS TO THE COLLECTION

Since this important collection was made known in the San Diego community, other donors have made contributions of postcards to Special Collections. In 1993 a collector in La Jolla donated nearly 1,000 postcards that are housed in separate boxes at the end of the Adams Collection. Most of these cards are arranged by geographic location. Smaller donations also have been received. For instance 21 views of U.S. planetariums were added recently as were 10 postcards of pre-1930's Tijuana and San Diego. All postcards are incorporated into the John R. and Jane Adams Postcard Collection, although photocopied images are attached to the donor's file in the event identification of their gifts is needed. Postcards are not purchased through regular acquisition funds. University funds are utilized for the labor involved in processing this large collection and making it accessible. Funds from Dr. Adams and the University have purchased the necessary acid free postcard boxes as well as the polypropylene sleeves.

USE OF THE COLLECTION

Several researchers have noted that further indexing and cross-referencing would increase scholarly utility of the postcards. As this is extremely labor intensive, it is unlikely that additional indexing can be accomplished without grant-funded assistance. Possible sources of grant funding are being explored. The digitization of the postcards to make them available on a CD-ROM or laser disk is being considered as are other means of electronic access. Copyright issues must be explored thoroughly to ensure that appropriate permission is obtained, or that any intellectual property rights have expired, before disseminating these graphic images electronically.

The Adams Collection is now being utilized by some students and scholars in their research projects. A student needing photographic images of tourist sites in Baja California found appropriate illustrations in the collection. A graduate student researching changes of downtown San Diego streets was able to plot the location of businesses by using postcards as well as city directories. Drama students look at costumes on postcards for guidance in their design projects. Students researching San Diego regional history find the collection a pictorial treasure trove for images of industry, the military presence, development of neighborhoods, agricultural areas, land use changes, and innumerable other topics. One SDSU scholar of Mexican history, Paul Vanderwood, utilized postcards depicting the United States-Mexican border during the Mexican Revolution in his book *Border Fury*. A pictorial history of Baja California in postcards is being prepared for publication by the author.

Postcards are frequently incorporated into exhibits mounted by Special Collections. The centennial of the postcard was celebrated in early 1993; postcards have accompanied books and other printed materials in exhibits on Peru, the art of Mexico, women workers, and women's costumes. When the 25th anniversary of the first women's studies program established in the United States is celebrated in fall 1995, depictions of women on postcards will be displayed prominently, along with archival records of the department.

Usage of the Adams Collection could be enhanced by increased knowledge of its existence and its utility. By making this resource more widely known, it is hoped that the Adams Collection will be more heavily utilized by students and faculty on the San Diego State University campus and other researchers and scholars. Patrons are welcome to use the Adams Collection in person Monday through Friday from 10:00 a.m. to 3:00 p.m. Inquiries about the Adams Postcard Collection are welcome through letters or telephone calls (619-594-6791).

The "Historic Picture Postcard Collection" at the Fiske Kimball Fine Arts Library, University of Virginia

Jack Robertson

INTRODUCTION

The Philadelphia architect, Wilson Eyre (1858-1944) and a circle of his friends traveled extensively in Europe during the latter 19th century and first decades of the 20th. In the course of travels these men avidly collected picture postcards not simply as keepsakes but also as a form of pictorial documentation of the cities and historic architectural monuments that informed their taste and design style. The extensive collection, numbering over 20,000 cards, came into the possession of John Herring, a longtime administrator at the University of Virginia, who, upon his retirement in 1988, donated the collection to the Fiske Kimball Fine Arts Library.

COLLECTION DEVELOPMENT

Over the past six years, two dozen other gift collections, ranging from several dozen to several thousand items, have been added to the core collection so that the Library's Historic Picture Postcard Collection now contains approximately 28,000 cards. Donors have included wealthy travelers, architects, landscape architects, art historians, and librarians, and the collection reflects this diversity in taste and professional orientation. All of

[Haworth co-indexing entry note]: "The 'Historic Picture Postcard Collection' at the Fiske Kimball Fine Arts Library, University of Virginia." Robertson, Jack. Co-published simultaneously in *Popular Culture in Libraries* (The Haworth Press, Inc.) Vol. 3, No. 2, 1995, pp. 59-66; and: *Postcards in the Library: Invaluable Visual Resources* (ed: Norman D. Stevens) The Haworth Press, Inc., 1995, pp. 59-66. Single or multiple copies of this article are available from The Haworth Document Delivery Service [1-800-342-9678, 9:00 a.m. - 5:00 p.m. (EST)].

59

these recent gifts have been received as a result of direct solicitation. The Library is the frequent beneficiary of donations from individuals with distinguished collections of books and slides. Interestingly, it does not occur to these individuals that picture postcards, especially old ones, would also be of use to the Library. I have begun making the point directly to all potential donors that these "ephemeral" items are valuable and welcomed. We have never purchased picture postcards with library materials acquisition funds.

COLLECTION SCOPE

Early on in processing of the Wilson Eyre collection, certain subject scope criteria were established. The strength of this collection were cards depicting buildings, architectural details, and urban vistas. These subjects fit the Library's established goal of supporting, with texts and images, the University's Architectural History graduate curriculum. Although there are cards from over fifty countries worldwide, the great strength of the collection is views from Italy, France, Great Britain, and the U.S. with 4,000 to 5,000 items for each of these countries.

Cards depicting works of art and decorative arts were excluded from the scope of our collection because, for the most part, the Library's collection of published monographs and serials provide larger numbers and much better quality images of the same works. In cases where painting or sculpture are integral to a building, however, picture postcards are retained. In the course of processing the cards, we discovered around two hundred cards depicting "ethnographic" views of people in costume within an architectural context that were also retained.

ORGANIZATION

The organization of the cards is based on a geographical hierarchy consisting of a five field string: country–region–district–city/site–individual building. The following paragraph is excerpted from the "Processing Procedures" guidelines:

> For each country, the political and/or administrative subdivisions are a set of nesting categories (fields) that range from the largest area (the country name) to the smallest (the individual site). Although these subdivisions differ for each country, and in the case of the U.S., for each state, use of these divisions allows us to group together sites

of a particular area in the filing system. This practice provides a limited regional context; it also allows us to handle sites which are not located in a specific town such as English country houses, French chateaux, and American estates.

These designations are derived from standard geographic or cultural reference tools including the following core titles that we are used to establish entries in our geographic authority file: *The Times Atlas of the World; Webster's New Geographical Dictionary; National Gazetteer of the United States of America; Treasures of Britain and Treasures of Ireland;* and volumes in the series *A Phaidon Cultural Guide.*

The geographic hierarchy used for filing and labeling the cards has the major advantage for processing in that the structure of data elements is consistent and the information for any given postcard view/site is easily authenticated. On the other hand, the resultant filing order is NOT easily browsable because library patrons or staff, seldom remember that, in order to find Blenheim Palace they need to think of the following "geographic hierarchy":

Great Britain–England–Oxfordshire–Woodstock–Blenheim

Fortunately, the *WordPerfect* files into which the postcards' geographic designations are stored allow us to re-sort the data elements in the fourth and fifth fields, in this case Woodstock and Blenheim, to provide easy alphabetic retrieval through a printed finding aid. A very useful benefit of having all cataloging information in formatted *WordPerfect* files is the ease and speed with which adhesive labels for every card can be generated by the transfer of information into a file formatted to print labels.

The geographic lists also provide information about the number of postcards available in the collection for each entry. For example:

Italy–**ABRUZZI**–Aquila–Sulmona @12
Italy–Abruzzi–Pescara–Pescara @9
Italy–**APULIA**–Bari–Alberobello @1
Italy–Apulia–Bari–Bari @22
Italy–Apulia–Bari–Castel del Monte @1
Italy–Apulia–Brindisi–Brindisi @21
Italy–Apulia–Brindisi–Fasano @3
Italy–Apulia–Brindisi–Laureto di Fasano @4
Italy–Apulia–Brindisi–Selva di Fasano @4
Italy–Apulia–Foggia–Foggia @7
Italy–Apulia–Lecce–Lecce @21
Italy–Apulia–Taranto–Taranto @17

There are approximately 50 cities for which there are more than 100 cards in the collection, in these cases every building or view has been cataloged. Appended to this article is a copy of the "Guidelines for Dividing Material by Category and/or Individual Building & Site." The following is an abbreviated form of the building-specific cataloging for the city of Washington, DC:

WASHINGTON, DC

General–Panoramas @4

Churches

–Cathedral of Sts. Peter and Paul (National Cathedral) @4
–National Shrine of the Immaculate Conception @1
–Old Pohick Church @2
–Old St. Johns Church @2
–Sacred Heart Church @1

Cultural Structures

–Arts and Industries Museum, Smithsonian Institution @2
–Folger Shakespeare Library @2
–Library of Congress @7

Entertainment and Recreation Structures

–Kennedy Center for the Performing Arts @9

Government Structures

–Capitol Building @11
–Pan-American Union Building @5
–Old Post Office Department Building @2

Hotels

–Ambassador Hotel @1
–Mayflower Hotel @2
–Watergate Inn @1
–American Red Cross Building @2

Monuments

–Jefferson Memorial @3
–Lincoln Memorial @7
–Memorial Continental Hall @1
–Sherman's Statue @1
–Washington Monument @6
–Red Cross Memorial (**SEE:** Medical Structures–American Red Cross Building)

Parks and Gardens

–Botanical Garden @1
–Dumbarton Oaks @3 (**SEE ALSO:** Palaces–Dumbarton Oaks)
–Meridian Hill Park @7

USE OF THE COLLECTION

The use of the collection has been minimal to date. Individual items from the collection have been used as supplementary illustrative material in several architectural exhibitions both in Charlottesville at the University of Virginia and in Richmond at the Virginia Historical Society. Half a dozen graduate students in the architectural history program have used approximately two dozen postcards as sources for 35mm slides to use in class presentations. Several times the postcards have served in meeting needs of researchers for a broad range of illustrations; for example, the collection contains over one-hundred cards from the Chicago "A Century of Progress Exposition" that provided images for a study of futuristic architecture. This large and rich resource is not used very much at all. This calls into question the allocation of staff resources to maintain and enlarge the collection.

PLANS

The point raised above emphasizes the need to plan very carefully for the future of the collection of historic picture postcards. Without elaboration of cataloging access and, ideally, access to the images themselves, it seems unlikely that this collection will continue other than as a "frozen asset" used little more than it has been in the past.

There are, however, very exciting possibilities to improve access and, therefore, increase use. The Fiske Kimball Fine Arts Library has recently inaugurated its Digital Image Center which is utilizing technology to collect, catalog, and disseminate either medium- or high-resolution images of art and architectural works. As the capabilities for processing images improve (i.e., scanning large numbers of slides, or possibly postcards, in less labor intensive batch jobs) the prospects for devising a project to digitize the postcard collection become very attractive. The groundbreaking work now being done in the Digital Image Center in archiving and processing image collections within a standards compliant structure will serve as the foundation for other image processing initiatives including the postcard collection. Special funding will be required to undertake large-scale processing projects such as this, but the benefits to a very wide user community by means of the WorldWideWeb will be, I believe, a compelling argument for this type of project.

If you have questions or comments about the Historic Picture Postcard Collection, please contact:

Jack Robertson, Fine Arts Librarian,
Fiske Kimball Fine Arts Library
Bayly Drive
University of Virginia
Charlottesville, VA 22903
(804) 924-6601
jsr8s@virginia.edu

APPENDIX

Guidelines for Dividing Material by Category and/or Individual Building & Site:

In cases where a great deal of material exists for a given city/town–for example, Rome, Florence, Venice, Paris, London, New York, Washington DC–a fifth field should be utilized to fill names of individual buildings, sites, or monuments. When possible, the individual buildings should be listed by name under the appropriate categories–as listed below. Individual buildings, sites, or monuments should be clustered according to the following usage guidelines; include along with the category designation in the Architectural Sites Headings List the parenthetical "including" notes from the list below. Also, when needed, add parenthetical notes–ahead of the "including" note–for the common building name in the appropriate language for the country in field (1.)–e.g., ITALY–LATIUM–ROMA–ROME–PALACES (Palazzi), or –CHURCHES (Kirchen).

NOTE: include with the heading the notes following the term in parenthesis; DO NOT include in the listing the usage notes given below in brackets.

GENERAL–COSTUMES
GENERAL–LANDSCAPES [use for landscape views without any
      buildings or city/town views; identify the landscape as precise-
      ly as possible and fill in fields (1.), (2.), and (3.) OR (1.) and
      (2.) OR even just (1.) if only a country can be determined.
GENERAL–MISCELLANEOUS
GENERAL–PANORAMAS (including aerial & broad inclusive views)
[NOTE: Always file the "GENERAL" headings at the beginning of
      any additional entries for a specific geographic entry, that is,
      out of alphabetic sequence as they appear in this listing.]
capitols SEE: GOVERNMENT STRUCTURES
CEMETERIES (including tombs, catacombs, mausoleums, etc.)
CHURCHES (including cathedrals, basilicas, chapels, baptisteries,
      convents, monasteries, etc.)
COMMERCIAL STRUCTURES (including stores, shops, banks,
      offices, businesses, skyscrapers, etc.)
CULTURAL STRUCTURES (including museums, libraries, galler-
      ies, temporary exhibitions & expositions, etc.) SEE ALSO:
      ENTERTAINMENT & RECREATION STRUCTURES
ENTERTAINMENT & RECREATION STRUCTURES (including
      theaters, opera & concert halls, amusement parks, etc.) SEE
      ALSO: CULTURAL STRUCTURES
FORTIFICATIONS (including walls, ramparts, forts, castles, forti-
      fied gates, etc.)
FOUNTAINS
gates SEE: FORTIFICATIONS

APPENDIX (continued)

GOVERNMENT STRUCTURES (including capitols, courthouses, post offices, etc.)

HOTELS (including inns, motels, etc.)

HOUSES **SEE ALSO:** PALACES [use for "anonymous" and vernacular structures]

INDUSTRIAL STRUCTURES (including factories, warehouses, mills, etc.)

libraries **SEE:** CULTURAL STRUCTURES

MEDICAL STRUCTURES (including hospitals, clinics, sanato[a]ria, etc.

Monasteries **SEE:** CHURCHES

MONUMENTS (including memorials, commemorative sculpture & arches)

museums **SEE:** CULTURAL STRUCTURES

PALACES (including mansions, villas, etc.) **SEE ALSO:** HOUSES

PARKS & GARDENS [including botanical gardens and garden pavilions & other structures integrated into an urban park setting; DO NOT USE for parks/grounds/gardens associated with a country house or villa–use instead the heading, PALACES, and specific structure name.]

religious structures **SEE:** CHURCHES (for all types of Christian buildings); **SEE:** TEMPLES (for all types of non-Christian buildings)

RIVERS (including bridges, piers, embankments, canals, islands, etc.) [i.e., include here views of the water traversed with its proper name, e.g., "–Bridges–Thames River"

SCHOOLS & COLLEGES (including universities, academies, etc.)

skyscrapers **SEE:** COMMERCIAL STRUCTURES

SQUARES & OPEN SPACES

stores **SEE:** COMMERCIAL STRUCTURES

STREETS

TEMPLES (religious structures other than Christian)

TOWERS [including detached church steeples & bell towers, lighthouses, etc.,] **SEE ALSO:** FORTIFICATIONS

TRANSPORTATION STRUCTURES (including airports, train depots & stations, etc.)

walls **SEE:** FORTIFICATIONS

world's fairs **SEE:** CULTURAL STRUCTURES

[revised 2/25/92]

[revised 11/10/92]

Reprinted with permission.

Why Aren't You Here?
Postcards in the Popular Culture Library

Alison M. Scott

The Popular Culture Library (PCL) opened its doors as a specialized branch collection in the Bowling Green State University Library in 1969. Popular culture as a distinct academic discipline was, at the time, emerging from three related, but different, academic specialties: folklore, consumer studies, and mass culture studies, all of which were related to the emergence of area studies as an "interdiscipline" in the 1960s. The PCL's founders hoped to help fulfill the University Library's primary role as the provider of bibliographic materials for support of the university curriculum, for as academic interest in popular culture grew, so did the need for research and teaching materials. Through the persistence and dedication of the PCL's founder, Ray B. Browne, its first librarian, William B. Schurk, and its many other staff members, donors and supporters, the PCL has overcome the persistent and unfortunate notion that "popular" is a synonym for "worthless." In just twenty-five years, the PCL has grown from a single, nearly empty room to a collection of over 100,000 books, nearly 1,000 periodicals, and more than 1,000,000 special collections items filling the entire fourth floor of the Jerome Library. It serves an active, international body of scholars.

The general, and often unexamined, assumption that "popular culture" as a descriptive category relates primarily to creative or imaginative productions, such as fiction, graphic arts, mass media productions, or leisure activities, such as sports and hobbies, has been a primary factor in the evolution of the PCL's holdings. The collection as a whole can be adequately, although not entirely accurately, described as a collection of mate-

[Haworth co-indexing entry note]: "Why Aren't You Here? Postcards in the Popular Culture Library." Scott, Alison, M. Co-published simultaneously in *Popular Culture in Libraries* (The Haworth Press, Inc.) Vol. 3, No. 2, 1995, pp. 67-71; and: *Postcards in the Library: Invaluable Visual Resources* (ed: Norman D. Stevens) The Haworth Press, Inc., 1995, pp. 67-71. Single or multiple copies of this article are available from The Haworth Document Delivery Service [1-800-342-9678, 9:00 a.m. - 5:00 p.m. (EST)].

67

rial relating to what Americans do for fun. Nevertheless, the still-growing collections of the PCL fully represent and reflect the tripartite origins of the critical study of popular culture. Twentieth-century American mass culture, or mass-produced culture, constitutes the bulk of the collection that includes, in particular, the monographic and periodical collections relating to modern genre and series fiction, graphic arts (including comic books and cartoons), mass media productions (movies, television and radio), and sports. Folklore and the related area of material culture studies constitute another significant percentage of the monographic, periodical and special collections that include materials documenting collectors and collecting, handicrafts, arts and crafts, games and hobbies, interior and house decoration, wit and humor, holidays and celebrations, travel and tourism, automobiles, commercial archaeology, popular religion, parapsychology and the occult. Consumer studies represents another important, and growing, proportion of special collections materials that include mail-order catalogs, travel brochures, commercials on film and videotape, and manuscript and archival collections documenting the interaction of the creative imagination and the marketplace.

From Lester Chadwick's 1924 series novel, *Baseball Joe, Captain of the Team*; or, *Bitter Struggles on the Diamond* to Frank Miller's 1992 graphic novel, *Robocop versus the Terminator*, each part of the PCL's collections is an important aspect of the whole. As a whole, those collections contribute to the PCL's fundamental mission: to acquire, preserve, and make accessible to students, scholars and researchers primary research materials documenting late-19th- and 20th-century American popular culture. One of the most important parts of that whole is the Postcard Collection that is an assemblage of over 62,000 individual items, gathered together from hundreds of individual donations into a single special collection. The materials in that collection offer resources for the investigation of graphic evidence documenting virtually every aspect of modern popular culture.

Consider just one of the items in this collection. The image on the front of the postcard, printed in sepia tones without any identifying caption, is of a man wearing a baseball uniform, standing on trampled, muddy ground, swinging a bat. Behind him, two touring sedans are parked in front of fairground sheds and low trees. The back of the postcard carries a one-cent stamp, the September 24, 1921 postmark of the Peculiar, Missouri, post office and the following message, addressed to Mr. and Mrs. A.E. Wills of Letts, Iowa:

> Hello Joe! how are you all? I am at home now. season is over for this
> year we are all well and getting along O.K. dads trile comes up next

wk. am glad I am here Bub. I was sold to Rochester N.Y. for N. year. some advancement isnt it. will write later to you. Thos Wills[1]

The photograph on the postcard has been identified as a picture of Rogers "Rajah" Hornsby (1896-1963). Hornsby served as player/manager with the St. Louis Cardinals, the New York Giants, the Boston Braves, the Chicago Cubs, and the St. Louis Browns between 1915 and 1937, and was elected to the Baseball Hall of Fame in 1942. At the time this card was postmarked, Hornsby was just reaching the peak of his career. He led the league in batting average from 1920-25, in runs batted in from 1920-22 and again in 1925, and was voted the most valuable player in 1925 and 1929.

The researcher who identified Hornsby was deeply disappointed to find that Thomas Wills, the sender of the postcard, "left few footprints in the sands of time."[2] Extrapolation from the juxtaposition of the text of the message and the picture of a baseball superstar, however, lead us to believe that Wills was a player in the minor leagues. Future study may uncover more traces of Mr. Wills, now that we know to look for him.

This single card, considered as a "documentary" object, has depths as yet unplumbed. The Postcard Collection, in conjunction with the documentary, monographic, and periodical resources of the PCL as a whole, has a potential for research that is virtually unparalleled.

The Postcard Collection consists, as noted above, of approximately 62,000 cards. There are no limits on the kinds of cards collected, and the PCL is as interested in acquiring used postcards as in "fresh-from-the-press" cards. All the cards in the collection do, however, have some pictorial or graphic content. The only items that are routinely excluded from the collection are cards that have no printed images (other than postage values) such as the blanks issued by the U.S. Postal Service.

A vast preponderance of the PCL's holdings were acquired as gifts, and the Postcard Collection is no different in that respect. Its content has been shaped almost entirely by donors. Current additions to the collection also depend entirely upon what supporters are generous enough to provide; luckily, they have been very generous. Recent acquisitions range from the 1993 series of postcards with images taken from the dust jackets of *The Oxford Sherlock Holmes* designed by Ivan Allen, to a photograph in black-and-white of Detroit's Shrine of the Little Flower, postmarked 1936 to a "colorized" photograph of Broadway Street, Fonda, New York postmarked 1912, to an embossed, gilded chromo depicting two turkeys and two American flags in the gondola of a dirigible with the motto, "Thanksgiving Greetings" postmarked 1908.

As with all the other research collections in the PCL, the Postcard

Collection is stored in a stack area that is closed to members of the public. Researchers using the collection are accommodated in the Library's supervised reading room. This helps ensure the safety and security of the collection, while it also provides for the maintenance of order in the physical arrangement of the collection. To facilitate the fullest use of the Postcard Collection, supporting materials, including the periodical *The Postcard Collector* and available reference works, are acquired.

The history of the PCL is that of an institution whose collections and ambitions have grown faster than its budget. Storage needs, for example, are resolved as creatively and inexpensively as possible. The immediate needs of the Postcard Collection have been met by recycling equipment from another department in the university library system: that collection is now housed in metal cabinets that were originally acquired by the Microforms Department for housing microfiche cards. Standard postcards fit handily inside these drawers, while oversize cards are stored flat in archival-quality cardboard boxes. To prevent abrasion to the graphic image, each card is placed inside an acid-free paper sleeve, which also allows every item's proper location within the collection to be noted without defacing the card itself.

Postcards in the collection are sorted either by geographical location or subject, based solely upon the image that the card carries. The majority of cards–at least two-thirds of the total–are imprinted with views of specific locations. These cards are filed by the most specific geographical or political designation available, using a current gazetteer as the authority for the place names and political entities that constitute the primary filing elements. The photograph of the Shrine of the Little Flower will be found under "United States–Michigan–Detroit," just as the picture of Broadway Street will be found under "United States–New York–Fonda."

Arrangement by subject, which is also based upon the imagery that a postcard carries, follows very general descriptive categories. These include such headings as sports, greeting cards, actors and actresses, and humor. The chromo of the two turkeys may be found under the heading of "Greeting Cards–Thanksgiving" and *The Oxford Sherlock Holmes* series under "Literature–Mysteries."

This system, which does not have enough complexity or depth to be awarded the name of "cataloging," has advantages and disadvantages. Its primary advantage is that it facilitates unequivocal decisions about where any individual card belongs. This allows student assistants to handle most of the sorting and filing, and, in these days of fiscal stringency in publicly-funded higher education, this is no small benefit. The major disadvantage is that this system does not facilitate access to alternative points of interest.

Since the specific location or the general subject is the sole access point for any card, there is no way to ascertain any additional information about the contents of the collection, short of examining each card every time a particular question arises. It would be useful to have access to the names of persons, places, and things pictured on cards, as well as to correspondents, printers, and printing techniques. As the staff of the PCL is able to take fuller advantage of the power of personal computers, an attempt will be made to remedy these limitations through increased indexing of alternative access points. Ultimately, the finding aid for the Postcard Collection will be accessible through the Internet.

At the present time, the usefulness of Postcard Collection is more potential than actual. Nevertheless, the collection has proved itself to be a valuable resource for scholars working on a variety of projects. These have included research into the history of highway signs and advertising, the popularization of *art nouveau* in the United States, and the iconography of American sports, as well as searches for practical solutions to problems in graphic design. Possible uses of the Postcard Collection range from documentation for historic preservation projects, to the study of the celebration of holidays, to patterns in the representation of ethnic stereotypes, to the persistence of topiary in public parks. The possibilities are virtually endless. The only limits to the collection's potential for scholars working in many areas lies in the ability to make them aware of the resources of the Postcard Collection, and their willingness to investigate its riches.

We now know to look for Tho[s] Wills. Who knows what else we will discover along the way in our collective researches in the Postcard Collection that will deepen our understanding of popular culture?

A standard message supposedly found on many postcards is–"Having a wonderful time. Wish you were here." The staff of the PCL does wish that more researchers were here. Our postcard message to scholars studying many aspects of popular culture would be: "Have a wonderful collection. Why aren't you here?"

NOTES

1. Thomas Wills to Mr. & Mrs. A.E. Letts, September 24, 1921, "Sports–Baseball" category, Postcard Collection, Popular Culture Library, Bowling Green State University, Bowling Green, Ohio.

2. Private communication, Steven Bryan Bieler to the author, December 1, 1993.

THE USE OF POSTCARDS

Sites Abroad:
Picture Postcards
and a Late Nineteenth Century
Woman's Sketchbook of the Grand Tour

Claudia Hill

Picture postcards are an untapped source which can prove surprisingly useful in art historical research. In this instance, early twentieth century European postcards provide useful corroboration of facts in analyzing a late nineteenth century woman's sketchbook[1] of the Grand Tour. A description of the sketchbook and discussion of its date and attribution are the subjects of the first half of this essay. The second half of this essay deals with the use of the postcards to identify drawings and confirm cultural, historical and literary associations with particular sites sketched.

The small sketchbook measures 6 1/4 × 8 1/4 × 3/4 inches. Its compact size would have made it extremely portable, permitting the artist to withdraw it rapidly and make quick sketches of memorable vistas along the journey. The sketches could have been used as studies for more com-

[Haworth co-indexing entry note]: "Sites Abroad: Picture Postcards and a Late Nineteenth Century Woman's Sketchbook of the Grand Tour." Hill, Claudia. Co-published simultaneously in *Popular Culture in Libraries* (The Haworth Press, Inc.) Vol. 3, No. 2, 1995, pp. 73-87; and: *Postcards in the Library: Invaluable Visual Resources* (ed: Norman D. Stevens) The Haworth Press, Inc., 1995, pp. 73-87. Single or multiple copies of this article are available from The Haworth Document Delivery Service [1-800-342-9678, 9:00 a.m. - 5:00 p.m. (EST)].

plete works[2] or treasured as pictorial souvenirs upon return home. The durable materials of which the sketchbook was made would have allowed for rough handling during a voyage.

The sketchbook has hard front and back boards covered in linen with remnants of two, thin linen strips to serve as ties. The 76 smooth, heavy-weight linen pages contain drawings only on the front of the pages perhaps due to the media employed by the artist. Graphite is the predominant medium, although there are instances where pen and ink, brush and wash or white chalk have been used. The freedom and unfinished quality of the majority of the sketches indicate that the drawings were made on site.

The date "1890" is inscribed in two places in the sketchbook.[3] The first inscription reads "Harriet Blake Andover Mass./-1890-U.S.A." (1r) and the second, "Steerage./Steam Ship./Catalonia/July 12./1890" (2r). To the right of this latter inscription is a drawing of passengers engaged in a variety of activities on the deck of a ship. The mast of the ship dominates the sketch and its large, billowing sail frames the composition (2r) (Illustration 1).

The dates of the voyage would have been consistent with those of the Catalonia.[4] Built in Scotland in 1881 and scrapped in Italy in 1901, this ship made transatlantic crossings between Boston and Liverpool from 1883 onwards. The ship, with three masts, one funnel and an iron hull, was owned and operated by the Cunard Shipping Line. Evidently, the greatest volume of passengers for the transatlantic voyage came from the period between April and September.[5]

Both historical information about Harriet Blake (1860-1940) and the artistic style of other works by her leave no doubt that it was she who drew the illustrations in the sketchbook. Blake lived in close proximity to Abbot Academy, a women's school.[6] According to the school's alumni records, she attended the Academy as a day student from 1879-1880.[7] Her mother, Mrs. Reverend Joseph Blake, graduated from the same institution in 1839 and her sister, Susan, worked there as a substitute teacher of literature.

Topographical scenes were the subject of other artistic works by Blake. Two of her sepia-toned etchings, owned by the Andover Historical Society, depict well-known buildings in the town; the residence of Harriet Beecher Stowe and the Andover Chapel.[8] The artist's signatures on both etchings strongly resembles that in the sketchbook. Blake also drew illustrations for a single issue of a literary publication for which her sister contributed an article.[9] In fact, her drawing of a sailboat in the magazine, accompanying a poem about Glengariff,[10] strongly resembles a drawing in the sketchbook of this Irish resort town (5r).

Blake apparently completed her studies at Abbot Academy in 1880.

ILLUSTRATION 1. Deck of the Catalonia Steamship, Pen and Ink Sketch (2r), July 12, 1890, Harriet Blake's Sketchbook, Private Collection

Steerage.

Steam Ship.

Catalonia
July 12.
1890.

Two years later, she was studying drawing and painting at the School of the Museum of Fine Arts, Boston.[11] The next six years were spent first as an apprentice in wood engraving, etching and mezzotint to the painter and engraver, William Baxter Palmer Closson (1848-1926), then later as his assistant. Blake received a scholarship to attend Cowles Art School in Boston from 1890-91. This scholarship may have provided the funds Blake needed for her Grand Tour.

The Grand Tour, an extended tour of European places of cultural, historical and literary significance, was generally taken by British aristocratic youth for educational and acculturational purposes. The Tour usually entailed visits to France, Germany, Italy and Switzerland. As an American, Blake would also have wanted to see England, Ireland and Scotland. All of these countries were part of her itinerary which may be determined from inscriptions in her sketchbook.

The inscriptions which accompany most drawings are dated and identify the general vicinity of the sketch. They reveal that over a seven week period, Blake's Grand Tour covered a large number of European cities and towns. At the onset of the tour, Blake appears to be traveling through July 17 from the south of Ireland to the north. She sketches the landscape as she passes through Brandon (4r), Glengariff (5r), Killarney (8r), and Ballybofey (9r). Apparently, Blake crossed the North Channel into Scotland, for the next drawing which is dated July 21 is of Edinburgh Castle (10r).

In the Scottish capital, Blake visits John Knox's house (12r), Holyrood Palace and Abbey (12-13r) before traveling to England to see the Melrose Abbey (14r), the city of Carlisle (16r), and the ruins at Kenilworth (17r). She probably departs from an English port to the Continent since the last sketch is of an inn located in Stratford-upon-Avon, England on July 23 (18r).

Over a week passes before Blake produces another drawing with the dated inscription "Aug. 1/Cologne./From Steamer." She appears to be traveling up the Rhine River towards the Alpine mountains. Sketches of sites in Germany date from August 1 through 9 and include a river scene at Bingen (24r), parks at Wiesbaden (25r), a building in Heidelberg (26r), the Stuttgart Castle (27-30r), and the gardens at Munich (33-35r). Drawings of boats and locks at Lindau (36-41r) occupy the artist's interest from August 11-12.

By August 13, Blake travels to Lucerne, Switzerland (45-49r). The Alpine ridges of Switzerland are the subject of many of Blake's drawings from August 13-18. She journeys to the Brünig Pass (50r), then towards the majestic mountains at Interlaken (51-54r), and Lake Thun (55r). She sketches the town of Chamonix, France on August 20 (58-61r) followed by views of the lakes of Lugano (64r), the villages of Menaggio (66-67r) and Bellagio (68r), and Lake Como (69-70r). The final drawings are of the Cathedral at Como, Italy (71r) and a drawing of the cityscape of Venice (72r).

Though Blake may have visited other countries on her Grand Tour, the drawings are so closely dated as to suggest that this was not probable between July 12 and August 24. However, there remain questions as to the ports where she embarked and disembarked. The last drawing in the sketchbook was of Venice, but this does not necessarily mean that Venice was the end of Blake's European tour, as the artist could have commenced a second sketchbook.

In the sketchbook are two unidentified drawings of buildings, presumably in Switzerland. The first drawing is executed in pen and ink with ink wash.(53r) (Illustration 2). In the foreground of the sketch is a Romanesque-style building with a tower capped by a tall, sharply gabled roof. Immediately below the roof are two small windows which are positioned above a larger, circular window. The spire of another building appears in the background. Foliage surrounds the first building and mountain ranges can be seen in the background. The second drawing is a graphite sketch of the same architectural structures (54r) (Illustration 3). Partially obscured by vegetation, only the towers are visible in the far distance on the left. A mountain range extends to the right, and people appear to be haying in a field in the foreground.

The inscription "Interlaken/Aug. 16" on both sketches indicates that the buildings were probably located in that Swiss resort town. Picture postcards of Interlaken can assist in the identification of the buildings. Postcards dating as close as possible to the 1890s would be preferable in such comparisons since buildings may be torn down or altered. However, the earliest postcards of Interlaken which were available for research purposes date from the early decades of the twentieth century.[12] A number of these 3 1/2 × 5 1/2 inch postcards, printed on thin card stock, display photographs of buildings resembling those in the sketchbook.

The photograph on one postcard in particular bears a striking resemblance to the architectural structures in the sketchbook[13] (Illustration 4). In the photograph, a building having a tower with a tall, pointed roof and windows as depicted in the drawings is positioned to the left. The very top of another tower can be seen in the far left, rising over trees and shrubbery. A woman, with her back towards the camera, strolls along a tree lined road towards a young child who faces her. It seems as if both the photographer and Blake were looking at this building from the same angle, perhaps even on the same road.

The photographic image does not extend to the bottom of the postcard

ILLUSTRATION 2. The English Church, Interlaken (53r), Pen and Ink with Wash, August 16, 1890, Harriet Blake's Sketchbook, Private Collection

ILLUSTRATION 3. The English Church Seen from the Distance, Interlaken (54r), Graphite Drawing, August 16, 1890, Harriet Blake's Sketchbook, Private Collection

ILLUSTRATION 4. Postcard of the English Church, Interlaken, Early Twentieth Century

13564 Interlaken — English Church

and thus leaves a white border along that edge. On the border is printed "13564 Interlaken–English Church." The postcard has no postmark nor does it have correspondence. The writing on the reverse of the postcard instructs the sender to write correspondence on the left, the address to the right and to place the postage in the upper right-hand corner. The design element of the border and the division of the reverse of the postcard suggests that it dates from the early decades of the twentieth century.

The English Church is probably the Old Convent Church also known as the Old Monastery and Nunnery of Interlaken.[14] The spire rising behind this church may have been that of the Roman Catholic church nearby. The English Church was formerly a twelfth century monastery and nunnery which was suppressed in the sixteenth century. It was surrounded by old walnut trees and stood at the northeast end of an old tree lined avenue called Höheweg. From this avenue commanded a famous view of the snow covered mountain, Jungfrau.[15]

Protestant services were held in English in various parts of the English Church.[16] Blake, as the daughter of a minister, may have been inclined to attend one of these services. The English Church, though not distinguished architecturally, would also have been an attractive site to many English speaking visitors. Its popularity was reflected in the number of postcards of the site which were sold.

By examining other postcards of Interlaken, a geographical feature of a landscape drawing in the sketchbook may be identified. Blake sketched a snow covered mountain peak visible between the V-shaped opening of two pine covered mountains (52r). The drawing is one of the more complete illustrations in the sketchbook. The artist employs pen and ink with wash in the drawing. White chalk is used to emphasize the snowy peaks.

Photographs on postcards of Interlaken show numerous mountain peaks around the Alpine town. One snow covered mountain is repeatedly photographed rising between two smaller tree covered mountains with the town at its base. This mountain top appears on a postcard with the inscription "18452 Interlaken und die Jungfrau."[17] The distinctive shape of the mountain, Jungfrau, was visible from almost every point in the town. This was clearly the snow covered mountain in Blake's sketchbook. It is interesting to find that Blake's sketch of the mountain immediately preceded the two sketches of the English Church. Would she have sketched the mountain while standing on the old, tree-lined avenue?

A further discovery which a postcard has provided, regards a hotel mentioned in the sketchbook. While visiting Heidelberg, the artist made an unfinished pen and ink drawing of a four-storied building. In the left-hand corner of the drawing, she wrote "Heidelberg/From window at/hotel

Schrider(sic)/morning Aug 4" (26r). A picture postcard of the "Hotel Schrieder" in Heidelberg shows the large, four-storied hotel surmounted by a single flag on the roof.[18] In front of the hotel is a small, fenced in park with a sidewalk around its perimeter. Another four-storied, rectangular building faces the hotel at the left. The facade of this building is partially blocked by trees from the park.

The reverse of this 3 1/2 × 5 1/2 inch colored postcard is reserved for postage and the address. The postcard is addressed to "Miss Maude P. Angier/West Durham/North Carolina." On the postcard are four American postmarks of September 1905; one appears on the front and three on the reverse. A two-cent American stamp is pasted in the upper right corner. Apparently, the card had been posted in the United States and forwarded a number of times.

If Blake had looked out of a window on the left side of the Schrieder Hotel, she would have seen the facade of the second building which resembles the sketch that she made. The misspelling of the name of the hotel was one of a number of misspellings in the sketchbook including "Gute Nacht"(sic) (24r) for Gutenacht, "Lurgano"(sic) (64r) for Lugano, and "Belaggio" (sic) (67r) for Bellagio. The Hotel Schrieder was classified as a first-class hotel in 1903.[19] The building was ideally located in the residential quarter of Heidelberg and near the train station. The hotel may have been particularly welcoming to American visitors or accommodating to touring agencies.

Aside from the identification of buildings and geological formations, inscriptions on postcards can confirm cultural, historical and literary associations with particular sites. For example, a verse is often inscribed on early twentieth century postcards of Blarney Castle, Blarney, Ireland. Blake, too, has handwritten a few lines adjacent to her graphite drawing of the Castle's fortifying tower (3r). The square tower she has drawn has machicolations and its battlements have been partially destroyed. Dark shading along the right edge of the ruin seems to suggest foliage.

To the left of the drawing, Blake writes: "O Blarney Castle, my/darling!/You're nothing at all but stone,/And a small little twist of/ould ivy!/Och wisha, vllahoo, allagone"/. This verse has not yet been identified but it is possible that these words were part of an Irish folk song. This is the only instance in the sketchbook in which the artist has juxtaposed a drawing with a verse. Where the verse ends, the inscription continues with some information about the history of the tower.

Blarney Castle was built by Cormac MacCarthy in the fifteenth century and underwent many sieges. The great attraction of this site was the famous Blarney stone, purported to form part of the sill of one of the machicolations on the south side of the tower.[20] This magic stone, in a precarious location on the tower, was believed to deliver eloquence to any individual who would venture to lean over the side of the sill and kiss it. The ruins of the tower were surrounded by old groves and beneath these were natural caves.

A color postcard of the Blarney Castle tower resembles the drawing in the sketchbook.[21] However, the battlements appear intact, which indicates that the photographer may have taken the photograph from another angle or that the tower had undergone restoration. There is an abundance of foliage around the stone ruins as in the sketch. The photograph is reproduced as a circular image on 3 1/2 × 5 1/2 inch thin, card stock. The reverse of the postcard is divided in half between the area for correspondence and the space for the address.

The hand-drawn decorative elements on the front of the card include shamrocks, an Irish harp framed in an escutcheon and a shadow at the bottom right of the photograph. A poem fragment appears in the upper right hand corner of the postcard in a panel. It reads: "THERE IS A STONE THERE/THAT WHOEVER KISSES,/OH! HE NEVER MISSES/TO GROW ELOQUENT."

This fragment of a poem has been attributed to Father Prout, also known as Francis Sylvester Mahoney (1804-1866).[22] Prout, a former Jesuit Priest and a native of Cork, was known for writing witty verse. Blarney Castle is the subject of other works, most notably the eighteenth century Irish song "The Groves of Blarney,"[23] to which Prout's verses about the Castle are frequently appended.

Inscriptions on postcards of Stratford-upon-Avon commonly refer to William Shakespeare, as it was the town of his birth. A recurring subject of early twentieth century picture postcards of Stratford-upon-Avon is the "Shakespeare Hostelrie." This first-class inn, of indeterminate age, had every room named after a Shakespeare play.[24] A postcard of the inn reveals that the building had five gables, each with a shuttered window.[25] There are three stories and the shingled roof is capped by at least one brick chimney. In front of the half-timbered wood and stucco facade is an early automobile. The automobile, parked next to a narrow sidewalk which separates the inn from the road, appears to be one of the models produced by the English manufacturer, Thomas Humber, in the early 1920s.[26]

The postcard would date from the early 1920s if the date of the automobile is correct. This date seems to be consistent with the design of the postcard as well. Printed in white on the front of the postcard is "Antona"/155 Ye Olde Five Gables, Shakespeare Hostelrie. Stratford-on-Avon." There is no postmark nor correspondence on the postcard, but instructions for where to place the message and address are printed on the reverse.

On July 23, Blake sketched an "Inn on the way to Shakespeare's House" at Stratford-upon-Avon (18r). The charcoal drawing of a two-storied inn with a shingled roof extends the length of page. The inn has at least two brick chimneys and three gables. The windows in the gables all appear to have shutters. Between the inn and the road is a narrow walkway.

The inn sketched by Blake and the inn depicted on the postcard are not the same structure though it is possible that the hotel was remodeled. Blake's inn is a more modest structure having two floors and without the half-timbered facade. The quaintness of the inn may have been the reason why she has chosen to illustrate it in lieu of more well-known subjects such as Shakespeare's alleged residence, Anne Hathaway's Cottage, Trinity Church or views along the river.

Stratford-upon-Avon was an important stop on the Grand Tour for Americans. As early as 1815, the American writer Washington Irving wrote of his travels "I had come to Stratford on a poetical pilgrimage. My first visit was to the house where Shakespeare was born."[27] One estimate was that by the first decade of the twentieth century, 30,000 pilgrims traveled annually to see Shakespeare's house and about a fourth of them were Americans.[28]

American writers, such as Nathaniel Hawthorne and Mark Twain visited other cities on Blake's Grand Tour as part of their own European travels. Hawthorne traveled to Scotland around 1876 and described Queen Mary's apartments in Holyrood Abbey as "very dreary and shabby-looking rooms, with bare floors."[29] He proceeded to relate how the guide at Edinburgh Castle "showed us Mons Meg, a great old cannon, broken at the breech, but still aimed threateningly from the highest ramparts."[30] Edinburgh Castle (10r), the window through which the above mentioned cannon was fired, and an inscription carved over the door to Mary's room (11r) are all sketched by Blake.

Twain's desire to learn German and study art prompted him to go to Heidelberg in the late 1870s while tramping about Europe.[31] His travels through Germany included traveling on the Neckar River, which flows into the Rhine, to see the picturesque castle ruins and rocky cliffs along the banks of that river. He recounts a number of legends and songs of the Rhine related to the "Lorelei."

The Lorelei was a famous cliff on the Rhine river located between Bingen and Coblenz.[32] Since it was situated at a point where the river is dangerously narrow, shipwrecks were frequent occurrences. Legends sprung up about a siren who would supposedly lure unsuspecting sailors to their deaths by singing beautiful songs.[33] In the late nineteenth century, these legends and songs about the "Lorelei" were propagated and transmitted to foreign visitors as a result of the opening of the Rhine to international navigation in 1868.

While Blake does not specifically mention this cliff in her sketchbook, she does produce a number of drawings of the banks along the Rhine (21-24r). One of these drawings is of a rocky crag surmounted by a castle to the right with sailing vessels, and a small house along the river's bank. The graphite drawing is labeled "Bingen/Aug. 1.*st*" (24r). Inserted in the bottom left of the sketch is a small drawing of what is likely to be the moon reflected in the waters of the Rhine. The words "Gute Nacht." are written below this drawing.

A color postcard of rocky precipices jutting into a river has the words "Gruss von Rhein, Lorelei." or "Greetings from the Rhine, Lorelei."[34] The photograph is printed so as to allow for a white border around most of the image. In the photograph, a steam ship can be seen on the far left near the narrow gap in the river between two sheer cliffs. The 3 1/2 × 5 1/2 inch postcard is printed on thin card stock and postmarked the first of June '01 on the reverse.

The handwritten message is crammed into the white border on the front of the postcard. The message reads:

> A glorious trip down the Rhine, stopping at Rüdesheim (National Denkmal, very fine), Coblenz, Bonn, where we saw the house where Beethoven was born, the graves of Niebuhr, Schumann & Schiller's wife and son. Friday on to Holland. M.E.N.

The writer of this postcard visits the "National Denkmal a national monument commemorating the founding of[35] the German Empire in 1871. The monument, also known as the Niederwald Memorial, was built at the top of a hill at Rüdesheim just across the Rhine from Bingen. The names of the individuals mentioned were famous for their contributions to history, music and literature; Barthold G. Niebuhr, a historian who laid the foundation for critical review of historical sources, the composers Ludwig van Beethoven and Robert Schumann, and the writer Friedrich von Schiller. The location of the graves was in the Old Cemetery, Alter Friedhof, in the northwest quarter of Bonn.[35]

The correspondence on the postcard describes some of the activities of a visitor who traveled on the Rhine River near Bingen. Blake too, may have visited this monument, the home of the composer, or peered at the graves of well-known individuals on her travels up the Rhine. Given her interest in seeing Shakespeare's house, it is likely that she would also have wanted to see where Beethoven lived. The handwritten message together with the photograph of the steamer chugging up the river past the Lorelei cliffs provide a more complete picture of what Blake's experiences along the Rhine would have involved.

While the postcards of the Lorelei, the Shakespeare Hostelrie and Blarney Castle contribute much information about the cultural context surrounding the locations visited by Blake, the postcards of the Schrieder Hotel, Jungfrau and the English Church provide nearly contemporary photographs of the sites that she sketched. It is remarkable how often her choices of subjects for her sketchbook correspond with the choices that photographers made in producing postcards for mass consumption. Blake is following in the footsteps of Irving, Hawthorne, Twain and countless other Americans who journeyed across the Atlantic to see sites abroad. It is fortunate that her small sketchbook survives to give us a charming and personal pictorial record of a late nineteenth century Grand Tour.

NOTES

1. The sketchbook, formerly belonging to Charles and Kelly Wiltse, Hanover, NH, is now in a private collection.

2. Color notations made on some of the sketches may have been intended to enable the artist to make accurate color renditions at a later date, (see 16r and 39v).

3. Another date appears in the watermark: "BRYON/WESTON'S/LINEN RECORD/1887" (50r).

4. Eugene W. Smith, *Passenger Ships of the World. Past and Present* (Boston, MA: George H. Dean Company, 1978), 52.

5. Francis E. Hyde, *Cunard and the North Atlantic 1840-1973: A History of Shipping and Financial Management* (Atlantic Highlands, NJ: Humanities Press, 1975), 63.

6. Harriet Blake is listed as residing at 9 Abbot Street in a house owned by Mrs. Reverand Joseph Blake in *The Andover Directory 1897-8. A Complete Index to Residents, Business, Streets, etc. of the Town and Other Useful information* (Shirley, MA: AB. Sparrow & Co., 1897), 42. Also living at the same residence was Susan M. Blake.

7. Alumni Records, Archives, Oliver Wendell Holmes Library, Phillips Academy, Andover, MA. Abbot Academy operated as an independent school until financial problems forced the school to merge with Phillips Academy in 1973, when the all boys school became co-ed.

8. Blake's etchings "The Stowe House" (1939.30) and "The Chapel" (1939.29) were the gift of Alice Jenkins to the Andover Historical Society. They are framed in similar manner and measure 3 × 5 inches and 5 1/2 × 3 3/8 inches respectively.

9. Julia Drinkwater et al. *The Andover Magazine*, [1890s]. Andover Historical Society.

10. Ibid, 3.

11. Alumni Records, Archives, Oliver Wendell Holmes Library, Phillips Academy, Andover, MA.

12. This approximate date was determined from postmarks, handwritten dates and the postcard design. Design features on early Swiss postcards allowed for a blank space on the front for a short message. After around 1902, messages were allowed on half of the side reserved for the address. See: Frank Staff, *The Picture Postcard & Its Origins* (New York, Washington: Frederick A. Praeger), 54 and 66.

13. Special Collections and Archives, Rutgers University Libraries, New Brunswick, NJ.

14. Karl Baedeker, *Switzerland and the Adjacent Portions of Italy, Savoy, and the Tyrol. Handbook for Travellers*, 10th edition (Leipsic: Karl Baedeker, 1883), 155. The English Church was also mentioned in Baedeker's *Switzerland*, 23rd edition, 1909, 197.

15. Baedeker, *Switzerland*, 1909, 197.

16. Ibid, and Baedeker, *Switzerland*, 1883, 155.

17. Special Collections and Archives, Rutgers University Libraries, New Brunswick, NJ.

18. Special Collections Library, Duke University, Durham, NC.

19. Karl Baedeker, *The Rhine from Rotterdam to Constance. Handbook for Travellers*, 15th revised edition (Leipsic: Karl Baedeker, 1903), 264.

20. John Cooke, *Handbook for Travellers in Ireland*, 8th edition, revised and edited (London: Edward Stanford, 1912), 389.

21. Special Collections Library, Duke University, Durham, NC.

22. Justin McCarthy, ed., *Irish Literature*, Vol. V-VI (New York, Bigelow Smith, 1904), 2441-2. The verse also appears in Cooke's *Handbook*, 1912, 388.

23. Ibid, 2439-2441. The song "The Groves of Blarney" is attributed to Richard Millikin of Cork around 1798 or 1799.

24. Karl Baedeker, *Great Britain. Handbook for Travellers*, 7th edition, revised and augmented (Leipzig: Karl Baedeker, 1910), 263.

25. Curt Teich Postcard Archives, Lake County Museum, Wauconda, IL.

26. Joseph H. Wherry, *Automobiles of the World* (Philadelphia: Chilton Book Company, 1968), 209-210.

27. Washington Irving, *The Sketch-book of Geoffrey Crayon, Gent.* (New York: G.P. Putnam and Son, 1869), 346.

28. Baedeker, *Great Britain*, 1910, 263.

29. Sophia Hawthorne, *Passages from the English Note-Books of Nathaniel Hawthorne*, Vol. II (Boston: James R. Osgood and Company, 1876), 38.

30. Ibid, 41.

31. Mark Twain (Samuel L. Clemens), *A Tramp Abroad* (Hartford, CT: American Publishing Company, 1889), 136-147.

32. Karl Baedeker, *The Rhine from Rotterdam to Constance. Handbook for Travellers* (Leipsic: Karl Baedeker, 1903), 88.

33. See F. J. Kiefer, *The Legends of the Rhine from Basle to Rotterdam* (Mayence: D. Kapp [1869]).

34. Special Collections Library, Duke University, Durham, NC.

35. Karl Baedeker, *The Rhine from Rotterdam to Constance. Handbook for Travellers* (Leipsic: Karl Baedeker, 1903), 47.

Researching the View Cards
of Mount Vernon

Barbara L. Anderson

Collecting postcards often creates an intense desire to actually see the sights and scenes that appear on those cards. Occasionally, the reverse is true. A visit to a famous historical site may help develop a greater interest in the view cards of that location. A visit to Mount Vernon, the estate of George Washington, lured me into a closer examination of the Mount Vernon cards already in my collection, and eventually led me to broaden that collection. In reviewing the cards, I noted a wide range of publishers, many different numbered series, a diversity of styles and widespread cancellation dates.

Mount Vernon, the most photographed home in America, has generated thousands, perhaps millions, of postcards since the estate was purchased in 1853 by the Mount Vernon Ladies Association (MVLA). Would it be possible to document the greater portion of the cards produced, and where would I obtain the necessary information required to develop a checklist of Mount Vernon postcards?

I began by contacting the MVLA, requesting archival information about Mount Vernon view cards. Did they have a complete collection of all cards featuring the Mansion and grounds? Did they have records of the publishers they employed to produce the cards? What changes in the exterior architecture had been made over the years, and when were they made?

I received useful information from an intern at Mount Vernon that included a record of postcards produced of the Mansion (exterior and interior views), a few notes about changes to the exterior, and the fact that the MVLA did not have a complete collection of all the cards. The postcard production records provided to me were sketchy, with wide gaps in

[Haworth co-indexing entry note]: "Researching the View Cards of Mount Vernon." Anderson, Barbara L. Co-published simultaneously in *Popular Culture in Libraries* (The Haworth Press, Inc.) Vol. 3, No. 2, 1995, pp. 89-93; and: *Postcards in the Library: Invaluable Visual Resources* (ed: Norman D. Stevens) The Haworth Press, Inc., 1995, pp. 89-93. Single or multiple copies of this article are available from The Haworth Document Delivery Service [1-800-342-9678, 9:00 a.m. - 5:00 p.m. (EST)].

89

the chronology and no mention of numerous publishers who had produced as many as 20 different series of cards.

I furthered my research by purchasing Mount Vernon cards at every available opportunity; and through two postcard publications, I solicited listings from other collectors which contributed to an ever-expanding list. As I acquired new cards and information, I sorted the views by publisher and attempted to date the cards. If used and cancelled, dating was a simple matter, since most postcards are addressed and mailed within a short time of purchase, if used at all.

If no postmark was present, and most cards were not mailed, the general outline for dating postcards proved useful. Postcard authorities have developed the following system for pinpointing the date of publication of older postcards.

PIONEERS: Mailed or published prior to July 1, 1898, before the effective date of the Postmaster's Act of 1898. These are governmental postals and required two cents for postage.

PRIVATE MAILING CARDS: Published between 1898 and December 24, 1901. Imprinted on the reverse of the card is "Private Mailing Card–Authorized by Act of Congress, May 19, 1898." The cost to mail was one cent.

UNDIVIDED BACK: Published before 1907. No message was allowed on the reverse. Cost to mail, one cent.

DIVIDED BACK: All cards published after 1907 had divided backs; the right side for the address, the left for the message.

WHITE BORDER ERA: Many cards published between 1915-1930 had a white border around the image.

LINEN ERA: From 1930 to 1945, views were printed on a linen-textured stock. Coloration was hand-applied to the negative and unattractive or undesirable features such as utility poles, people, vehicles, etc., were airbrushed out.

PHOTOCHROMES: 1939 to present.

Other aspects of postcards are often useful in dating. For example, city zone numbers were implemented in May of 1943 and Zip Codes started in July of 1963.

My research into the postcards of Mount Vernon has produced three published articles to date. "The View Cards of Mount Vernon" was published in the November, 1993 issue of *The Postcard Collector*, a monthly magazine now being published by Landmark Publications. That article focused on a general history of the Mansion and discussed a mere handful of the various publishers who produced cards of Mount Vernon. The archival records of the MVLA were outlined, and various interesting sidelights obtained from these records were noted. Space considerations only allowed eight postcards to be illustrated, including the very first postcard produced by the Detroit Publishing Company in 1901.

Information about defunct publishers is extremely difficult to obtain. Many companies simply went out of business and left no record of their activities. Letters to various postcard authorities netted no useful data, but networking with other collectors occasionally provided valuable information. I had acquired a series of eight cards showing sketches of various exterior scenes around the estate. The drawings were signed by Elizabeth O'Neill Verner. Her name was mentioned in the MVLA chronology and as a result of featuring one of her cards in the *Postcard Collector* article, I was contacted by a Verner collector. He was able to provide me with considerable background material about this artist, that in turn, led to an article about her work. "Elizabeth O'Neill Verner" published in the April 25, 1994 edition of *Barr's Postcard News*, a weekly tabloid newspaper.

Barr's Postcard News also published "Washington's Home: Curt Teich and Mount Vernon View Cards" in their July 19, 1993 issue. In this piece I directed the readers' attention to the Curt Teich cards, and was able to provide in-depth information about the Mount Vernon cards printed by the Curt Teich Company.

The Curt Teich Publishing Company of Chicago printed millions of view cards during their existence and fortunately their records were preserved. A call to the Curt Teich Archives at the Lake County Museum in Wauconda, Illinois, provided me with a complete listing of all the postcards produced featuring the Mount Vernon estate. These photocopies of the original production records proved invaluable.

Curt Teich was primarily a printing company which worked in conjunction with publishers who had a contract with a client to produce view cards. The Teich records indicated the publisher in most cases, and the Teich numbering system enabled me to chronicle all the cards that the company produced. The Teich listings also helped in dating their cards since the original records, except in the case of the earliest cards, noted specific production dates. Teich experimented with several numbering systems and finally settled on a workable designation in early 1930. In many cases, the records even noted the quantity of cards printed, ranging from 3,500 to 25,000.

Architectural alterations to the exterior of the Mansion assisted in dating early cards. Assuming that these features are visible in the image, the removal of a porch on the south end in 1931, and the removal of a roof balustrade in 1936, provide solid visual evidence of a general time frame for the issuance of a card.

When Martha Washington died in 1802, many of the furnishings and artifacts in the Mansion were sold. During the intervening years, the MVLA made rigorous efforts to recover some of the original furnishings and appointments. Researching the changes in the various rooms of the Mansion could provide additional chronological evidence for dating. Assuming that careful records have been kept of changes and replacements, one could pursue research into the date of cards depicting interior views, using the MVLA archives. This project remains to be accomplished.

Having accumulated extensive listings of the postcards of Mount Vernon, the first task to be completed involves setting up well organized lists of the cards issued by each different publisher. Many companies produced multiple series of cards over a period of several years. As changes occurred in the decor of the individual rooms, the MVLA clearly contracted for new series of cards showing these alterations. Separate lists for each series from each different publisher will be formatted. Each sheet will contain headings for such basic data as Publisher (if known), Printer (if known), Type of Card (Private Mailing Card, undivided back, white border, linen, chrome, continental chrome, color, black and white, etc.), Artwork (photographic, drawing, painting, reproduction), Numbering System, Date (specific or range), and Notes (cancellations noted, miscellaneous information). Following these general headings will be a listing of all cards and any numbers that might be present.

The Postcard Collector article led to interesting and enlightening correspondence with a representative of the I & M Ottenheimer Publishing Company of Baltimore, Maryland. The company had produced cards of Mount Vernon in the early 1900's, and in spite of changes in their operation, is still in existence. The Ottenheimer representative provided me with color photocopies of Mount Vernon cards from his personal collection and, more importantly, copies of the original black and white photographs that were used to produce the postcards.

In the process of studying the cards, I came to the conclusion that negatives of many images had obviously been used by many different publishers. Some cards feature identical images, but the reverse side carries the imprint of different publishers/printers. Companies undoubtedly sold or traded their negatives to another firm. On the reverse of the black and white photographs received from Ottenheimer, for example, a notation indicates that they had been obtained from the Leet Brothers Company, another publisher who produced copious quantities of Mount Vernon views. This evidence confirms the fact that negative and plates were bought and sold.

The end result of researching Mount Vernon postcards will be a monograph. The market for this kind of publication will be narrow indeed, but in the interests of furthering scholarly research on postcards, it seems worthwhile to pursue the project. A potential outline for such a manuscript might include the following sections:

- *Why?* An explanation of why I undertook the study and the nature of the initial inspiration.
- *History of Mount Vernon.* Background information about the original property, the acquisition by the MVLA, and general data regarding the estate itself.
- *Research process.* A detailed discussion of how I proceeded to study Mount Vernon postcards.
- *Format explanation.* A discussion of the format for listing the cards by publisher. The goal here is a user-friendly checklist.

"Patriotic and Profitable": The World War I Postcards in the Hoover Institution Archives

Elena S. Danielson

During World War I, picture postcards, already popular since the 1890s, became a fundamental means of mass communication and persuasion, as well as an instrument for private and governmental fundraising in pre-radio Europe and Russia.[1] During the first massive modern war in history, the millions of young men sent into the battlefield depended on postcards to reassure relatives they were still alive. The advantages of postcards over traditional letters were instantly obvious to all: speed and ease. Lacking an envelope, the cards rapidly passed through military censorship, and the tiny space provided for a message alleviated the pressure on tired troops to write anything lengthy.

The explosion of postcard publication at the turn of the century is well represented in the holdings of the Hoover Institution Archives at Stanford University, that document political and social change in the twentieth century. Scattered throughout the 5,000 collections are postcard images from around the world. Some are of a tourist nature with local color such as carefully posed natives. Others fix the appearances of buildings and cityscapes long since destroyed. Many have a strong political content. Of the latter category the most interesting set is an accumulation of 12,000 World War I era postcards, now located together in what is called the "World War I Pictorial" collection of the Hoover Institution Archives. Approximately 5,000 of the 12,000 cards were printed in Germany, another 5,000 or so in Russia, and the balance are primarily American, Austrian, British, Dutch, French and Hungarian.

[Haworth co-indexing entry note]: "'Patriotic and Profitable': The World War I Postcards in the Hoover Institution Archives." Danielson, Elena S. Co-published simultaneously in *Popular Culture in Libraries* (The Haworth Press, Inc.) Vol. 3, No. 2, 1995, pp. 95-107; and: *Postcards in the Library: Invaluable Visual Resources* (ed: Norman D. Stevens) The Haworth Press, Inc., 1995, pp. 95-107. Single or multiple copies of this article are available from The Haworth Document Delivery Service [1-800-342-9678, 9:00 a.m. - 5:00 p.m. (EST)].

95

The "World War I Pictorial" collection is an artificially created assembly of visual materials that were acquired from various sources. The majority of the cards were purchased soon after the armistice, most of them within a few years of the founding of the Hoover Institution in 1919. There is evidence that some of the materials were secured in large lots. A vast number of German postcards came in the 1920s from a private dealer named Friedrich Mönkemöller, an engineer living in Bonn. Many of these German cards have handwriting on them, and cancellation markings, although the Feldpost cards did not require postage stamps as such. The Russian cards, which do not have handwritten text, bear a rubber stamp marking from the library of the Tsarist governmental office overseeing publishing. It is very likely that the Russian cards were purchased in a lot from the new Soviet government by the Hoover Institution's very successful first Russian curator Frank A. Golder in about 1921-22. The fact that the majority of the cards are either Russian or German reflects the interests of the founding curators.

While the German publishing industry had already developed the postcard as an essential element of middle class life by the 1880s, the Russians caught up quickly. The Russian government had joined the Universal Postal Union by 1872. Privately published cards became legal c.1894, years after they were common in Germany, but about the same time that Great Britain permitted private cards. Swedish, German and French companies continued to market cards in Tsarist territory, but Russian chromolithograph capability achieved a very high quality of its own by the turn of the century. Russian postcard art did not come out of a vacuum, but rather built on a colorful folk tradition of broadsides called the "lubok" that combined text and imaginative woodblock pictures. The lubok persisted right up to the time that publishers came out with lithographed replacements.[2]

Although it is difficult to estimate how representative the Hoover collection is, or what percent of the total output is included in it, a survey of these wartime cards produces two immediate conclusions. The first is the impressive number of images produced during the war and the speed with which cartoons, photographs, and paintings were printed up and distributed both on the homefront and in battlefields. Among the 12,000 cards there are certainly a good number of duplicates or cards so similar as to function as duplicates, but the number of unique images is a tribute to the power of profit in wartime publishing that must have employed a huge number of artists, print shops, and design studios, both private and government sponsored. The blatant propaganda and often crude patriotism of the cards did not in any way diminish their popularity. The Great War created an enormous market for an already burgeoning industry.

Secondly, beyond sheer quantity, the collection is remarkable for documenting the stunning inappropriateness of the images. This is a subject that bears closer examination. With the exception of straightforward photos of bombed out buildings that are really in the realm of reportage, the postcard pictures are typically engaging, entertaining and completely out of step with reality. Important social movements are totally excluded, probably by censorship either official or self-imposed. Text and images often do not match well. In general, the motives of the artist, the designer, the publisher, the government and the buyer of the cards are at odds in very complex ways. Great caution must be exercised in using postcards as direct documentation of social trends. The size of the "World War I Pictorial" collection is sufficient to illustrate the complexity of this pocket sized poster art. The following examples from the Hoover collection are intended to show the value of taking the time to untangle the mixed motives of Great War postcards. Two of the most obvious conclusions are the essential self-delusion of patriotic cards, and the way the cards reflect the interaction between cultures in violent collision such as Russia and Germany in World War I. It is also useful to see how the cards function within a larger printing and publishing market that includes posters, political stickers, and even candy wrappers that together create a lively, national pictorial culture. Well made postcard and stamp albums hint at the intended permanence of this shared medium as a coffee table fixture, and the leisure of an earlier age to assemble and appreciate such private, family collections.

After a brief survey of the range of the collection a closer look at two specific examples, one German and one Russian, will show how an artist's patriotic sketch once it is widely distributed in card format, becomes an icon of sorts whose meaning is easily manipulated and even inverted in times of social upheaval.

The main categories of cards for both countries include photographs and painted portraits of important military leaders, the text of proclamations and patriotic songs, paintings and photographs of battle sites, inspiring quotes, genre paintings of hearth and home, scenes of battle, aerial warfare, ships at sea, and satiric cartoons.

The penchant for self-delusion is most obvious in the large category of satirical cartoons, often too crude to appear as wall art, although they were commonly reproduced in newspapers and illustrated journals. Imaginative and amusing Russian cartoons trivialize the German enemy as a fat, beer-swilling, sausage-eating fool. The observation balloons which gave the

Germans such an advantage are depicted as oversize Wurst. Russian Cossacks stomp on Prussian cockroaches. (In Russian the words for Prussian and cockroach sound similar enough for the pun to work.) From most of these cards it would be impossible to guess that the battlefield defeats of the Russian army set the stage for massive mutinies that eventually forced the abdication of the Tsar and set the stage for the Bolshevik seizure of power in November 1917. The seriousness of the threat is usually masked by a cavalier confidence and wishful thinking. French and British cartoons are very similar in chauvinism, though the drawing styles represent different traditions. In one French caricature, a band of German troops is trying to surrender, while the cool French soldier tells them to wait until he has finished writing a letter home. Clearly, these are scenes that just never actually happened.

Especially inappropriate are the sentimental drawings of cute Russian children playing war. One child in a Russian uniform is beating up a smaller child in a German uniform with a miniature spiked helmet. At their feet a toy Rheims Cathedral is knocked over. Prior to August 1914 several artists had established a following with a series of charming children's scenes. These artists simply adapted their style to the wartime situation, turning innocent kitsch into a shallow callousness. The military catastrophe that led to revolution and a humiliating withdrawal from the conflict is expressed in just a few, mostly cheaply printed postcards in the collection of uncertain provenance.

German postcards are equally unrealistic. Scenic postcards from the Eastern Front make invasion seem like another innocent form of tourism. By the 1890s the German "greetings from" (Gruss aus) postcard had become a standard for travelers, rather analogous to the American "Wish you were here" cards. This tourist card style continued without a pause when shooting started. Charming landscape paintings and photos depict the Masurian Lakes, the site of a ferocious battle that sent the Tsarist army reeling in defeat but at great cost to the Imperial German army. The simplicity of the identification "German printshop, Warsaw" belies the violence that made the operation possible. A photo card shows a German soldier slogging through a field where tired Polish women are trying to keep the farms going while their men are at war. The text is about the dashing German soldier meeting local beauties. The obvious incongruity and falseness of the text is not of consequence in wartime. In a cartoon verging on self-parody, a wholesome young German soldier, looking exactly like a boy scout, cheerfully tries sign language on a baffled couple wearing embroidered peasant clothes. In the caption the soldier says to himself "If only I knew how to say 'beer' in Wallachian."

An entire series of stylish paintings show German soldiers dancing mazurkas with colorfully dressed "local" Polish beauties. In the same series, soldiers with very minor injuries are tended by slender and attractive German nurses who are entranced by the men's tales of valor. Married soldiers come home on R and R to stylish wives and loving children in picture perfect homes. Girlfriends playfully attach little bouquets of wildflowers to the spike on the helmet of departing German fiancés. The series was published as "Lustige Blaetter," or funny pages, by Wennerberg and Eysler of Berlin. For all the brash swagger these stylish cards do not achieve the level of arrogance and pompousness found in the World War II German cards, instead they function as naive morale boosters not conspicuously different from the braggadocio of British, French or American cards. The flirtatious Wennerberg girls are as wholesome and lighthearted as the American girls painted by Howard Chandler Christy, just less given to wearing men's uniforms.

German Feldpost produced its own special, often improvised types of cards. In some cards the picture side was clearly left over from peacetime supplies, and the address side was printed for battlefield conditions. Many of the designs are rapidly drawn sketches of the battlefield printed up in great haste. In postcards sent to the field, the individual message was so clearly unimportant compared with the act of sending a tangible greeting, that the address side frequently left no room for a message at all, just labeled spaces for detailed regiment and battalion numbers to insure that the card would reach the particular soldier. The card's purpose was to arrive, not relay any personal words. Soldiers used these cards to keep in touch when they were separated in different units. The importance of the field post cards is reflected in the cards themselves. There is a photocard showing German field artists at work, and a cartoon showing the postcard printers working harder than the other military personnel. One painting shows the mobile Feldpost as a covered wagon in the midst of bombed out buildings where happy troops gather. The printer of one clearly improvised Feldpost card from northern France is given as "Landsturmdruckerei Briey im Kriegsjahr 1914."

Various German charitable organizations sold Feldpost cards to raise money. These are more expensively printed in full color by studios in major cities. The address side of the cards provided exact information on what percentage of the profits went to the charity, typically 15% of the 10 Pfennig unit price. Often the cards reproduced elaborate academic oil paintings of German ships or planes destroying specific British ships including merchant vessels, paintings reproduced and sold in order to raise money for injured German veterans. A Professor Willy Stoewer painted endless sea battles, and scenes of U-Boat romanticism. The unembarrassed pride in destroying the enemy is not diminished by the casualties on both sides. A Red Cross card set sponsored by Kaiser Wilhelm II was sold with a preprinted five Pfennig stamp. Another Red Cross series designed for use by prisoners of war features carefully posed photos of luxurious conditions in which POWs play pool in immaculate recreation halls, live in requisitioned palaces, and sleep in comfort.

Ironies are evident throughout the collection. On occasion the publisher and the postcard seem contradictory. Many printers in Tsarist Russia had Germanic last names, although the families may have lived in Russia for generations. Anti-German cartoons appear regularly on Russian cards printed by such expatriate German family companies. Only one of the non-Bolshevik cards in the collection carries an anti-war subtext. It is a reproduction of a well known Russian painting "The Apotheosis of War" that depicts a stack of skulls and eerie, sinister crows. (The painting created in 1871 by V.V. Vereshchagin is now in the Tretyakov Gallery.) Reproduction of museum artwork, such as we are familiar with today, was already well established in turn of the century Russia. Thinly disguised as a Russian art reproduction, this image is one of the very few anti-war cards to be represented in the collection. This card's troubling message is compounded by that fact that it was published by the Mehnert Company of Moscow. More research would be required to determine whether this printer came from the same Mehnert family so torn by double loyalty that one Russian born member went to Germany and enlisted in the Kaiser's army. Russians of German background were systematically persecuted in the course of the war although experts agree that the overwhelming majority were loyal to Russia.

Both German and Russian postcards are well represented by patriotic and religious kitsch, and combinations of the two. Christ or the Virgin comforts fallen soldiers on the field in Russian cards. Easter eggs cheer Russian soldiers. Holiday greetings were a direct continuation from pre-war traditions with a military twist. From the cards one would guess that Christmas in a German trench was a jovial treat. "Beste Weihnachts und Neujahrswuensche" (Best wishes for Christmas and New Years) says a card showing soldiers firing heavy cannons, in a vignette bordered with a cheerful Christmas garland, published by the Austrian Red Cross. Family sentiment comprises another huge category of kitsch in wartime.

As war progressed the jolly facade gave way to bitter satire, still predictably unrealistic. Early cartoons might show Russian Cossacks skewering German soldiers on their swords as shashlik. Once such humor is no longer viable, a Russian cartoon shows a German soldier skewering a

Russian baby in an image that anticipates the most terrifying scene in Eisenstein's World War II classic film "Alexander Nevsky."

Germans responded to Allied cards depicting Huns killing babies and raping local women. One card shows a kindly German soldier still wearing his dagger while tending a French infant. The printed caption reads "Unsere 'Barbaren' im Feindesland: Fuetterung des kleinen Feindes." (Our "barbarians" in enemy territory: feeding the little enemy.) On the verso is a penciled notation in the spiky German handwriting of the era: "Ein Idyll, wie es haeufig zu sehen ist, bei uns in Feindesland, Frankreich, Maerz 1916." (An idyll that can be frequently seen among us in enemy territory France, March 1916.) One can only speculate how the writer reconciled armed invasion with appalling civilian casualties and concern for "little enemies."

The greatest artistic effort went into government fundraising. Both German and Russian war bond advertisements offered an illusory 5 1/2% interest. These war bond posters were routinely reduced to postcard size. The same images were further reduced to sticker size, and printed up as perforated stamps, much like medical fundraising stamps in post World War II America. The postcards had several obvious advantages over both posters and stamps. The postcard has two useable sides so combining text and image has greater possibilities. Long admonitions to buy bonds and send shrapnel against the Germans graced the address side of postcards with poster images on the front. Ornate folklore designs on the address side of Russian postcards reinforced the patriotic theme of defending Mother Russia and the unique Russian culture. The heavy paper stock of postcards made them more durable than either posters and stamps, and the fact that they could be mailed circulated the images in a unique way. Whole newspaper pages and proclamations were reduced to tiny type on postcard stock, also as quite unreadable stamps.

Most, but not all of the postcard art was steeped in various degrees of hypocrisy. Among the dozens of Russian publishers from the major cities of the empire that are represented in the Hoover collection, one printer stands out by virtue of the aesthetic integrity and technical quality of the artwork. The potentially clichéd patriotic scene of St. George slaying a dragon is presented with fresh verve by the artist M.A. Vrubel, and printed in gorgeous color by A. A. Levenson. In another card, what could be an embarrassingly sentimental woman in traditional Russian attire is raised above kitsch by the subtle technical brilliance of the color lithography, also by Levenson. The same firm departed in style for an anti-German card with a bold cabaret scene in garish red. A. A. Levenson advertised his Moscow firm as a "rapid printer." He specialized in timely formats:

newspapers, theater posters, race track tickets, invitations, and postcards. A lavish, limited edition company history, published in 1903, provides an overview of his operation.[3] On page 32, the book illustrates each of 14 colors that go into one art card. A printed postcard on page 39 looks so real one is tempted to pick it up. Examples of 10 color chromolithographs are shown on page 61. The book includes photographs of new printing machinery, said to come from the United States. Even today it would be difficult to match the quality of the printing, which makes use of the best paintings being created in the Russian Silver Age and reproducing them in carefully mixed inks with unusually delicate shades. Even the tiny stamp versions of cards printed by Levenson retain detail and shading, judging by several specimens preserved in the Hoover Institution's "Stamp Collection."

Russian war loan appeals sometimes reverted to old loyalties with figures of ancient helmeted Slavic warriors. A surprising number of the government sponsored war loan posters showed heroic factory workers, presumably the target audience for fund raising. In one entitled "Everything for the war," a graceful young woman confidently if somewhat delicately operates heavy industrial machinery in a munitions factory. The Hoover Institution has examples of this appeal in poster, postcard and stamp versions. It was published by the government department overseeing small credit and loans. The same publisher produced a war loan appeal by the artist R. Zarrin showing a similarly refined young man working a lathe with the caption "Patriotic and Profitable–Subscribe to war loans at 5 1/2%." There was still some expectation that the war loans would be repaid with interest, patriotism at a self-serving profit margin. This factory worker, whose stylish grooming and serene expression would look more appropriate in a drawing room than a factory, is worlds away from the dynamic socialist realist proletarian worker that would burst forth in Soviet art in just another year.

The contradictory illusion of combining patriotism and profit in the war loan effort can easily be transferred to the inherent conflict of interest in the propaganda cards that advertised the bonds. The millions of cards, mailed free from the field, made the pictures well known to a huge popular audience. The following two examples trace the fate of nationalist symbols.

By far the most popular and probably most widely circulated German poster of World War I shows a soldier in black face camouflage and bright eyes staring ahead with an almost mystic gaze.[4] He is wearing the steel helmet introduced in 1916 to replace the impractical spiked helmet, that had a leather base, like old American football helmets. By the way he holds on to a beam, he has the look of one defending an embattled homeland, clearly not the posture of an aggressive invader. The text reads "Helft uns siegen! zeichnet Kriegsanleihe" (Help us Win! Sign War Loans) (see Illustration1). This distinctive outline of the helmeted defender with glowing eyes became an emotion laden icon during the second stage of the war. It was produced in huge quantities as posters of various sizes, and as a postcard for mass distribution. The compelling image was designed by Professor Fritz Erler, and the card was published in Munich, by Kolortiefdruck der Muenchener Graphischen Gesellschaft Pick & Co. The dark, helmeted outline was used repeatedly during the troubled interwar period and throughout World War II in different permutations to rally German nationalism. In World War II the postcard industry flourished again to distribute poster images of helmeted heroes by Nazi artists such as Ludwig Hohlwein and Mjolnir. Perhaps because of this wide distribution, the Allies picked up on the shape of the helmet with its curved neck guard, inverted the meaning, and used it as a symbol of evil. Even today the symbolism of evil can be seen in the same profile adapted in figures such as Darth Vader.

The concluding example comes from an honest attempt to raise funds for injured Russian soldiers in a straightforward way that surprised all parties by its popular success. Charitable organizations in both Germany and Russia sold postcards to raise funds. At the outset of the war, as injured Russian peasant soldiers streamed back from the front, concerned civic leaders intensified these fundraising efforts, despite some opposition to initiatives outside of centralized control. In August 1914 the city fathers of Moscow asked an eminent art professor at the Moscow School of Art, Architecture and Sculpture to make a drawing for a collection drive to benefit the war wounded. The artist, Leonid Pasternak, father of poet Boris Pasternak, was known for his quick sketches from life that were both realistic in an academic sense but marked by forthright individuality and understated intensity. His drawings of his friend, the writer Leo Tolstoy, were especially successful. Leonid Pasternak accepted the commission, but explained that he was unfamiliar with military uniforms and asked to have a soldier come to his studio. The resulting sketch from life is direct and unpretentious. A weary soldier, weighted down by his experiences, leans against a wall and holds a cloth to a bleeding head wound (see Illustration 2). A.A. Levenson printed up the drawing both as a postcard with no text which was sold to raise funds and as a poster to advertise the drive. The postcard shows signs of being produced in great haste, even for a "rapid printer." There is no typesetting or text on either side, no marked space for a stamp, only the small compressed diamond with the Levenson logo. Pasternak remembers that the card was expensive. It was collected apparently as art and as a donation to a worthy cause, rather than as a means of communication. The card version in black ink on buff stock has a finer line while the poster was drawn over with a bolder stroke to show

ILLUSTRATION 1. Postcard version of "Help us Win! Subscribe to the War Loan" by Fritz Erler that was widely used in a variety of postcards and posters in Germany during World War I. (World War I Pictorial Collection/ Hoover Institution Archives, Public Domain)

ILLUSTRATION 2. Postcard of "The Wounded Soldier" by Leonid Pasternak that, in a variety of formats, was successfully used to raise funds for those injured in the war in Russia at the start of World War I. (World War I Pictorial Collection/Hoover Institution Archives, Public Domain)

up better in the large format. Done on the largest lithographic stone available, each poster was in effect an original. The poster text is in fluid handwriting that says "To Help the War Victims 20-21 August, Moscow." The poster, but not the card, has red ink to show the blood from the wound. Pasternak's sketch struck a cord with the public. The poster was plastered all over the city and led to the sale of hundreds of thousands of cards. Stamps and candy wrappers were also printed. The public responded to the patriotism, and the charity reaped the profits for the wounded. In 1915 the English magazine *The Studio* issued a special edition of the print known as The Wounded Soldier. The picture was reproduced all over Russia as well, a remarkable success for a simple motif that does not incorporate any obvious attention grabbing devices.

Even this direct and accessible drawing was not without its ideological complications. Reportedly Tsar Nicholas II was not as happy with the Pasternak card as the Moscow citizens were. He felt that the tired soldier was a slander against the Russian fighting man. While certainly not the artist's intention, there was some logic to Nicholas' strictly political reaction. Nicholas' enemies, the Bolsheviks, used a pirated version of the picture in 1918 for an anti-imperialist, anti-war poster without bothering to inform the artist. Pasternak had never intended his postcard to be used this way. When Pasternak asked about his copyright, the new Soviet authorities informed him that it had been nationalized along with all forms of property. He was asked to provide more drawings for the new regime. Although Leonid Pasternak, like his son Boris, was not unsympathetic to the stated ideals of the new communist ideology, he never again produced propaganda art.[5]

The mix of patriotism and profit is never an easy one; yet somehow the spontaneity of the image, the quick if misdirected wit, the often high quality draftsmanship and printing of Great War cards catch the eye. With even the most intelligent and honest postcards, the meaning can be turned inside out when the image is caught up in the crosscurrents of war propaganda, such as in these last two examples. While the confluence of political sentiment for a mass audience and an artist's individual aesthetics defies simple explanations, often it is the tension between the two that gives political postcard art its unusual fascination.

NOTES

1. I would like to thank Professor Peter Paret of the Institute for Advanced Study at Princeton, New Jersey, for his encouragement of my interest in World War I postcards and their relationship to political poster art. Professor and Mrs. Viktor Bortnevski both graciously helped me with translating and interpreting Russian cards.

2. A quick look at typical reference books indicates that the Russian postcard industry is less well understood in the West than the German one. John Lafflin writes in *World War I in Postcards* page 175: "If Russians had postcards during

the Great War, they did not reach the West." At least 5,000 reached the Hoover Institution Archives. Richard Bartmann asserts in his otherwise accurate and fascinating *Picture Postcard Encyclopedia of Russia* that Russian war cards did not attain "the unlimited yet refined degree of hate and contempt that character-ized the German, French and Austro-Hungarian cards of these years." He would find the Hoover Institution's set of Russian cards on a par with the nationalistic hatred found in the propaganda of other countries.

3. A.A. Levenson *Tovarishchestvo skoropechatni A.A. Levenson: Istoricheskii ocherk i opisanie masterskikh 1881-1903.* Moscow: Levenson, 1903. A copy of this book is located in the art collection of the Hoover Institution Library.

4. For an analysis of this oddly enduring symbol see Peter Paret *Persuasive Images: Posters of War and Revolution from the Hoover Institution Archives* p. 44 and 108-109.

5. See Stephen White *The Bolshevik Poster* pages 14-15. The Hoover Institu-tion has an example of the postcard in the "World War I Pictorial" collection. The original poster (RU/SU 1066) and the Bolshevik version (RU/SU) 2284 are in the "Poster Collection."

SELECT BIBLIOGRAPHY

Bartmann, Richard *Picture Postcard Catalog: Russia, 1895-1917* Erlangen: xero-graphic reproduction, 1986.

Bartmann, Richard *Picture Postcard Encyclopedia of Russia* Erlangen: xero-graphic reproduction, 1992.

Jahn, Hubertus F. "Aspects of Patriotic Culture in Russia During World War I" *Ethnic Groups* 10:187-200, 1993.

Jahn, Hubertus F. *Patriotic Culture in Russia During World War I* Ph.D. disserta-tion, Georgetown University, 1991.

Laffin, John *World War I in Postcards* Gloucester: Alan Sutton, 1989.

Levenson, A.A. *Tovarishchestvo skoropechatni A.A. Levenson: Istoricheskii Ocherk i Opisanie Masterskix 1881-1903* Moscow: Levenson, 1903.

Paret, Peter, Beth Irwin Lewis and Paul Paret *Persuasive Images: Posters of War and Revolutions from the Hoover Institution Archives* Princeton, New Jersey: Princeton University Press, 1992.

Pasternak, Leonid *The Memoirs of Leonid Pasternak*, (translated by Jennifer Bradshaw with an introduction by Josephine Pasternak) London: Quartet Books 1982.

A Russian Impressionist: Paintings and Drawings by Leonid Pasternak, 1890-1945 Washington, D.C.: Smithsonian, 1987.

White, Stephen *The Bolshevik Poster* New Haven and London: Yale University Press, 1988.

Willoughby, Martin *A History of Postcards: A Pictorial Record from the Turn of the Century to the Present Day* London: Bracken Books, 1994.

Zariankin, IU. et al., ed. *Moskva na starinnykh otkrytakh* Moscow: Skorpion, 1992.

Learning from Medical Postcards

John K. Crellin
William H. Helfand

Popular beliefs and attitudes affect health care. They not only play a role in shaping political forces, but they can also influence physician-patient relationships and even play a major role in determining an individual's self-care practices. A good way to explore popular beliefs is through the popular arts, where images invariably provide a mirror for prevailing convictions. Comic strips, sheet-music covers, posters, valentines, advertisements, postcards and related printed media represent and illustrate relationships between popular culture and health. Each provides examples of images showing insights into attitudes about health care; of all these media, illustrated postcards probably provide the largest sample.

In addition to their value as an inexpensive means of communication, postcards are an ideal teaching tool because of the evocative way they reflect popular ideas and practices.[1] We have chosen three areas to investigate how postcards throw light on health-care attitudes: ideas about the treatment of common conditions, evidence concerning stereotyped views of medical settings, and finally, to emphasize educational roles for postcards, indications of problems in physician-patient communication.

TREATMENT OF COMMON ILLNESSES

During the period of the golden age of postcards, from about 1900 to 1914, many popular beliefs held that ill-health and chronic illness were based on impurities in the blood, or on debilitated or "run-down" condi-

---

[Haworth co-indexing entry note]: "Learning from Medical Postcards." Crellin, John K., and William H. Helfand. Co-published simultaneously in *Popular Culture in Libraries* (The Haworth Press, Inc.) Vol. 3, No. 2, 1995, pp. 109-120; and: *Postcards in the Library: Invaluable Visual Resources* (ed: Norman D. Stevens) The Haworth Press, Inc., 1995, pp. 109-120. Single or multiple copies of this article are available from The Haworth Document Delivery Service [1-800-342-9678, 9:00 a.m. - 5:00 p.m. (EST)].

tions. Postcards served to reinforce these concepts in various ways (see Illustration 1). For example, the proprietors of Winox, a well-known tonic in the 1920's, published postcard photographs of well-known actors and actresses accompanied by testimonials proclaiming that "Winox is a very good tonic and very valuable in cases of over-fatigue and nervous strain," as well as numerous variations on the same idea.[2] Widespread interest in tonics, a popular dosage form with large numbers of competing products available, is also reflected in the promotion of ales and stouts such as Burke's Stout ("As Good for the Well and Strong as for the Convalescent") and Guiness's Extra Stout ("Guiness is Good for You").

Tonics were also a source for postcard humor. An English comic card mailed in 1906 shows an overweight man napping in the open air. A testimonial on the card reads: "Dear Sir, I was troubled, with insomnia. I took one bottle of your "Nap" Tonic and sleep from morn till night. PS Send another bottle." In another postcard, a little girl notices a skeleton pinned to a bedroom wall; her friend explains, "Oh, they stuck that up to show me what I'd look like if I didn't take my cod liver oil."

Laxatives were viewed as another means of "purifying" the body, a notion that at times suggested going beyond cleaning the gastro-intestinal tract. The postcards, however, focus on constipation, rather than cleansing, which is no surprise given the long-standing preoccupation with the bowels and regularity among physicians and the public. A number of general home medicine books as well as "specialist" texts such as Bernarr MacFadden's *Constipation. Its Cause, Effect and Treatment* (1927), blamed innumerable ailments on constipation and associated autointoxication. Comic postcards have continuously exploited the problem. One postcard published in the 1950's shows a couple viewing a portrait of a king:

> It says here that he sat on the throne for 25 years!
>
> Blimey—the old Devil must have been constipated.

Many comic cards refer to familiar laxatives in their quips about body motions. One card shows an employment officer talking to a client:

> So you work part time packing Epsom Salts. Anything else?
>
> I get relief Sir.

Postcards also comment on the potency of laxative medications, the most popular of which has always been castor oil. As the farmer rushes to his outhouse, his wife observes, "I kept a-tellin' you that wasn't cough medicine, paw." Or as his doctor leaves, the bedridden patient tells his wife, "That silly fool of a doctor told me to take castor oil and stay in bed–It's impossible!" Some popular postcards question the difference between a laxative (castor oil, Epsom salts or Crazy Water, depending on the card) and a bottle of whisky. The answer given is that "One's a TALKIE, the other's a MOVIE."

In addition to comic examples, advertising postcards, using various marketing strategies, address the public's preoccupation with constipation. A postcard view of the Ex-Lax Exhibit in the Hall of Pharmacy at the New York World's Fair (1939), includes the phrase "scientific control," suggesting the authority of science behind the product. In the main, postcards advertising laxatives stress efficacy and reliability.

Comic postcards are also a good source for therapies that have gone out of style. Images published during the first 25 years of this century highlight various self-treatments which are no longer popular. One relatively common therapy depicted on early postcards is the mustard plaster, used in the treatment of respiratory infections. Another is mustard foot baths, a procedure in which the feet are soaked in hot water medicated with mustard. The practice was once widely known for treating feverish head colds. The caption on a postcard of a child shown with a package of powdered mustard next to the basin, says "Hope this finds you better than it leaves me at present." Another depicts a forlorn soul, his feet in a bucket of hot water noting "I've been praying so long for a letter from you that I'm suffering from a sore throat." This card, mailed from Manchester, New Hampshire, in 1925 has a message on the back which offers an added prescription, "Guess I will have to make some iodine and gargle."

FRUSTRATIONS WITH THE MEDICAL SETTING

One waits too long to see the doctor; the office is cluttered with out-of-date and often uninteresting magazines; the doctor's fees are too high and the pharmacist's prescription costs are exorbitant. All these chronic problems of less than adequate medical care are reflected in postcard images from the earliest at the turn of the century to those currently available for sale. Not only do the problems not go away with the passage of time, but they are also not unique to one country. A man with an ax stuck in his head is scornfully asked by the nurse, "Do you have an appointment?" Another with an arrow protruding from his front and back asks the direction to go for help and is scornfully told by the nurse to "just follow the arrow." A skeleton, slumped in a chair, is advised by the nurse that he "can see the doctor now."

ILLUSTRATION 1. Comic postcards are a good source for images of out-dated therapies; this one showing the proper use of mustard foot baths.

I've been praying so long for a letter from you that I'm suffering with a sore throat!

Reprinted with permission.

Postcards also consider costs. In one, a physician hands a patient "a prescription to reduce your weight," and receives the reply, "Never mind, Doc, your bill will have the same effect." A bed-ridden patient requests a reduction in the doctor's bill because he "gave the 'flu' to the whole neighborhood." A French postcard contrasts treatment given to a wealthy patient and a poor patient with the same illness. For the former, the situation is very serious, the cure will be slow but certain, and consultations will be necessary twice a day; for the poor patient, it is not serious at all, cure is immediate, and all that is required is rest, fresh air, and exercise. Further consultations would be useless. Even in an age of extensive third-party involvement in medical care, similar differences endure.

To some extent, these postcards, critical of such bothersome medical practices, reflect a public disquiet with certain facets of medicine which have been on the increase in recent years. The demise of American medicine's "golden age," a period of high social esteem and prestige of physicians, plus admiration for their work, during the first half of the twentieth century, has many causes. Certainly among them are increasingly high fees, perceptions of greed, a decline in the priestly role of physicians and their concern for patients, and perhaps a general erosion of professionalism.[3] The increasing scientific content in the practice of medicine has also served to expand the estrangement between practitioner and patient. In earlier postcard images the physician is formally attired; in later cards he (or increasingly, she) wears a white coat.

Ambivalence towards medicine in the early decades of the century often focused on the increasingly conspicuous and steadily enlarging group of practitioners, the specialists; postcards have frequently commented on the specialist's role. Particular attention has been given to psychiatrists, a group which has probably occasioned more ambivalence than any other group of medical practitioners. The scrutiny devoted to them goes beyond the psychiatrist's couch, a symbol which became a part of medical folklore as soon as it was introduced, and has been widely used by postcard and other caricaturists. It is not easy to generalize about the spectrum of twentieth century attitudes towards psychiatry, shaped by such factors as attitudes towards mental illness and overall expectations of medicine. However, the considerable number of postcard illustrations of psychiatrists does indicate a general acceptance of them by the 1930's, even if accompanied by an element of suspicion of psychological and psychoanalytical concepts. Such suspicion persists. A 1987 comic card by Jennifer Berman, for example, depicts "a Rogerian counselor" who dominated parties with "psychobabble."

Surgeons have also been frequently caricatured. Despite advances in the use of anesthesia and analgesics in the nineteenth century, it is the patient's fear of pain that is most often expressed in postcard images of surgeons and surgical scenes. In comic postcards, the surgeon is invariably a "butcher," often holding an ax or a saw rather than the delicate instruments more commonly employed in operations (see Illustration 2). Gender issues are also evident in surgical scenes, with male practitioners operating on attractive female patients. Postcards of obstetricians, ophthalmologists, and from the turn of the century when X-rays were still a novelty, radiologists also exist, but those other specialties are rare. There are, of course, a large group of postcards for related professions, nurses, dentists and pharmacists.[4]

Lay ambivalence and changing attitudes towards the physician can be seen very clearly in a long-lasting group of postcard images, that of children playing doctor. These generally provide a positive view of medical care. Over the years a good number of such series have been published in France, England, Germany and the United States, presenting photographic mock-up scenes of a little girl nursing a baby doll, visited by a little boy dressed as a doctor. One such card carries the caption, "There'll be no work for the undertaker." A beautifully photographed series of six postcards of such children, entitled "The Doctor," points out the growing importance of specialists in the years before the first World War (see Illustration 3). Here the doctor is a young boy dressed in full morning suit, displaying the impeccable manners of a 'gentleman physician.' The cards provide captions for the doctor's visit, and suggest positive attitudes towards the physician:

> Good morning Mrs. Brown! Ah, the little girl not very well.
>
> Bronchitis you think? Just let me examine her.
>
> I don't quite know whether it's diphtheria, teeth or chilblains?
>
> A very serious case, I think we had better call in a specialist.
>
> But in any case, I came provided with suitable medicine.
>
> Good afternoon, Mrs. Brown. I shall of course call daily in the future.

"Romantic" postcards of the same period, examples of which include photographs of staged scenarios of handsome young male doctors making house calls on appealing young female patients, also suggest positive aspects of medical care. They universally imply optimism that medicine can indeed cure, an attitude reflective of medical, surgical and therapeutic

ILLUSTRATION 2. Fear of the surgeon is reflected in this exaggerated Italian image.

Reprinted with permission.

ILLUSTRATION 3. One of many images in sets of postcards of children playing doctor, a genre that has gone out of style in recent years.

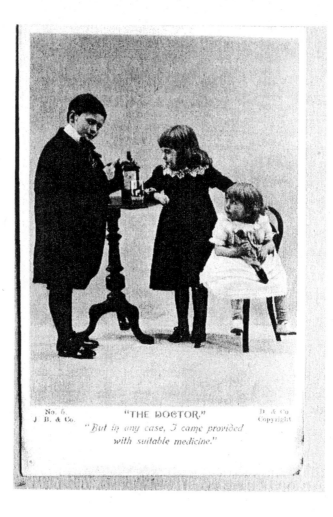

Reprinted with permission.

advances of the time. In these series the physician is always male and the patient always female. Related series have a female nurse attending a male patient, but the romantic objective of the postcards is the same.

Today, unfortunately, it is impossible to find postcards such as those in the series of children playing doctor. Instead, the dealer's racks now contain many postcards published since the early 1960's of surgeons holding bloody saws and other frightening instruments, of dentists inflicting more pain than is necessary, of patients done in by bureaucracy, and of physicians in compromising situations. A 1992 Jennifer Berman comic card illustrates a common situation; it shows a physician talking to a patient: "I can see by this 'big growth' in my country club fees that you'll need surgery. Which organ are you least fond of?"

PHYSICIAN-PATIENT COMMUNICATION

The early decades of the twentieth century were years of significant medical developments. One of the consequences was that medical language became further specialized, and as a result, talking to doctors became more of an issue for many patients. The patient's failure to adequately follow the physician's directions is not uncommon, and in capitalizing on such misunderstandings, postcard artists have used such experiences to highlight the incorrect administration of medicines through malapropisms or other errors in understanding (see Illustration 4). For example, a woman holding a bottle of medicine she has just received from her doctor comments "the doctor says as 'ow I wanted a 'opium' medicine as I'm a bit consecrated." Another shows a patient sitting in a tub of water. When his doctor asks what he is doing there, he replies "didn't you tell me to take me medicine three times a day in water?" In a variant of this, the physician asks a farmer if he had taken the box of pills which were sent, and received a perplexing reply, ". . . I did, but I misdoubt the lid hasn't come off yet." Parenthetically, it should be noted that both of these cards of misunderstood directions are shown in the patient's home, illustrating a practice which has regretfully also gone out of style, the doctor's house call. Modern postcards continue to illustrate the same type of problem; in one a young woman tells her doctor, ". . . those birth control pills you gave me must be too small, doctor, they keep falling out."

Another postcard shows a nurse telling a woman that Mr. Jones had his tonsils removed, thus eliciting the reply, "Oh dear, I'm so sorry because Mr. Jones was so fond of children." A variant of this card presents two working class women gossiping over the garden fence:

They have taken away my old man's appendix.

What a pity, and 'im so fond of children too.

To be sure, these images and messages often reveal social class differences between physicians and lay people, frequently shown by differences in attire and demeanor. In one, a top-hatted and morning-suited physician asks a cleaning woman if she has taken her husband's temperature, and she answers, "Yes, sir, I put the barometer on his chest, it went up to very dry, so I gives him a pint of beer and he's gone to work!" A final example offers a more elaborate jumble:

> O! Larry asthore, sure it's yerself ought to
> be the proud man to-night. The doctor says
> ye have bad information on the brain with
> sevare indigistion of the lungs and a touch of
> new-mown hay which may any minuit turn
> to a guitar of yer pedestrian organs, so he is
> coming to telescope ye to-morrow.

Certainly these causes of misunderstanding, the failure to hear correctly, the lack of comprehension of technical terms, and the misinterpretation of the physician's advice are problems which have always been with us. Though the examples presented on the postcards are mundane and often overly simplistic, they are a pertinent reminder that communication has become more complex in recent years largely because of increasing sophistication in many areas of diagnosis and therapy.

CONCLUSION

Whether consciously or unconsciously, purchasers of postcards often identified themselves or their intended recipient with the image or subject matter of their purchase; this is corroborated by messages on the card which reinforce the image. To give but one example, the message on the back of a postcard view of a hospital comments, "This is where I'll be soon if I don't stop overeating."[5] The commercial success of illustrated postcards from their inception at the turn of the century suggests that they are a sensitive indicator of everyday attitudes, as are the cartoons which have appeared in magazines such as *Puck, Punch* and *The New Yorker.* Since the purposes of postcards differed, and the audience to which they

ILLUSTRATION 4. An example of the difficulties some patients have in understanding the physician's directions.

"What on earth are you doing?"
"Oh, just swigging off a dose of medicine. The doctor told me to take it three times a day in water"

appealed was generally less sophisticated, they offer a perspective rarely found in contemporary books and periodicals.

Ultimately, the postcards are able to offer comments on prevailing opinions about self-care and the physician patient relationship. Their study adds an insightful dimension to that coming from surveys and the published literature of the day.

NOTES

1. In addition to their frequent use as lecture aids, they are also effective as exhibits. One of us has used postcards regularly in small exhibitions in the Health Sciences Library, Memorial University of Newfoundland.

2. Unless otherwise noted, this and other postcards discussed in this paper are in the collections of the authors.

3. Burnham, J. C. "American Medicine's Golden Age: What happened to it?" *Science* 215:1474, 1982.

4. Postcards of nurses have been discussed in two books by Cynthia O'Neill *A Picture of Health*, (S. B. Publications, Loggerheads, Shropshire, UK, 1989) and *More Pictures of Health* Meadow Books (distr. By Witley Press Ltd., Hunstanton, Norfolk, UK, 1991). Pharmacy has been reviewed in two publications by J. C. Crellin and W. H. Helfand, "The Pharmacy in Comic Postcards" *Pharmacy in History*, 23:107-13, 1981 (#3) and "Picture Postcards, a Resource for the Social History of Pharmacy." *Pharmacy in History*, 25:116-30, 1983 (#3). Dentists are treated in a continuing series of articles by Ben Z. Swanson in the *Journal of the History of Dentistry*.

5. Postcard in the hospital postcard collection of the Moody Medical Library, Galveston, Texas.

Graphic Images and Publisher Exploitation of Yellowstone Park in Postcards: "Viewing the Marvelous Scenes in Wonderland"[1]

Richard Saunders

When collectors of American postcards gather to discuss their hoarded treasures there are three implicit jokes among them: Niagara Falls, Washington D.C., and Yellowstone National Park. The humor stems from the commonness of the cards. There are hundreds of images from each place and even before mid-century literally tens of millions of cards were produced and sold. Virtually every postcard publisher included at least a few images of these three sites in their visual stock. While it makes for good humor, such breadth of deltiological activity also provides an intriguing documentary history–especially for Yellowstone National Park. Yellowstone postcards were more than simple sidelines to business, they were for one publisher a substantial industry in themselves. Ever since the initial first-hand accounts of park features were spun into the tales of American fur trappers, the Yellowstone area has inspired and amazed tourists from across the world. While the area of Yellowstone National Park was one of the last major geographic discoveries in North America, because of the uniqueness, variety, and scale of its geologic features, Yellowstone has become one of the most visually exploited landscapes and one of the most photographed places on earth.

PRE-CARD SOUVENIRS

That "truth is stranger than fiction" is truly a cliché in Yellowstone. Souvenir postcards of the Park are based–sometimes badly–on the docu-

---

[Haworth co-indexing entry note]: "Graphic Images and Publisher Exploitation of Yellowstone Park in Postcards: 'Viewing the Marvelous Scenes in Wonderland.' " Saunders, Richard. Co-published simultaneously in *Popular Culture in Libraries* (The Haworth Press, Inc.) Vol. 3, No. 2, 1995, pp. 121-139; and: *Postcards in the Library: Invaluable Visual Resources* (ed: Norman D. Stevens) The Haworth Press, Inc., 1995, pp. 121-139. Single or multiple copies of this article are available from The Haworth Document Delivery Service [1-800-342-9678, 9:00 a.m. - 5:00 p.m. (EST)].

mentary credibility of photographs. Souvenir photography was nothing new. Carte de visite, cabinet, and larger photos decorated the walls of many Victorian-era homes, and stereoptican views were popular parlor diversions.[2] The first photographer in Yellowstone was William Henry Jackson, who accompanied the first Hayden expedition into the Yellowstone area. His photos contributed substantially to the weight of the case made before Congress to establish Yellowstone as a public reserve in 1872.[3] Another young photographer, F. Jay Haynes, followed Jackson into the Park a decade later and eventually landed a federal concession for making and selling commercial photographs in the park. Jay Haynes issued the first pictorial souvenirs of the Park in 1883. These were drawings done after Haynes' photos, lithographed in four-tone grey to one side of a single leaf, folded into a 3 1/2 × 5 1/8 inch cover.[4] Both of these photographers eventually expanded their business interests to include postcards, and their companies–the Detroit Publishing Company and F. Jay Haynes (later Haynes Picture Shops and Haynes, Inc. under his son)–became giants in postcard publishing for Yellowstone. In many ways the history of postcards in Yellowstone is the story of F. Jay and Jack E. Haynes.

POSTCARD BUSINESS BEFORE 1917

Congress authorized the U.S. Post Office's production of single-sided Postal Mailing Cards barely a year after the establishment of Yellowstone as a national reserve. The same act authorized the circulation of printed cards as business mailing forms at a comparable domestic postal rate–one penny. For twenty years the post office distributed and carried postal cards before the first private pictorial postcard was issued for the 1893 World Columbian Exhibition. The commercial production and distribution of pictorial "private mailing cards" had to wait for five more years until authorized by an act of Congress May 19th, 1898.[5] Despite this official beginning, the earliest pictorial postcard with Yellowstone images was produced and distributed a year earlier. A card by Albert Rayier, copyrighted 1897 and produced by the Oakland Journal printing plant, shows a montage of eight Yellowstone scenes printed in black halftones and is postmarked from Mammoth Hot Springs, Wyoming in August the same year.[6] This card was one of a series that Kayser produced that included subjects from several western states.

Jay Haynes got a look at some of the early montage postcards before 1899 and set about to design a card of his own for his other Yellowstone business venture, a newly-organized tourist transportation concern, the Monida & Yellowstone Stage Company. After correspondence with Poole

Bros., a Chicago printing company, he placed an order in April for 5,000 cards. It was a montage similar to the Kayser card, but of five images arranged around a map of the park. Unfortunately further correspondence does not survive and no record of payment to Poole is recorded in the invoices or ledgers of Haynes companies–the cards may never have been delivered. By mid-May and with the tourist season fast approaching, Haynes was getting anxious. The last concrete evidence of the transaction is Haynes inquiry about when the first card shipment would arrive.[7] As a card of this description has not been discovered to date, Poole Bros. may not have delivered the cards at all.

The same year ten of W.H. Jackson's images of Park features appeared among the first commercial postcards issued by the Detroit Publishing Company in 1899.[8] The cards were an important departure from earlier cards (their experimental F series of 1898) and set the stage for virtually all postcards produced thereafter. First, the images were delicately colored rather than black and white halftones; second, they had a single vignette image on each card leaving a white border for writing, rather than a montage of several images. The reason for this departure was obvious. Detroit's Yellowstone cards were made up into sets of ten and sold in a single package. Why sell one card with ten images when ten cards each with a single image would sell just as well?

Obviously the most substantial market for Yellowstone postcards would be with tourists in the Park itself or in transit to or from the park. Postcard sales in Yellowstone would be dependent on summer tourism as tourism in Yellowstone Park is dependent on the seasons. The Park was open to public travel only from mid-June to the middle of September. Business in Yellowstone operated on a parallel schedule, and was tightly under control of the Department of the Interior who issued concession licenses to service industries: hotel and camping companies, transportation companies, and in-park stores. Since the production of postcards was approved in May, barely a month before the commencement of the 1898 season, the likelihood that any postcards were distributed in the Park–other than the example above referred to–is virtually nil, since little opportunity existed for concessionaires to secure reproducible images and contract with a printer for card production.

The Detroit Publishing Company cards appear to have been distributed in the Park on a small scale through the 1899 season and caused a stir among Park concessionaires. The distributor for the Detroit sets was probably the powerful Yellowstone Park Hotel Company. W.W. Wylie had some of Detroit's cards overprinted for his Wylie Camps Company, which operated a string of tent-camps in the park.[9] Haynes' own lithographed souvenir folders had always sold well, but it was obvious that with penny postcards Jackson and Detroit Publishing had upped the ante for the souvenir business. The potential retail volume of photographic postcards promised was an opportunity that Haynes must capitalize on to maintain his business in the Park. At the close of the 1899 season the photographer began planning to produce his own set of colored souvenir cards, intending to compete /directly with Detroit's set.

From his winter base in St. Paul, Haynes first approached the Taber Prang Art Company of Boston. Prang had pioneered the process of chromolithography in the United States and had produced and published the first color reproductions of the Park features, Thomas Moran's watercolors from the Hayden expedition, in 1876.[10] When Detroit Publishing obtained exclusive rights to a new German photo-chromolithographic process made directly from photographic negatives the accuracy of the image and the quality of the color reproduction rose dramatically, largely due to Detroit's insistence on absolute registration for the color separations for each image. The highest expression of this art was the series of photo-chromolithographs produced 1898-1906 that eventually bankrupted the company.[11] With practically their first postcards Detroit Publishing Company set the benchmark in postcard production quality. Prang continued the older color-reproduction process that relied on whole-tone colors that tended to be rather flat (something akin to the printing on today's cereal boxes), printing color onto a photographic image rather than using a color separation process. Haynes was dissatisfied with the sample Prang returned and the cost estimate of $17.50 per thousand cards and declined to pursue them as a source.[12] He also approached the Philadelphia company of J. Murray Jordan about reproducing postcards in single-colored half-tones, but apparently decided against the arrangement.[13]

Detroit Publishing Company's cards had sold well the season before suggesting that they would do as well or, without competition, better in the future. As the 1900 travel season approached Haynes began to be pressed for time. Though the correspondence does not survive he was finally able to find a printer capable of producing cards that met his expectations no further afield than his own city. In late June of 1900, St. Paul printing firm Brown & Bigelow billed Haynes $1,563.13 for 61,500 "3 color Reproductions" (including overs). Haynes had all the cards made up into sets sold in a separately printed envelope.[14] Selling individual postcards was a later development.

By the end of the 1900 season there is no question that Yellowstone postcards were a success. The new source of potential revenue opened an economic interest in Yellowstone outside the small circle of Park concessionaires. Cards published by Franz Huld and H.A. Rost, both New York companies, have been discovered with Yellowstone postmarks from the 1900 season.[15] Almost immediately the postcard craze that had swept Europe a decade earlier descended on Yellowstone concessionaires and businessmen in the surrounding communities. Within five years not only F. Jay Haynes and Detroit Publishing were publishing Yellowstone postcards, but E.C. Kropp, H.H. Tammen Company, and half a dozen other major publishers had entered the market. There existed an ineffectual check on unrestricted marketing in Yellowstone in that businesses had to have a federal license to operate within the Park, but little or nothing was done to regulate competing products or services beyond controlling the licenses. The licensing arrangement kept card sales in the park limited to a small number of specific store owners, but postcard distribution in the Park was simply a contractual arrangement between a concessionaire and a publisher.

In 1908 Jay's son Jack Haynes moved up from work as a summer employee to join his father in the Yellowstone business in a substantial fashion. As Jay became increasingly drawn into the operation of the Monida & Yellowstone Stage Company (later the Yellowstone-Western Stage Co.), Jack assumed ever more responsibility for the photo business. In 1908 Haynes issued the first fifty cards in the 100 Series–a set of postcards with images arranged "touristically" in the order that features would be encountered by tourists in a trip through the Park. The enormous success of the 100 Series (which eventually included more than double the initial one hundred cards) laid the foundation for Jack's increasing success in later years.

Haynes was very careful not to allow his cards to be sold anywhere else but in the park itself. "I do not think I would care to have [my postcards] placed with the News Company in the east," he had informed Prang in 1900. "Most of my customers come from the east and will buy more liberally in the park of subjects they have not seen displayed in the eastern news stands." Though Haynes' photos were licensed to railroads and other advertisers everywhere, no photos were released for publication, and Jack continued his father's policy into the 1960s.[16] Haynes was correct. The policy intentionally created for the traveler a unique source for Haynes' popular Yellowstone images on postcards. The Haynes' cards never did sell outside of Yellowstone National Park–but their photographic images did. He was correct about the context of card purchasing in the Park, but as it turned out his exclusive license for in-Park sales of photographic images hurt his emerging postcard business. Jay's unwillingness to distribute his own cards into the large markets of the East left a graphic void that other publishers were only too willing to fill.

Because of the complexity of photography before the invention of the dry plate negative, only "official photographer" Jay Haynes was really in a position to secure the quality and range of images needed for successful Yellowstone card publication. As he was nearly the sole source of good photographic images of Yellowstone, using Haynes' widely distributed photographs was obviously the simplest method for a postcard publisher to secure images of the Park. Haynes was not so slow as to miss this point. Almost immediately after publishing his own cards he apparently arranged a licensing agreement with Milwaukee card publisher E.C. Kropp to allow Kropp to use and market Haynes photographs of Yellowstone on postcards in the East. Only on the cards produced by Kropp is Haynes credited as photographer. Other publishers were not as scrupulous about appropriating Haynes' images for their cards.

Prior to the development of color photography any colored postcard had to be produced from lithographic stones and later etched zinc plates. The original source might be a detailed photograph, but the finished card was very often heavily retouched–sometimes leaving only the barest suggestion of photographic accuracy–to add any colors, enhance the visual image, wipe out unwanted details, or disguise the source of the picture. Prior to 1909 there was no enforceable copyright restriction on graphic images, consequently plagiarism was rampant among postcard publishers. Due to his position as "official" Yellowstone photographer Haynes was typically the victim. Several Eastern publishers produced full Yellowstone series of their own, mimicking Haynes' 100 Series and often simply reproducing his pictures. Using many of Asahel Curtis's images shot for the Northern Pacific Railroad, Bloom Bros. issued the Y.P. Series in the 1910s for distribution along the NPRR route. Tammen, relying somewhat on C.B. Joslin's pictures, and Acmegraph each produced sets of Yellowstone cards, some of which were images unpretentiously plagiarized from Haynes.

Comparing images between publishers and time periods it is possible to trace the use of popular images. Perhaps the best example of the extent of publishers' unabashed use of a good image began as a Haynes photo, negative number 10162. This is one of Haynes' most famous photos, taken in 1905 upon completion of Old Faithful Inn. The massive log inn regally occupies the background; in the foreground is a man (a young Jack E. Haynes, Jay's son, specifically) standing beside the steaming cone of Beehive Geyser, just across the Firehole River from the Inn. This image was first used on postcards in a series of Haynes' monochromatic collotype cards produced in Germany in 1905. Before ten years were out the same image appeared in the stock of other publishers. Acmegraph used the image,[17] and the American News Company issued two different color variations at different times.[18] In the mid 1920s Bloom Bros. had the decency to try to retouch Jack Haynes out of the picture when issuing the cropped image on their card, but Jack's ghost is still there–the plate retoucher neglected to remove the entire figure. His legs and torso are gone, but against the bank of the river Jack's disembodied hat, head and collar can still be seen.[19]

Within the concession licensing system then in place, any of the Park's concessionaires could distribute postcards in the park or contract with a single publisher to distribute theirs. Postcards had become a substantial source of income and Haynes thereby did not enjoy a graphic-product monopoly that a strict reading of his concession license could have entitled him to. By 1910 Park tourism and profits had increased to such an extent that the Department of the Interior sought to raise ground rent and franchise taxes accordingly. Haynes protested, but sought to use the opportunity to corner the pictorial souvenir market–which included the increasingly lucrative postcard market. Haynes boldly proposed to the park superintendent to approximately quadruple his franchise tax to the government, but in exchange sought departmental sanction for an undisputed monopoly for producing and distributing anything exhibiting Park scenery.[20] He was turned down. Competitor's Yellowstone postcards–many with his own photographs–continued to be shipped into and distributed in the Park by other concessionaires. Haynes' most insistent complaint to the Department of the Interior was that other Park concessions were profiting from postcard images pirated from Haynes and on which sales he could not make a profit. A good example of the scale of his problem surfaced in 1912. The Wylie Permanent Camps Company was a popular alternative to the expensive hotel accommodations in the park, and one which provided a substantial market for postcards in the park. Haynes supplied cards from his 100 Series to company superintendent A.W. Miles, but Miles supplemented the Haynes stock with additional cards from Acmegraph. Haynes bought a set of the Acmegraph cards and then matched them one for one from the cards in his own series. Fully half of Acmegraph's set were his own plagiarized images.[21]

Jay Haynes turned the entire Yellowstone picture concession over to son Jack in time for the 1915 season and thereafter concentrated on running his very lucrative passenger service. One of Jack's first actions was to beard National Park Service director Stephen Mather with a resurrected complaint of injury to his business from others' sale of pictorial souvenirs.[22] The complaint was a valid one, other concessionaires made no secret of selling postcards in their stores or hotels and their actions clearly compromised the license granted to Haynes. His letter was probably one that factored strongly in Mather's decision to call all Yellowstone concession owners together at the end of the 1916 season. In a series of meetings held in Chicago, Mather (a believer in the value of regulated monopolies) proposed to reissue to concessionaires exclusive licenses for particular industries, and instructed them to divide the economic territory and consolidate businesses to eliminate competition. In the negotiations that followed the hotels, tourist camps, transportation, general stores, and souvenir concessions were consolidated. Assets were traded and sold. Jay Haynes was instructed to divest his entire park interests and retire from business in Yellowstone altogether. Jack was finally given the exclusive right over pictorial souvenirs, including postcards, that his father had sought for a long time. This right extended to production, brokering, and marketing all graphic souvenirs sold in the Park, specifically including postcards. Other concessionaires could sell cards provided that they were secured from Haynes. Cards sold outside the park obviously remained uncontrolled. Regarding Haynes' business specifically, the consolidation was intended to cut the in-flow of plagiarized images by drying up the market, thereby insuring that publishers would have to at least produce their own images for Yellowstone cards. Part of the deal involved the sale of postcard stocks held by other concessionaires. Haynes acquired the Detroit "Photostint" cards that the hotel company had been selling along with cards from the Wylie and Shaw and Powell camps.[23]

Haynes' maintained a substantial stock that could be delivered almost at will. He was quite willing to let others in the Park distribute his cards, and neither Jay nor Jack balked about buying cards from other publishers to distribute. At other times Jay bought cards from Grey News Company of Salt Lake City, E.C. Kropp of Milwaukee, and F.A. Rinehart of Omaha, among others.[24]

YELLOWSTONE POSTCARD PUBLISHING OUTSIDE OF YELLOWSTONE

Detroit Publishing Company's earliest cards attracted attention to Yellowstone outside the park, too. Yellowstone was uniquely American and was a graphic image as distinct as the Statue of Liberty. Yellowstone enjoyed steadily-rising popularity as a tourist destination. In 1899 nearly ten thousand people traveled through the Park (less than a single day's total presently). The majority of these constituted the "carriage trade" of the eastern cities: upper-middle class businessmen and their spouses, members of the professions, financially secure leisure-seekers. These people had money to spend, and were the great harbingers of America's consumption society of the next century. A product that could capture their attention would sell well. The opportunity was not lost on printers and the transportation industry nationally.

Though they never intended to sell the cards in the Park itself, many other publishers employed a few Yellowstone images as part of a larger whole, illustrating a tour of America for instance. These cards seem to have been typically sold singly along major transportation routes and in large terminals. E.C. Kropp even generated the same cards for more than one market. A pair of Kropp's Yellowstone images usually found on common backs for U.S. mailing have also been examined with a unique back that has only been seen canceled in coastal seaports. Yellowstone was thus employed as a scenic draw for foreign tourists. English publisher Raphael Tuck produced several Yellowstone cards that seem to have been sold only in travel terminals. Postmarks on Tuck's Yellowstone cards seem limited only to larger cities on the seaboards (Portland, San Francisco, Boston, New York and others). For Tuck, the lure of "far away places" was the draw. Postcards sold in railway and steamship terminals were not just pictorial mementos of where one had been, but also served as illustrative advertising for where one could potentially go (by implication, go via the line that was selling the cards). The unique thermal and scenic wonders of Yellowstone were ideal images on both counts.

Not all publishers were interested in selling their cards in the Park itself as there was good business in selling to tourists en route. Businessmen in many gateway communities such as Gardiner and Livingston, Montana, also issued postcards, typically for sale in their stores or by arrangement with other local retailers or in neighboring communities. Many of these cards pictured things found in Yellowstone–such as animals or flowers–which by *association* could be interpreted by the tourist as being in the Park. Gardiner, Montana, store-owner W.S. Berry published a series of floral cards and animal cards, sold very well in Gardiner and in Livingston.

Throughout postcard history a few publishers produced a bare handful or only a single Yellowstone card, almost always for sale in a local establishment but often hundreds of miles from Yellowstone. American Oil Company produced one card of Old Faithful for its American Scenery Collection; Auburn Post Card Manufacturing Co. in Indiana published three views of snowfall against Yellowstone buildings in 1959, and the same year Far West Studios in Virginia City, Montana, produced one view of Pilot and Index peaks; Chicago's C.R. Child produced a card showing the old "lunch counters" where bears rooted through hotel kitchen garbage; Dan Grigg Enterprises in Mitchell, South Dakota, produced one shoreline view of Yellowstone Lake; H.O. Schilling Advertising Consultants produced a promotional card for the Circle R Motel in West Yellowstone; Dude Larson of Kanab, Utah, and Charles M. Russell were two artists who contributed a single Yellowstone image to their publishers; Great Falls druggist M.P. Horan's card of the Lower Falls was nonetheless printed in Germany, Omaha News Company produced a similar view; Petley Studios in Phoenix, Arizona, included a West Yellowstone view in their stock; E.C. Waters' boat of the same name was featured on the card produced by the Tanner Souvenir Company of New York, another New York firm known only as T.P. & Co. produced a series titled "Picturesque America Series," and numbered their image of the Lower Falls as n.922. Dozens of others could be cited.

Cards produced in this fashion were probably either short-term speculative ventures or commissioned for a particular business.

POSTCARDS AFTER 1916

Even after Jack Haynes was granted a concession contract for illustrated Yellowstone souvenirs, it was not until 1930 when he could capitalize on the sympathy of powerful friends in the National Park Service that he could stand fully on the strength of his paper monopoly. Denver's H.H. Tammen Company had not taken kindly to the loss of their lucrative in-Park market. In April, 1916 the *Denver Post* carried an editorial that lambasted Mather's concession arrangements. The column was picked up by the *Livingston Post*, one of the Park-area's local newspapers.[25] Publishers were clearly not happy about the potential loss of market that a monopoly could bring.

Under the terms arranged in the 1916 reorganization and the explicit directions of Stephen Mather, Haynes bought all the back-stocked cards carried by the hotel company (Detroit Publishing Co.), Hamilton General Stores (Bloom Bros.), and the camping companies (apparently H.H. Tammen Co. and Acmegraph) and contracted directly with postcard publishers to thereafter distribute their cards in the park.[26] Tammen brazenly continued to publish pirated Haynes images, and even approached the Yellowstone Park Transportation Company directly in 1919 asking them to secure Haynes' prints from which to produce an updated set of cards.[27] Bloom Bros. acted similarly and tried to get Haynes prints through C.A. Hamilton of Hamilton General Stores.[28] Haynes was generally able to restrict the flow of his new images to postcard publishers by carefully copyrighting each image, but the older Haynes images continued to be used illegally.

Even after business had been restructured, due to competition from other concessionaires Haynes continued to market his cards at a disadvantage. After a decade of marginal business returns, the Department of the Interior auditors noticed his bottom line and suggested he raise his prices. Haynes pointed to unlicensed competition as the real issue and found a protector in former Park superintendent Horace M. Albright. Albright succeeded Stephen Mather as the director of the National Park Service in 1929 and was well aware of the unfair competitive nature of Yellowstone business, fueled substantially by the automobile. Automobiles were explicitly barred from the Park until August, 1915. By the later 1920s a decade of automobile tourism had created a revolution to business in the national park. Where once every tourist passed by (and typically bought at) Haynes' hotel picture stands when checking in at the desk, automobiles steered an ever-larger number of tourists to the auto camps and cabins. Large stores were built by Hamilton and others to capitalize on the influx of self-guided auto tourists. These locations as well as the unlicensed trade in postcards and other illustrated souvenirs undercut Haynes' business severely. Haynes finally played his hand by petitioning the park superintendent and the National Park Service for the right to compensate his picture-business losses by establishing his own chain of general stores.[29] Superintendent Roger Toll suggested to Albright that the decennial concession negotiation for Hamilton's and Pryor's stores be used to force the competition issue with the concessionaires generally. Albright concurred, and at the end of the 1930 season under federal aegis Haynes was able to sign agreements with the other concessionaires that they would abide by the terms of the leases. This gave Haynes Picture Shops the exclusive right to distribute not only postcards, but "photographs, . . . cameras, motion picture machines, films, developing and printing service, lantern slides, pictorial folders and other items consisting primarily of views, photographs or reproductions of photographs, . . ."[30] The results were dramatic. In the 1937 season Haynes sold 1,879,880 cards of his own production in addition to brokering an unspecified (but substantial) number of other publishers' cards.[31] Under these arrangements Haynes began to turn a consistent profit.

During the "linen" postcard period (1930s and 1940s, so named for the finish of the card stock used for cards) and into the photochrome era (post-1950) little changed in Yellowstone's economic structures until closure of Haynes Inc. in 1966. Though he moved his headquarters from St. Paul to Bozeman, Montana, in 1945, Haynes continued to both publish his own cards and to retail as well as broker cards from other publishers. Haynes even dropped his own set of floral cards in favor of marketing the superior floral set made by Harrison Crandall, Grand Teton National Park photo concessionaire.[32]

A direct result of the 1930 concession agreements, Bloom Bros. ceased publishing Yellowstone cards at all in 1931.[33] Other producers quickly followed suit. By the mid 1940s Haynes was the sole publisher of a full line of Yellowstone postcards, though as noted previously, other publishers often released a few images for their own purposes. In 1951 Haynes made a major technological shift in Yellowstone card publishing that changed the entire graphic presentation of his postcards and insured his monopoly on Yellowstone images sold in the park. Rather than hand-painting black-and-white positive images (photographs) and then producing cards by a lithographic duo-tone process using zinc plates, Haynes began shooting color-film transparencies and had his new cards printed by offset-lithography from four-color separations. His concession meant that since no one else could sell cards in the Park, publishers had no real reason to create new Yellowstone cards at all. A few local businesses in border communities continued to have cards made for sale in their own locations, but these fall into the genre of advertising and postcard sales were incidental to business, not the heart of it.

In the explosion of tourism after World War II the relationship between tourism and postcards changed radically. By this time boxed sets of cards were less important than cards marketed singly, and postcards were becoming less important than amateur photography. Jack continued the "touristic" arrangement of images in his card series, but now they were displayed in revolving racks. Personal cameras had become standard tourist equipment, consequently a box of postcards was not needed to record the trip. Where once they had been the only way that cards were sold, postcard sets by the 1950s became the simplest way to dispose of unwanted or overstocked single cards. At this time Haynes Inc. was marketing approximately 3 million postcards in its 100-day business season–an average of 30,000 postcards daily. The majority was the new photochrome stock, but as late as 1960 Haynes was still selling back-stock of the old lithographed linen cards. By 1957 better than half of Haynes' gross sales was in retailing film and film processing to tourists, and the percentage was climbing.[34]

In 1962 Jack Haynes passed away after nearly six decades as "Mr. Yellowstone." His widow and business partner, Isabel Haynes, continued to manage the family concern for five more years and took over the selection and publication of postcard images. The last postcards published under what still remains as the longest-held park concession contract, commemorated the golden anniversary of the National Park Service in

1966. In 1967 Isabel Haynes sold Haynes Inc. to another concession, Hamilton Stores. During its tenure in Yellowstone National Park the Haynes family had actively participated in all the major periods of American postcard material history. Nearly thirty years later postcards have by no means disappeared, but their place in tourist experience has changed significantly.

SOME CONCLUSIONS

Demographics of Postcard Mailing

It would be useful to determine for various periods the ratio of cards mailed in Yellowstone and elsewhere, but given the tens of millions of Yellowstone cards produced there is no way that an accurate sampling of postmark cancellations can be made. The conclusions herein are drawn from the three largest and most complete private collections of Yellowstone postcards, as well as from examining the stocks of some postcard dealers specializing in Yellowstone cards. Based on this imperfect representation of the whole there seems to be an inverse relationship of Yellowstone and border community postmarks on cards before and after the Second World War. Park tourists of every period had essentially three options for cards purchased in the park: they could mail them from the park; could take them home and post them when convenient (like greeting cards); or could keep them unused as mementos, loose or perhaps pasted into an album.

Compared to photochrome cards of the 1950s and beyond, a high percentage of the earliest Yellowstone cards–particularly Haynes' cards, sold only in the park–are either uncancelled or mailed somewhere beyond the park or its border communities. Clearly until the First World War most Yellowstone postcards are found without cancellations, and the majority of postmarks on Yellowstone-image cards are from outside of Montana or Wyoming. From then until roughly 1946 the majority of postmarks found on postcards with Yellowstone images still seem to be from outside the park and its border communities though the ratio is somewhat more even. After 1946 the relationship practically inverts, with few cards remaining uncancelled and far more cards sporting postmarks from Yellowstone itself than from other locations. The comparative dearth of Yellowstone postmarks when compared to the high number of "foreign" postmarks on cards only sold in the park suggests that in the earliest years of the century postcards were treated as were any souvenirs, that is as something to be carried away and kept.

There is a simple empirical fact that hints at the reason for the change: self-guided tourism, which in Yellowstone was colloquially called "sage-brushing." Prior to 1916 practically all of the tourists who passed through the park were escorted through on one of the stagecoach companies and stayed in one of the Park's hotels or the permanent camps. In 1916 the Secretary of the Interior mandated the cessation of horse-drawn stages and the change to motorized busses. The same year saw the first full season that automobiles were permitted in the Park, and also the commencement of one of the first coast-to-coast roads, the Yellowstone Trail. With the conclusion of World War I came the Good Roads Movement and the democratization of travel through the automobile. Following a precipitous plunge in tourism during World War II, Yellowstone tourism after 1946 skyrocketed as GI's returned home to meet their working wives. Automobiles that had been a luxury before the War now became a necessity, and individual ownership facilitated a huge upswing in automobile tourism nationwide.

Changing Scope of Postcard Sales

Until a regular winter tourist season was established in the 1970s, Yellowstone's business season was limited to merely 100 days during the summer. Costs had to be recovered and profits secured in that time. During the 15, 100-day seasons between 1900 and 1914 visitors to Yellowstone totaled barely over a quarter-million people. At the same time, from surviving printers' bills, Haynes produced and sold at least 3,100,000 postcards. Statistically, *every* visitor to Yellowstone between 1900 and 1914 would have bought 1.6 sets plus a few loose cards–and during this time Jay Haynes did not have a monopoly on postcard sales. By 1937 circumstances and tourism had changed drastically. Annual tourism nearly totaled 500,000 visitors and Jack Haynes enjoyed a postcard-distribution monopoly in the Park. In 1937 Haynes sales of his 1,879,880 postcards had dropped to a per-tourist average of less than four cards. As tourism thereafter climbed exponentially, postcard sales continued to climb but the average number of cards purchased per tourist still fell. In 1951 Jack Haynes wrote to Montana's U.S. Representative protesting Postal Bill H.R. 2982, which intended to increase the postal rates for both commercial and U.S. Mail postcards. The length of the Yellowstone tourist season had not increased over what his father had enjoyed forty years earlier, but Jack estimated that in the same 100 day tourist season the 24 Haynes Picture Shops and outlets were retailing approximately 3,000,000 postcards and $15,000.00 in stamps (primarily penny stamps for card mailing).[35] Thus, tourists in 1951 purchased an average of two and a half postcards each.

Today with nearly 3 million annual visitors a rough average of postcards-purchased to park visitors has still fallen and does not even reach one to one.[36]

Reviewing the figures one can only conclude that early postcards were enormously important products in the Park and were a vital part of experiencing Yellowstone. But the scope and trend of sales also implies something about the changing experience of twentieth-century tourism itself. The automobile made possible a greater number of Park tourists to buy cards, but the coincident popularity of the camera contributed to the printed postcard's obsolescence as a documentary format. A peripheral market existed for privately-published cards as Yellowstone cards were issued within broader series or for specific locations rather than as individual series. Outside of the Park's gateway communities that peripheral market may no longer exist.

Social Expectations Reflected in Postcard Images

The span of publishers, cards and years in the collections examined confirms that demand for some images–for example, thermal features such as geysers–remains fairly constant, though cards' forms may change. On the other hand, postcard presentation of man-made features–such as camp and hotel accommodations–have changed over time. Before 1908 scenes of the grand hotels and spotless camps were fairly common. Haynes even published a five-card "Wylie Series" for that company. After the First World War images of the hotel interiors became gradually more abundant, perhaps suggesting that "sagebrushing" in auto camps was not the sole way to see Yellowstone. The post-War explosion of tourism affected even Haynes' monopoly of card publishing. With the shift to photochromes in the 1950s the hotel images took a back seat to depictions of the modern vinyl and chrome conveniences of cabins, stores, and cafeterias catering to tourism's new automobile democracy. As the 1980s approached civilized progress became more intrusive and less of a virtue, overcrowding became more of an issue after the Park's centennial, the ecology movements of the 1970s were having an effect on public psyche. Postcard images again changed. Landscapes become dominant over specific features, close-up images of specific wild animals become increasingly common, and man-made objects such as camps and hotels virtually disappear into the background if they are seen at all. Graphic consumption in Yellowstone postcards thus mirrors the ethos of outdoor travel and reflects the consumption priorities of travelers in whatever time they may be. The same type of study could–and probably should–be conducted for other locales.

Stepping back even further, the creation and distribution of postcards was an important social documentary record for Yellowstone, especially before 1950. Modern fine art portrays increasingly less about our existence and more about our ethos. By the 1870s the place of oil and watercolor art as documentary media has been supplanted by the camera and the halftone print. F. Jay Haynes built his Yellowstone concession on the cumbersome realities of 19th century photography. Tourists were unwilling to be burdened with the glass plates, developing tents and chemicals, and tripod setups necessary to take photographs. Haynes' photographs and stereographs were thus convenient documentary records as well as artistic renderings. As postcards began to be published at the turn of the century, sold as boxed sets, they began to supplant inexpensively the handfuls of documentary photographs bought by tourists, and photographs began to be more often bought and displayed as art. But the demands for postcards changed as photography changed. With the wide adoption of hand-held cameras tourists could take their own photographs, capitalizing on their own perspectives as tourists. Sets of cards became less important as tourists photographed sites themselves. Postcards gained a different significance to travelers as individual cards became a convenient form to be exploited as they were intended–an inexpensive communication medium. By the 1920s Haynes in-park photo processing was becoming increasingly important business. Card sales were still rising, but compared to the numbers of tourists percentages of cards bought per tourist was declining. A glance at present Yellowstone postcards will suggest that they have now become an art form themselves and amateur photographs and videorecordings have essentially supplanted postcards as a documentary form. Park visitation has skyrocketed, and as tourist-wielded cameras became more commonplace the importance of the postcard itself as a documentary medium has declined to the point that it would be impossible today to find a set of postcards "touristically arranged."

As historical interest moves deeper into twentieth century history, scholars must understand and contextualize the experiences and forms of expression unique to the century. Obviously this cannot be done without substantial collections of primary sources from which to work. For Yellowstone, as well as other tourist destinations, postcards provide one economic perspective of scenery as a consumable commodity and adds an edge to simple statistical figures of park attendance.

Other than as curiosities to the biographer or family historian, or as collectibles, individual postcards are typically perceived to have little value. However when collected carefully for a specific area the collective entity becomes a significant and revealing documentary record and a socioeconomic window. What remains to be done for Yellowstone and other locations is a systematic content analysis of images and publishers to reveal precisely what images were being published, and compare how images reflect changing social priorities and expectations. In general the dynamics of postcard production hints at the market and interest-driven cultural values of the times; photo-illustrated cards provide a pictorial record of a community and its self-concept; a survey of postmarks suggests the scope of particular regional markets and travelers; and the record of image and publishers may be coupled to other primary sources to understand a facet of business history that has been often overlooked. Specifically, a study of postcards with Yellowstone National Park illustrates the value–intrinsic and economic–that Yellowstone holds.

NOTES

1. Laura E.A. Batson to Mrs. Robert L. Laylor, 1901 Jul. 9, from postcard in the possession of Jack and Susan Davis, Bozeman, Mont. I am deeply indebted to the Davis's, collector Tom Mulvaney, and deltiographer Kathie Burke for the use of their extensive collections and for sharing their extensive knowledge in the preparation of this article.

2. General sizes for carte de visite is 2.5 × 4 in., cabinets 6 × 9 in., and stereoptican cards varied from 3.5 to 4.5 × 7 in.

3. Aubrey Haines, *Yellowstone National Park: Its Exploration and Establishment* (Washington: National Park Service, 1974), 103-104. The negatives of the earliest official expeditionary photographer, T.J. Hine of the Barlow-Heap expedition, were consumed in the Chicago Fire, leaving Jackson's photos as the "first."

4. *Yellowstone National Park*, (Fargo, N.D.: Photographed and publ. by F. Jay Haynes, c1883). According to a note in some copies the lithography was done in Germany by Louis Glaser, possibly under the arrangement of the U.S. distributor for Glaser's work, Wittemann Bros. of New York. The Leipzig company printed postcards for Haynes between 1905 and 1913. This type of viewbook was fairly common and was often issued by railroads or growing Western communities.

5. An act establishing the use issuance of "United States Postal Cards" was signed in to law 1872 Jun. 8, but the details were not established until 1873 Apr. 15, standardized to 5 1/8 × 3 inches. Frank Staff, *The Picture Postcard and Its Origins*, (New York: Praeger Publ., 1966), 86, 60.

6. Albert Rayier, "Greetings from Yellowstone Park," private collection. The printer is noted in the engraving on the card, "Oakland Journal Print," and is copyrighted 1897.

7. See Haynes Studio Ledger, Coll. 1502, books 173, 187-190; the correspondence is in the Yellowstone-Western Stage Company ledgers, Coll. 1502, book 127, p. 39, 40, 67, Burlingame Special Collections, Montana State Univ.-Bozeman. At this point processing is not completed for the Jack E. Haynes papers, Coll. 1504. Box and folder locations are given where available, otherwise folder titles are given.

8. Nancy Stickles Stechschulte, *The Detroit Publishing Company Postcards*, (Big Rapids, Mich.: The Author, c1994). Detroit was then known as the Detroit Photochrome Company which later became the Detroit Publishing Company. The nine YNP postcards were from the second series, issued by DPC in 1899, known to collectors as the G Series.

9. Yellowstone postcard collection, MSU–Bozeman.

10. Ferdinand V. Hayden, illus. by Thomas Moran, *The Yellowstone National Park*, (Boston: L. Prang & Co., 1876).

11. Jim Hughes, *The Birth of a Century*, (London: Tauris Parke Books, 1994).

12. FJH to Prang, 1900 Mar 10, 15, 16, Coll.1501, bk.7, p.254, 420, 448, MSU-Bozeman.

13. FJH to J. Murray Jordan, 1900 Mar 19, Coll.1501, bk.7, p.448, MSU-Bozeman.

14. That is, "three Color . . ." not "three-color. . ." The early Haynes cards did not carry his name and were monochromatic halftones. See bill of 1900 Jun 26, Coll 1501, bk. 187, p. 108. An earlier bill for "50,000 mailing cards" dated 1900 Jun 11 was superseded by the later bill (Ibid, p.118); F. Jay Haynes Papers, "Revised Register, 1900," MS Coll 146, bx 22 fd 6, Montana Historical Society, Helena. Haynes listed the ten images supplied to Brown & Bigelow as "Eagle Nest Rock, Cleopatra Terrace, Silver Gate, Golden Gate & Bunsen Peak, Gt. Falls of the Yellowstone, Grotto [Geyser], Old Faithful [Geyser], Hot Springs Fishing Cone, Grand Canyon Grand View, Giant Geyser."

15. Cards from these publishers were probably bought by west-bound travelers, carried to the Park and then mailed. Neither publisher had a Yellowstone series or enough images to attract a concessionaire's need for a wide range of images.

16. FJH to Prang, 1900 March 10, Coll.1500, bk. 7, p.420; JEH to H.H. Hays, 1917 Feb 12, Coll.1504, bx 5, fd 16, MSU-Bozeman.

17. Acmegraph Co., "Old Faithful Inn from Beehive Cone," #6500.

18. Acmegraph, "Old Faithful Inn, Yellowstone National Park, Showing Beehive Glaciar [sic]," #1211 and #5482.

19. Bloom Bros., "Old Faithful Inn. Yellowstone National Park," Y.P. 61. Haynes' image was later replaced with one from the NPRR after the new wings had been added to the Inn in the 1920s.

20. FJH to Maj. H.C. Benson, 1910 Apr 16, Coll.1500, bx 8, fd 35, MSU–Bozeman.

21. "[Postcards] Bought from Wylie, 1912," Coll.1500, MSU-Bozeman.

22. "Copy of paper handed Mr. S. Mather at residence of Col. Brett by JEH," 1915 Jun 7, Coll. 1504, MSU-Bozeman.

23. Coll.1504, bx 7, fd 14; Coll.1504, "Yellowstone Park Hotel Co."

24. Coll.1501, bk 173, p. 176; bk 188, p. 230, 239; bk 189, p. 22, MSU-Bozeman.

25. 1916 Apr 20; Coll. 1504, bx 11, fd 2.

26. Stephen T. Mather to JEH, 1916 Jun 6, Coll.1504, bx 11, fd 8; [Harry Child] to Mr. Livingston, 1917 Feb 1, Coll.1504, bx 7, fd 14; JEH to Detroit Publishing Co., 1920 Feb 16, Coll. 1504, bx 7, fd 14.

27. Coll. 1504, "Tammen Co."

28. JEH to C.A. Hamilton, 1921 Mar 5, Coll.1504, bx 10, fd 22. Boston's Metropolitan Lithograph and Publishing Co. was also turned down by Haynes (J.E. Haynes to MLPC, 1922 Jul 29, Coll.1504, bx 12, fd 6).

29. JEH to Roger Toll, 1929 Sep 10, Coll.1504, bx 15 fd 11.

30. "Agreement," 1930 Nov 1, Coll. 1504, bx 16 fd 4.

31. "Post card samples, 1937," Coll. 1504.

32. "Crandall Studios," Coll. 1504, bx 6 fd 16.

33. [JEH] to Horace M. Albright, 1931 Mar 30, Coll.1504, bx 17 fd 2.

34. See totals figured for the Secretary of the Interior for franchise contract negotiations in Coll. 1504, bx 34.

35. JEH to Wesley D'Ewart, 1951 Apr 18, Coll.1504, "Teich & Co.," MSU–Bozeman.

36. Chip Rhinehart (card purchaser for Hamilton Stores), personal communication to author, 1994 Dec.

A View of Main Street:
The Use of Postcards
in Historic Preservation

Loriene Roy

INTRODUCTION[1]

What has become of the frank, five-a-nickel postcards? . . . They
arrived from the next town up the line, or from across the continent,
inscribed for all to see: "Your Ma and I stopped at this hotel before
you were ever heard of," or, shamelessly: "Well if she doesn't care
any more than that I don't either. See you Tues." On their tinted
surfaces were some of the truest visual records ever made of any
period.[2]

To some, the postcard is an emblem of an earlier, finer time. Postcards
draw others close to memory and, perhaps even, regret. Whether nostalgic,
humorous, deceitful, or literal, the picture postcard is finding a place in the
realm of study–as object of study and as partner in serious research.
Among the many uses of postcards is as visual evidence of the built
environment, an environment that is fragile and sometimes lost. The following article presents a brief discussion of architecture as a popular
theme on postcards. A definition of historic presentation is then followed
by an outline of the variety of documentary sources historic preservationists use in their work. Incidents that involved postcards in historic preservation efforts build a case for their potential usefulness. Finally, the
advantages and limitations of postcards as evidence are presented.

ARCHITECTURAL THEMES ON POSTCARDS

Nothing so attracts people in our time as the architectural wonders of
the past.[3]

[Haworth co-indexing entry note]: "A View of Main Street: The Use of Postcards in Historic
Preservation." Roy, Loriene. Co-published simultaneously in *Popular Culture in Libraries* (The Haworth Press, Inc.) Vol. 3, No. 2, 1995, pp. 141-158; and: *Postcards in the Library: Invaluable Visual
Resources* (ed: Norman D. Stevens) The Haworth Press, Inc., 1995, pp. 141-158. Single or multiple
copies of this article are available from The Haworth Document Delivery Service [1-800-342-9678,
9:00 a.m. - 5:00 p.m. (EST)].

Architectural themes have long been represented on postcards: the first picture postcard in the United States featured one of the buildings at the 1893 World Columbian Exposition.[4] The first picture postcard in Britain was of the Tower of London.[5] Since then, postcards have illustrated an abundance of built structures, from airports to zoos.[6] Local scenes were the most popular subjects of early postcards.[7] The earliest postcards made in the United States, the so-called pioneer cards manufactured from 1869 to 1898, featured multi-view collages that grouped vignettes of college campus scenes, public monuments, and structures such as courthouses.[8] Postcards were the canvass of local pride. The views selected epitomized images of modernity and achievement that the community wanted to project to the world, certainly to travelers and those receiving the postcards they mailed. Thus, the typical postcards–of courthouses, religious institutions, hospitals, schools, libraries, recreational facilities, and industry–were cap-sules of philosophy, solidifying a sense of community.[9]

TYPES OF POSTCARDS DEPICTING ARCHITECTURAL THEMES

To me there was something magical about those linen cards. The skyscrapers and monuments and bridges and beaches seemed so per-fect. And those skies! The most gorgeous robin's-egg blues gently fading into pale peach tinged with just a blush of coral, a few wisps of fluffy white clouds floating overhead; the perfect foil for the main subject of the card, be it a movie star's Hollywood mansion, a fabulous municipal fountain, a spectacular natural wonder . . . or a hotel.[10]

For convenience, postcards that might potentially be used for their architectural content can be grouped according to: date of manufacture; graphic process used; caption; material; topic or purpose, and view. Cate-gorizing by date arrives at an exact or approximate publication date for a card, based on such evidence as labeling, cancellation, printed copyright date, space reserved for private messages, attribution to a particular artist or company, and knowledge of photographic process. Thus, postcards grouped by date are described as pioneer cards (also referred to as souve-nir cards, mail cards, or correspondence cards, depending on their label-ing), private mail cards, undivided back cards, divided back cards, cards with white edges or borders, cards on linen-finished paper, and modern chromolithographic cards.[11] Another date-based grouping assigns post-cards to one of four categories: (1) pioneers; (2) early-century; (3) mid-century; and (4) late-century.[12] Such categorizations are used by collectors and dealers in evaluating the uniqueness or rarity of a card and, hence, its monetary value.

Postcards with architecture content have images that are either printed or are real-photographs. Some postcards are based on sketches and are intended to demonstrate an artistic rendering of a view or structure. Some postcards were created from early photographic processes, such as stereoptican views. Real-photo postcards include commercially mass-produced images as well as amateur created one-of-a-kind photographs. Some cards were initially based on photographs and then hand-tinted or retouched to differ from the original photograph. Included in this category are fanciful photomontages that superimpose photographs of varying scale, depicting oversize produce and creatures such as the famed jackelope. Alterations in photographs were also created using air-brush techniques to add desirable features, such as fair skies and clouds, or to remove distracting details such as utility wires and shadows.

When comparing the caption used on postcards, both the greeting and the font are distinguishing characteristics. Architectural features can sometimes be ascertained on "Greetings From" postcards, derived from the "Gruss Aus" or "Gruss Von" messages on early German-made cards.[13] The "Greetings From" heading followed by the state or city from which the message was sent or intended, can be printed in small font or as "Large Letters." In small text "Greetings From," the message is secondary to the view or other graphic. In "Large Letter" greetings, the text usually comprise the majority of the depicted graphic. Architectural structures are imbedded inside the large letters or appear as background.[14]

Most postcards were constructed from paper-based materials. Novelty postcards are those that demonstrate unusual physical qualities. A "hold-to-light" card of a building has transparent panels that appear to glow when the card is held up to a bright light source. Hinged-door postcards have panels that can be lifted to reveal additional graphics. Postcards may incorporate or consist largely of non-paper substances, including metal, leather, and cloth such as silk or velvet. The image of a structure may be gilded or outlined in tinsel or glitter.

Cards are sometimes defined by their topic and/or purpose. Commemorative cards were designed to coincide with a special event. Popular collectable souvenir cards depict international exposition grounds and their structures. Many other cards were manufactured to advertise a product, place, or company. Architectural evidence is found in postcards designed to illustrate non-architectural themes. Thus, streetscapes are evident in cards featuring vehicles such as fire engines, street cars, or trains. Various classification schemes might obscure the architectural usefulness of some cards. Cards that dealers might file under "celebrity" or "entertainment" might illustrate the homes of famous people.[15] Cards sold for their Indian Territory cancellation may depict residences or civic structures.[16] Architecturally based postcards sought by collectors include skylines, scenics, and large city views. Collectors may define their collecting interests more narrowly, focusing on specific towns or structures, or even architectural details, such as gargoyles. Collectable postcards feature structures such as aftermaths of disasters, amusement parks, arenas, asylums, ball parks, breweries, canals, castles, churches, court houses, covered bridges, dams, diners and restaurants, doctor's offices, drive-ins, factories, fire stations, gardens, gas stations, geodesic domes, hospitals, hotels, houseboats, libraries, lighthouses, parks, pharmacies, resorts, rest homes, roadside architecture, sanitariums, schools, skyscrapers, spas, stadiums, state capitols, tourist cabins, train depots, windmills.

Along with "Greetings From" cards, the most common category of postcards is the view card.[17] View cards provide a visual of an actual scene as distinguished from postcards that depict a portrait, imaginary setting, cartoon or caricature, or entirely textual graphic. Views can be multiple or single: showing one graphic or many. Long views–aerial or bird's eye, cityscapes, streetscapes, panoramics–show more than one structure. Single views illustrate, more commonly, the exterior features of a structure, or an interior view, or, through different camera angles, varying views of the building. Some views show lighted structures or night scenes.

Post cards can usually be placed in more than one category. There are pioneer view cards, novelty view cards printed on copper or aluminum, multiple vignette or view cards showing interior and exterior views of a structure, and cards with both real-photo and illustrated graphics.[18]

HISTORIC PRESERVATION: DEFINITION, PROCESS, AND SOURCES OF INFORMATION

There is no art as impermanent as architecture. All that solid brick and stone mean nothing. Concrete is as evanescent as air. The monuments of our civilization stand, usually, on negotiable real estate; their value goes down as land value goes up.[19]

As with many noble disciplines, historic preservation can be defined from a number of perspectives.[20] Historic preservation is an action or group of actions: "the act or process of applying measures to sustain the existing form, integrity, and material of a building or structure, and the existing form and vegetative cover of a site. It may include initial stabilization work, where necessary, as well as ongoing maintenance of the historic building materials."[21] These activities are more simply defined as connecting "the buildings of the past to the community's functioning present."[22] Historic preservation is defined by those engaged in these activities: "Historic preservation refers to the activities of those who attempt to save architecturally significant buildings from destruction."[23] Historic preservation is a philosophy of "meeting the past in a material way."[24]

Interest in historic preservation began in the 1960s in response to the destruction of historic urban centers in the guise of urban renewal when some cities razed historic structures and districts to create room for highways and shopping centers.[25] Reaction to the impact of urban renewal led to the passage of the National Historic Preservation Act of 1966 and the creation of state historic preservation commissions or offices (SHPO).[26] State commissions assumed many tasks, chief among them were three aims: to survey or create an inventory of the state's architectural heritage; to nominate appropriate architectural or archaeological properties to the National Register of Historic Places; and to serve as a resource in preventing the destruction of these resources, a task that includes their preservation and restoration. Historic preservation efforts often combine the talents and interests of city planners, architects, local historians, public historians, local preservation organizations, folklorists, historical and cultural geographers, architectural historians, archaeologists, cultural anthropologists, curators, museologists, chemists, engineers, realtors, archivists and librarians, and volunteers. The cross disciplinary appeal of historic preservation is also reflected in the range of organizations and professional associations involved. These include such diverse groups as the National League of Cities, National Conference of Mayors, National Association of Counties, International City Managers Association, American Planning Association, American Institute of Architects, American Society of Landscape Architects, American Society of Civil Engineers, The National Trust, American Association for State and Local History, Society of Architectural Historians, and American Association of Museums. Not mentioned are the hundreds of local, county, regional, state, and federal government agencies also involved.

Historic preservation efforts may be directed toward the restoration of a single public or private structure, such as a public restroom or private residence, or extended to embrace an entire city block or urban district. There is great interest in restoring "vernacular artifacts" of the recent past: gas stations, motels, and roadside architecture such as colossal storage reservoirs in the shapes of catsup-bottles or pineapples.[27]

There are three stages in historic preservation.[28] First are the processes involved in the identification and description of properties that are worthy of preservation. This involves data collection and analysis, the result of which is a written report called a survey. Surveys include such data as the provenance of a structure, including present and past owners; date of construction and architect and/or builder; a description of the architectural style; a description of the historic importance of the structure; and visual documentation, usually photographs.[29] Surveys are prepared for individual structures according to prescribed guidelines, such as those used in National Register nominations and documentation for the Historic American Buildings Survey (HABS) and the Historic American Engineering Record (HAER); the later, established in 1933 and 1969, respectively, are national projects to produce and collect architectural records.[30] The next process is that of evaluating the properties. The end product is an evaluative list, referred to as the inventory.[31] The final processes, based on a preservation plan stemming from the survey and inventory, apply technical practice to prevent the deterioration of destruction of the properties.

As with other types of historical research, historic preservation seeks answers to three main queries. It describes the past, to measure change over time, and to interpret the reasons for change and its impact.[32] In answering these questions, historic preservationists use both physical and non-physical research methods.[33] Physical evidence is centered on the structure itself. It includes gathering artifacts through archaeological excavation and testing such artifacts through experimentation such as the chemical analyses applied to paint and finishes and examination of saw marks, mortar, and wallpaper.

Non-physical methodologies include locating, creating, and interpreting written, oral, and graphic sources. Written sources are numerous. They include manuscripts: account books, diaries and journals, correspondence, and traveler's accounts. Print resources of use in historic preservation include newspapers, journal articles, county histories, gazetteers, city directories, trade catalogs, pattern books, and monographic works on communities, architects, architectural firms, and as case studies of buildings preserved or demolished. Legal documents such as deeds, land records, tax records, probate inventories, and building permits are sought as are government documents such as census material. Genealogical sources, such as church records, are useful. Finally, ephemera, such as broadsides and brochures often collected in scrapbooks, might be useful.

Oral history involves interviewing those who are knowledgeable about the history related to a site, area, or structure.

Graphic resources are paintings, daguerreotypes, tintypes, photographs, prints, paintings, drawings, maps, and other visual documents. Photographs are the best sources of documentary evidence since they, if available, capture an image of the structure as it was.[34] Prints evolve from artistic renderings and are found as engravings, etchings, wood cuts, and lithographs. These illustrations sometimes appear on borders of writing paper, on carte-de-visites, and on envelopes. Architectural drawings, prepared at various stages of a structure's development, include conceptual drawings, preliminaries, design and bid drawings, working drawings, as-built drawings, as well as those that show alterations, existing conditions, and restorations.[35] Other architectural drawings that are helpful are measured drawings, plans, elevations, sections, large-scale, and interpretive drawings such as cutaways and exploded views.[36] Measured drawings show scale and are annotated to explain alterations in a building. Maps–plat, bird's eye view, fire insurance, geological survey maps–are often used. Radiographs, infrared photographs, and computer enhanced photographs are sometimes obtained.

THE USE OF POSTCARDS IN HISTORIC PRESERVATION

Postcards, especially real-photo postcards, provide much the same documentary evidence as do photographs. They share the ability of photographs to convey attributes such as texture and three-dimensional projection and concepts such as context and spatial relationships.[37] Many postcards present generalities. The detail presented varies, depending on the production process and the condition of the card. Postcards are often used as illustrations in publications and media productions.[38] Postcards are used in historic preservation to: (1) serve as a starting point in research; (2) provide unique documentation; (3) supplement other evidence, and (4) educate.

Postcards Lead to Research

By providing evidence of the existence of structures and/or their elements, postcards can point to the need for conducting further research: "The collection of these cards leads from curiosity to information-gathering to research."[39] Postcards imply that a structure existed. A single postcard provides at least an impression, from one elevation, of a structure's character-defining features such as the facade, foundation, and roof. Researchers might study these elements in attributing structures to an architect or firm. Researchers have examined postcards of churches to compare steeple designs in an effort to trace architectural influence.[40] Long-views allow the comparison of nearby structures. An architect documented urban history, especially the development of skyscrapers, through the changing panoramic views portrayed in postcards.[41]

Postcards Provide Unique Information and Supplement Other Evidence

Postcards sometimes provide evidence that does not exist elsewhere, such as views of vantage points not recorded in photographs. Early views of downtown Houston, for example, exist largely on postcards.[42] A postcard provided the only early interior and exterior views of a fruit and vegetable market and was used as part of the site's National Register nomination application.[43] Postcards may illustrate the topography of an area, providing evidence of the geography of built-over areas. Postcards of a site before construction of a hydroelectric system provided engineers with information about the topography.[44] Postcards also document small communities often unavailable in other visual representation; postcards provide almost the only extant views of Traer, Iowa.[45] Postcards can supplement oral testimony: a postcard was the only record that collaborated oral evidence that a porch had been constructed on a residence under restoration in New Jersey.[46]

Postcards can be helpful in providing evidence of sequence and chronology. They can illustrate stages of construction and reconstruction. Postcards provided documentary evidence in the restoration of the Old Stone Fort in Nacogdoches, Texas and the Titus County (Texas) courthouse.[47] Postcards were consulted in the renovation of a church and hotel lobby in Maynard, Massachusetts.[48] Postcards taken over three to four periods, can illustrate the evolution of a building and the development of a site.[49] Postcards of a park in Massachusetts provided a visual representation of the middle period of the park's history, aiding its restoration.[50] Postcards document alterations such as additions, enclosure or removal of porches, and alterations in windows and doors. A librarian in Maine used an early postcard of the library building to determine where to locate a reconstructed war memorial plaque.[51]

Postcards can be studied for their presentation of architectural structures. They have been used in the study of church building construction, covered bridges, automobile culture, and in comparing architectural features of Masonic temples.[52] The National Park Service has also used postcards in preparing surveys of structures and grounds.[53]

Postcards contribute evidence of ephemera associated with structures or sites. Signage in a variety of forms are seen–as wall advertising, markers and plaques on or near structures, window displays, posted menus, sign boards, marquee, and seasonable signage. Study of signage examines the existence of signs, their location, content, size, lighting, style, and lettering. Postcards of Las Vegas streetscapes provided evidence in a study of the history of signage.[54] Shutters, awnings and canopies are shown. Postcards were used in a study of the introduction and transfer of electrification into rural areas.[55] Streetscapes capture views of street vendors, benches, plant holders, and bicycle racks. Postcards also document transitory information: prior names for streets and structures and sites of temporary relocations. In the late summer of 1992, Muscovites eagerly purchased packets of postcards of early streetscapes so they could restore pre-Communist names to streets and buildings.[56]

Interior views, more rarely available, show wall coverings, art works such as statues and murals, ceilings, stairways. and other elements of interior design. Wide interior views show the relationship between areas and their functions.

Images on postcards are used in renovating or constructing enclosures such as fences and walls. Postcards were used to date the front gates of an historic structure, the Hermitage, in Nashville.[57] The location and materials used in walkways, streets, and curbings are shown as is street lighting. Postcards have provided images of landscaping used during earlier periods on the grounds of the Tennessee State Capitol and in a study of park development in Chicago.[58] Types of foliage are discerned, allowing an assessment of the proportion of open space and foliage. As-built views show initial plantings; views taken at different seasons show annuals. Postcards show types of placement of garden furnishings and sculptural elements such as flagpoles, benches, trellises, pergola, and sun dials. Barns, garages, sheds, and other outbuildings appear.

Messages on postcards–either as printed text or added as correspondence–provide additional information about a structure, especially its use or how others perceived it. For example, a traveler in 1907 had this to say to a friend in Dorchester, Massachusetts about his time in Gadsden, Alabama: "Am leaving here to-night. Finest place to get away from I ever struck."[59] Other messages provide information about a structure's history: "This [Carnegie library, La Harpe, Illinois] stands where mother's house did."[60]

Postcard photographers capture difficult or unusual views. Wide angle views show context, even providing images of missing structures, and suggest the layout of paths and roads and the location of parks and bridges.[61]

Postcards Help Educate

Displays of and exhibits with postcards can be colorful, interesting, and approachable, adding a "nostalgic feel."[62]

Preservationists and architects use postcards in educating the lay public and also in marketing preservation proposals.[63] Staff in the National Trust's Main Street Program projected slides of postcards in presentations to the community to illustrate how town centers were altered after urban renewal.[64] Architects collect and study postcards in order to educate themselves as to how buildings contemporary with the ones they will be involved in reconstructing appeared.[65]

Limitations of Postcards

Postcards must be evaluated under the same criteria historians use to judge other documentary evidence.[66] The two most frequently mentioned limitations of postcards concern their portrayal of color and the accuracy of the image. While color postcards are striking visually, it is best not to trust the color process. Postcards of the same structure may show vastly differing color schemes, even when the postcards are duplicates of the same view, contemporary with each other and are possibly printed from the same negative. Changes in color might hint at polychromatic treatment. For example, difference in contrast between a wall surface and a rim implies that two different color paints were used to cover the different surfaces. The printed colors themselves should not be taken as evidence as to true or actual color. Instead, the postcard should be treated as a black and while photograph.[67]

Printed postcards, while they resemble photographs, can be altered, often at the request of those requesting the postcard, to make the image more striking.[68] Some postcards were retouched to add more modern features; hence, newer model automobiles might be added to an older postcard of a commercial establishment before reprinting.[69] An artist hand-colored a postcard street scene of Oklahoma City, adding the roof to a building under construction.[70] Older images of buildings might be altered to illustrate planned (and sometimes never completed) remodeling or additions. Postcards may be based on preliminary drawings; the final structure, if built, might have differed greatly from the image depicted on the postcard. There are, for example, postcards of the Carnegie Library of Pittsburgh that show a large auditorium and two tall towers at the rear of the building (see Illustration 1). Neither of those features were every built but those postcards are indistinguishable from other postcards of the same building as it actually exists (see Illustration 2). A common feature added was the American flag.[71] Distracting visual content–such as scaffolding, utility wires, and traffic lights–might be airbrushed out, as might entire buildings. Photographs were retouched or cropped so the resultant image eliminated potholes and rough roads. People were airbrushed out or added.[72] Even if unaltered, postcards do not often provide clear evidence of detailing. Gettys recommends listing known facts that are revealed on a postcard such as the evidence of other structures and events with known dates.[73] It is a good rule of thumb to always cross verify the textual and visual material presented on a postcard with other reliable evidence.[74]

The camera angle used by the photographer might introduce distortion in the image. Structures may be 'stretched out,' appearing larger or proportionally different from their actual dimensions. Many photographers, especially those capturing individual structures, recorded more foreground on postcards by lowering the camera lens. Foreshortening can omit roof forms. No view by itself will show all projections and openings. It is sometimes difficult to assess orientation of a structure from a postcard. Long-views omit minute detail. Skyscapes do not show detail at street-level.

Allmen states that dating a postcard can build on three assumptions:

1. Most postcards picture scenes contemporary with their issuance.
2. Most postcards are mailed contemporary with their production.
3. Most stamps are used contemporary with their issuance.[75]

She also provides advice on dating a postcard based on documentary evidence within the graphic; evidence of usage, including cancellation marks, postage, and messages; comparison of the postcard's physical structure with what is known about postcard manufacturing history; and knowledge of printing processes.[76] The obvious difficulty of dating postcards is that older views can be reprinted and not be representative of the structure's condition at the time the postcard was mailed. Sometimes older cards are promoted as contemporary cards.

Postmarks assist in dating a card although this is the date the card was mailed rather than the date it was manufactured. Gettys notes that postmarks are actually the most recent date of the postcard.[77] Dating can be ascertained by internal evidence, including signage and the style of clothing worn by individuals depicted in postcards. Sometimes the subject of the card–such as an anniversary or celebration–reveals the date.[78]

Another limitation of postcards concerns their availability and access. There is no definitive list of postcards; unique discoveries of heretofore unknown views continue to be made. Researchers must purchase cards from dealers, exchange duplicates with collectors or use the holdings of individuals, archives, or libraries. Postcards are organized according to various schemes; some collections, like the Curt Teich Postcard Archives, are well organized and provide reference assistance while other collections are not well organized and professional service may be limited. Since

ILLUSTRATION 1. Postcard representation of the Carnegie Library in Pittsburgh, PA, that includes towers and an auditorium from the original design.

518   CARNEGIE LIBRARY, SCHENLEY PARK, Pittsburgh, Pa   ILL. P. CARD CO., 118 CHAMBERS ST., N. Y.

From the personal collection of Norman D. Stevens.

ILLUSTRATION 2. Postcard representation of the Carnegie Library in Pittsburgh, PA, showing the building as actually constructed.

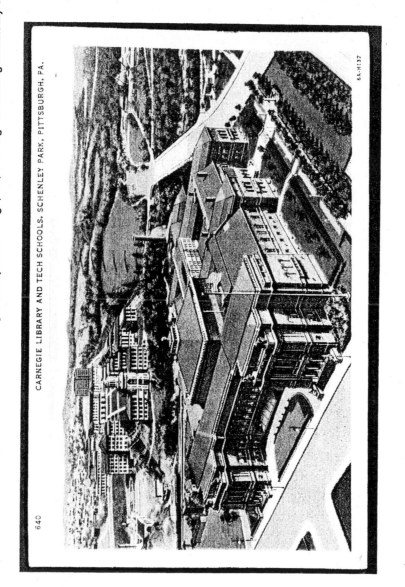

CARNEGIE LIBRARY AND TECH SCHOOLS, SCHENLEY PARK, PITTSBURGH, PA.

640

6A-H137

From the personal collection of Norman D. Stevens.

postcards date only from the late nineteenth-century, they are largely documents of twentieth-century culture.

SUMMARY[79]

Postcards were created for promotional purposes: to advertise a location. These often idealized views have evolved from tourist souvenirs to historic documents; they induce nostalgia and provoke research. Postcards are not the first and only source of evidence sought by those involved in historic preservation efforts. Yet they can add supportive documentation and sometimes unique information for those involved in nominating a structure or site for National Register status or restoring a structure to a particular period or date. Postcards have popular appeal. Copied onto slides, postcards are effective visuals in public education programs, especially those involving local history and preservation platforms. Postcards as artifacts add interest to displays and exhibits. Architectural postcards are often well composed views that work well as illustrations in publications. Postcards are widely available, even the oldest cards continue to be traded and sold. Their costs–even for real-photograph postcards–are often less than for copies of photographs.[80] Resurgence in the use and collection of postcards has been in part attributed to the historic preservation movement.[81]

NOTES

1. Many individuals kindly assisted me in understanding the role that postcards might play in historic preservation efforts. Those who willingly participated in interviews include Dr. Kate Adams, the Center for American History, The University of Texas at Austin; Drury Blakeley Alexander, The School of Architecture, The University of Texas at Austin; Wayne Bell, The School of Architecture, The University of Texas at Austin; Elena Danielson, Hoover Institute Archives; Philip Doty, Graduate School of Library and Information Science, The University of Texas at Austin; Meredith Eliassen, J. Paul Leonard Library, San Francisco State University; Janet Foster, Acroterion, Morristown, New Jersey; Dwayne Jones, Texas Historical Commission; Charlie Mackie, Heritage Society of Austin (Texas); John H. McClintock, Post Card History Society, Manassas, Virginia; Dr. Louis Marchiafava, Houston Public Library; Eric Paddock, Colorado Historical Society; Chuck Parrott, Lowell (Massachusetts) Historic Preservation Commission; Carol Roark, Dallas Public Library; Linda Roark, Texas Historical Commission; Mary Sarber, El Paso Public Library; Earle Shettleworth, Maine Historic Preservation Commission; Katherine Hamilton-Smith, Curt Teich Postcard Archives; and Sally Simms Stokes, University of Maryland. Many others provided

contacts and encouragement, including Patricia Bozeman, University of Houston; Lois R. Densky-Wolff, University of Medicine & Dentistry of New Jersey; Richard Engeman, University of Washington; Claudia Hill, Getty Center for the History of Art & the Humanities; Dr. Martha Norkunas, the Center for American History, The University of Texas at Austin; Gary Patillo, The Undergraduate Library, The University of Texas at Austin; Jack Robertson, University of Virginia; Richard Saunders, Montana State University; Norman D. Stevens, Storrs, Connecticut; and Chris Wolff, Morristown, New Jersey. Still others (John Awald, Dr. Eric Mogren, Will Moore, David J. Pence, Dave Pierson, Larry Reynolds) responded to requests for assistance posted on three electronic listservs, H-Local, H-West, and POSTCARD. Toni Loftin, Graduate School of Library and Information Science, The University of Texas at Austin, conducted the literature search and retrieved much of the textual material upon which this article is based.

2. Evans, Walker, "Main Street Looking North From Courthouse Square: A Portfolio of American Picture Postcards from the Trolley-Car Period," Fortune 37 (5) (May 1948): 102. I am indebted to Eric Paddock, Colorado State Historical Society, for drawing this article to my attention.

3. John Kenneth Galbraith, "The Economic and Social Returns of Preservation," In *Preservation: Toward an Ethic in the 1980s* (Washington, DC: The Preservation Press, 1980), p. 57.

4. Staff, Frank, *The Picture Postcard & Its Origins* (New York; Washington: Frederick A. Praeger, 1966), 60.

5. Ibid., 61.

6. For examples of other architectural themes recorded on postcards see books on collectibles (e.g., Allmen, Diane. *The Official Identification and Price Guide to Postcards*. New York: House of Collectibles, 1990) and books consisting largely of reproductions of postcards (e.g., Zaid, Barry. *Wish You Were Here: A Tour of America's Great Hotels During the Golden Age of the Picture Post Card*. New York: Crown, 1990). Also, the list of subscribers to the POSTCARD listserv describes the collecting interests of its members.

7. Gomery, J. Douglas, "A Short History of the Picture Postcard," *Marquee: The Journal of the Theatre Historical Society* 16 (2) (1984): 18.

8. Kaduck, John M., *Rare & Expensive Postcards, Book 1*, revised (Lombard, Illinois: Wallace-Homestead Book Company, 1982), 6-7.

9. Paddock, Eric. Interview with author, 16 December 1994.

10. Zaid, *Wish You Were Here*, 6.

11. Kaduck, *Rare & Expensive Postcards*, 93.

12. Allmen, *The Official Identification and Price Guide to Postcards*, 10.

13. Kaduck, *Rare & Expensive Postcards*, 9.

14. Allmen indicates that, during the 1940s and 1950s, more than one thousand localities in the United States were depicted on Large-Letter linen postcards. Allmen, *Official Identification and Price Guide to Postcards*, 46.

15. See example of card shown in Kaduck, *Rare & Expensive Postcards*, 64 and Allmen, *The Official Identification and Price Guide to Postcards*, 44.

16. See examples of cards shown in Kaduck, *Rare & Expensive Postcards*, 72.

17. Wilkinson, Billy R., "Academic Library Postcards," *College & Research Libraries News* 49 (10) (Nov. 1988): 648.

18. Monahan, Valerie, *An American Postcard Collector's Guide* (Poole, England: Blandford Press, 1981), 29.

19. Huxtable, Ada Louise, "Anatomy of a Failure," *New York Times* 17 March 1968, reprinted in *Goodbye History, Hello Hamburger: An Anthology of Architectural Delights and Disasters* (Washington, DC: The Preservation Press, 1986), 85.

20. See the following source for a thorough review essay on sources published on historic preservation. Carder, James N., "American Historic Preservation," *Choice* 20 (18) (April 1983): 1089-1090, 1092-1094, 1096, 1098, 1100.

21. Jones, Dwayne, *Guidelines for Drafting Historic Preservation Ordinances and Model Ordinance* (Austin, Texas: Texas Historical Commission, National Register Programs, Certified Local Government Program, 1988), 16.

22. Huxtable, Ada Louise, "Where Did We Go Wrong?" *New York Times* 14 July 1968, reprinted in Goodbye *History, Hello Hamburger: An Anthology of Architectural Delights and Disasters* (Washington, DC: The Preservation Press, 1986), 62.

23. Weinberg, Nathan, *Preservation in American Towns and Cities* (Boulder, Colorado: Westview Press, 1979), xv.

24. Kyvig, David E. and Myron A. Marty, *Nearby History: Exploring the Past Around You* (Nashville, Tennessee: American Association for State and Local History, 1982), 184.

25. Friedman, Mildred, "1970/1991 Doing the Right Thing," *Architectural Record* 179 (July 1991): 171.

26. *Texas Historical Commission Biennial Report: 1985-1986* (Austin, Texas: Texas Historical Commission, 1986), 35.

27. Rattner, Selma, "To Save the World we Built," *American Heritage* 38 (3) (April 1987): 91; Dorrance, William H. (letter), "More Menaced Americana," *Historic Preservation News* 34 (5) (October/November 1994): 7.

28. Stipe, Robert E., "Historic Preservation: The Process and the Actors," in *The American Mosaic: Preserving a Nation's Heritage* (Robert E. Stipe and Antoinette J. Lee, eds., Washington, DC: United States Committee/International Council on Monuments and Sites, 1987), 8.

29. Ziegler, Arthur P., Jr. and Walter C. Kidney, *Historic Preservation in Small Towns: A Manual of Practice* (Nashville: American Association for State and Local History, 1980), 16-17.

30. For an extensive treatment of the documentation involved in HABS/HAER see Burns, John A., ed. *Recording Historic Structures: Historic American Buildings Survey/Historic American Engineering Record*. Washington, DC: American Institute of Architects Press, 1989.

31. Jones, *Guidelines for Drafting Historic Preservation Ordinances*, 15.

32. Kyvig and Marty, *Nearby History*, 16.

33. For list of sources used in historic preservation see the following publications. Beeman, Cynthia J. and Bruce D. Jensen. *Remembering Texas: Guidelines for Historical Research.* Austin, Texas: Texas Historical Commission, 1992;

Burns, *Recording Historic Structures*, 32-33; Howard, Hugh. *How Old Is This House?: A Skeleton Key to Dating and Identifying Three Centuries of American Houses*. New York: Farrar, Straus, and Giroux, 1989; and *Research Tools for Historic Restoration*. Austin, Texas: Texas Historical Commission, 1986.

34. Favretti, Rudy J. and Joy Putnam Favretti, *Landscapes and Gardens for Historic Buildings: A Handbook for Reproducing and Creating Authentic Landscape Settings* (Nashville: American Association for State and Local History, 1978), 91.

35. Burns, *Recording Historic Structures*, 114-115.

36. Ibid., 147-165.

37. Ibid., 70.

38. See the Indicia column in issues of *Image File*, the quarterly journal of the Curt Teich Postcard Archives, for examples of the use of postcards.

39. Matthews, Marianne, "Antique Theatre Post Cards: Springboard to Theatre Research," *Marquee: The Journal of the Theatre Historical Society* 16 (2) (1984): 19.

40. Shettleworth, Earl. Telephone conversation with author, 14 December 1994.

41. "Every picture postcard that depicts a cityscape shows one stage in a historic process. It is the process of interdependent stages in which one change affects another. A comparison of postcards from different times can provide clues to a city's history." Adam Andreas, "Urban Histories: 3 for 25c," *Historic Preservation* 29 (July 1977): 29.

42. Marchiafava, Louis. Telephone conversation with author, 12 December 1994.

43. Densky-Wolff, Lois R. Electronic correspondence with author, 21 November 1994.

44. Shettleworth, Earle. Telephone conversation with author, 14 December 1994.

45. Mendes, Joel. Letter to Katherine Hamilton-Smith, 9 April 1993; Saunders, Richard. Electronic correspondence with author, 22 November 1994.

46. Densky-Wolff, Lois R. Electronic correspondence with author, 21 November 1994.

47. Roark, Linda. Interview with author, 23 November 1994.

48. Pierson, Dave. Electronic correspondence with author, 7 December 1994.

49. Alexander, Drury Blakely. Interview with author, 2 November 1994.

50. Parrott, Chuck. Telephone conversation with author, 16 December 1994.

51. Stevens, Norman D. Electronic correspondence to author, 6 July 1994.

52. Keister, Kim, "Wish You Were Here: The Curt Teich Postcard Archives Depict Americans as They Saw Themselves Through the First Seven Decades of the Twentieth Century," *Historic Preservation* 44 (March/April 1992): 61; Liebhold, Peter. Letter to Katherine Hamilton-Smith, 18 April 1993; Sennott, R. Stephen. Letter to Katherine Hamilton-Smith, 12 April 1993; Moore, Will. Electronic correspondence to author, 1 December 1994.

53. "Graham Foundation Grant Received," *Image File* 8 (2) (1991): 14.

54. Gust, Debra, "Notes from the Research Desk," *Image File* 8 (1) (1994): 10.

55. Keister, "Wish You Were Here," 59.

56. Danielson, Elena. Telephone conversation with author, 22 November 1994.

57. Gust, Debra, "Notes from the Research Desk," *Image File* 7 (3) (1993): 8.

58. Gust, "Notes from the Research Desk," *Image File* 7 (3) (1993): 8; Ranney, Victora Post. Letter to Katherine Hamilton-Smith, 18 April 1994.

59. Postcard, author's collection.

60. Postcard, mailed 28 August, 1906, author's collection.

61. Gettys, Marshall, "Historic Postcards as a Tool of the Preservationist," *Outlook in Historic Conservation* (Nov./Dec. 1982): [3].

62. Allman, *The Official Identification and Price Guide to Postcards*, 56.

63. "Graham Foundation Grant Received," 14.

64. Keister, "Wish You Were Here," 61.

65. Roark, Linda. Interview with author, 23 November 1994.

66. These criteria are: "authenticity, reliability, accuracy, credibility, and usefulness." Kyvig and Marty, *Nearby History*, 47.

67. Mackie, Charlie. Telephone conversation with author, 15 December 1994.

68. For an example illustrating manipulation of an original photograph in the production of a Curt Teich postcard see Keister, "Wish You Were Here," 59.

69. Gerosa, Emma. "America in 1926: The Rush to Be Modern," *Image File* 7 (4) (1993): 4.

70. Edwards, Jim and Hal Ottaway, *The Vanished Splendor: Postcard Views of Early Oklahoma City* (Oklahoma City: Abalache Book Shop Publishing, 1982), [3].

71. Gerosa, "America in 1926," 5.

72. Jennings, Jan. "A Most Modern Rendezvous," *Image File* 8 (2) (1994): 6; Zaid, *Wish You Were Here*, 34.

73. Gettys, "Historic Postcards as a Tool of the Preservationist," [2].

74. Monahan provides examples of two postcards, while they depict the same structure, record the differing heights for the building. Monahan, Valerie, *An American Postcard Collector's Guide* (Poole, England: Blandford Press, 1981), 39.

75. Allmer, *The Official Identification and Price Guide to Postcards*, p. 15.

76. Ibid., 16-19.

77. Gettys, "Historic Postcards as a Tool of the Preservationist," [2].

78. Gerosa, "America in 1926," 4.

79. Gettys described the use of postcards in historic preservation: "In summary, historic postcards are an excellent but frequently overlooked source of information for the preservationist. The information contained on the postcards is usually detailed and accurate and most commonly not available from other sources. When used in combination with traditional resources, the postcard adds a dimension to preservation research." Gettys, "Historic Postcards as a Tool of the Preservationist," [4].

80. Shettleworth, Earle. Telephone conversation with author, 14 December 1994.

81. Edwards and Ottaway, *The Vanished Splendor*, [1].

Metered Mail:
A Survey of Contemporary Poetry
Postcard Publishing

Timothy D. Murray

American research libraries have been engaged in the task of collecting
the work of contemporary poets for well over sixty years. In the process,
librarians have had to make decisions on collecting materials in a bewil-
dering array of formats, including small and fine press publications, little
magazines, anthologies, broadsides and other ephemeral publications, and,
for the truly committed, literary manuscripts.

The poetry postcard or poemcard, the generic name by which it is commonly known, is a unique hybrid of all of these formats. Poetry postcards
have been produced, largely since the 1960s, simply and inexpensively by
small presses, but they have also been printed in handsome letterpress
editions by some of the best-known fine press printers. Poemcards have
occasionally taken the form of little magazines, either as entire magazines
issued in the form of postcards or as special postcard issues. Poemcards also
appear among the manuscripts and papers of contemporary poets, to whom
they have been sent by friends or fellow poets as postcards. In such contexts
they present to the curator who has custody over them the dilemma of
determining which takes precedence, the printed poemcard or the holograph
message on its verso. Finally, the poemcard is probably most commonly
viewed by librarians, bookdealers, and bibliographers as a variant, more
ephemeral, form of the traditional poetry broadside.

To the postcard collector, the term "ephemera" is high praise indeed,
but to the research librarian, more often than not, "ephemera" conveys

[Haworth co-indexing entry note]: "Metered Mail: A Survey of Contemporary Poetry Postcard
Publishing." Murray, Timothy D. Co-published simultaneously in *Popular Culture in Libraries* (The
Haworth Press, Inc.) Vol. 3, No. 2, 1995, pp. 159-171; and: *Postcards in the Library: Invaluable Visual
Resources* (ed: Norman D. Stevens) The Haworth Press, Inc., 1995, pp. 159-171. Single or multiple
copies of this article are available from The Haworth Document Delivery Service [1-800-342-9678,
9:00 a.m. - 5:00 p.m. (EST)].

159

negative images and such materials seldom receive the comparable collection development, preservation, and cataloging attention that the rare book, the manuscript, or even the poetry broadside receives. I would argue, however, that the poemcard, though certainly ephemeral, merits consideration from research libraries which strive to build in-depth, or even representative, collections of contemporary poetry in all formats, and deserves to be collected, preserved, cataloged, and made available to scholars.

Before proceeding further, I should define exactly what I mean when I refer to poemcards or poetry postcards. First and foremost, the poemcard must approximate in size and shape the traditional postcard format. The standard dimensions of a postcard are typically 3 1/2 × 5 1/2; however, over the course of time all sizes and shapes of postcards have been produced and mailed through the world's postal systems. The publishers of poetry postcards have also engaged in such experimentation, and poemcards can be found in a variety of sizes. I am only considering unfolded, single-sheet printings whose publishers and printers actually characterize these productions as poetry postcards, as opposed to numerous other forms of broadside publications.

As to the poetry itself, I have limited this examination primarily to poemcards which print original work by contemporary poets or which present poetry in the context of the contemporary small and fine press traditions. Excluded in my definition of poemcard are typical greeting card poetry, jingles and advertising verse, musical lyrics, limericks, and most reprints of classic or popular poems of the past, regardless of whether they are printed on postcards. I am also focusing on poemcards published from the 1960s to the present. Although one can find examples of poetry postcards from earlier years, the genre really established itself during the 1960s. Finally, I have limited my survey to poemcards published by American presses, with some coverage of poemcards from Canada and the British Isles. These represent the presses with which I am most familiar. A truly comprehensive treatment of the poetry postcard would include work produced throughout Europe, Canada, Latin America, Australia and New Zealand, and Japan.

One other area which I am regarding as out of scope is the vast world of correspondence art–and its related genres of assemblage, collage, etc.– much of which is often specifically produced in the postcard format. The postcard format presents its own unique artistic challenges, and, of course, the lines that separate poetry and art are often quite blurred in the work of artists concerned with the visual experience of language. Unless such works meet the criteria I have outlined above, I have excluded them from this survey. I am also excluding manuscript poetry written on postcards. Literary manuscript collections, particularly those with correspondence from the 1950s and 1960s, often include original manuscripts written on postcards. As intriguing a topic for research as this might be, I have excluded it from this survey.

Although a search of library catalogs will turn up occasional examples of poetry postcards from the first half of the twentieth century, the poem-card, at least as I am considering it, first began to appear with regularity during the 1960s, a period which saw a tremendous renaissance in poetry and poetry publishing in the United States. In the 1960s, a phenomenal number of little magazines and small and independent presses were launched by a new generation of poets who felt excluded by, or simply were not interested in publishing their work in, the established magazines and presses. They discovered the means to print and publish their poetry, and that of their friends, quickly and cheaply. Poetry broadsides and other ephemeral publications–such as poemcards–were a particularly popular printing activity.

At the same time as small press and little magazine editors were publishing poetry as quickly and as inexpensively as possible, there was also a resurgence of interest in fine printing. An emerging group of printers, artists, and designers, some of whom had been weaned on mimeographed small press publications, were drawn to the traditional craft of letterpress printing. These new fine press proprietors, like those who preceded them, were particularly interested in printing contemporary poetry in handsome, limited editions that provided them the opportunity to combine their own craft and creativity with that of a poet.

The poetry broadside has been a popular format for printers, almost from the very inception of printing in Europe during the fifteenth century, and remains today a staple of both the small press and fine printing traditions. For the small press printer, the poetry broadside can be printed quickly, cheaply, and in large numbers. During the 1960s and 1970s, when political poetry was at its height, broadsides were printed and distributed by hand in the streets, on bulletin boards, and at rallies or concerts. They continue to be a popular method of promoting poetry readings and other events. For the letterpress printer, the poetry broadside can offer technical challenges, creative opportunities, and a certain freedom that the book cannot. It is out of the broadside format and from these two printing traditions that the poetry postcard was born.

In my examination of as many different poemcards as possible, particularly those which are housed in the collections of American research libraries,[1] I discovered several interesting trends. It is quite apparent, from the sheer number of poemcards listed in library catalogs, that since the 1960s small and fine presses have printed an astonishing number of poetry postcards. Few libraries, however, appear to house strong collections of poemcards apart from those produced by a few presses. A good many presses also appear to have issued poemcards in series, but, with few exceptions, rarely is the entire series found in a library collection or, for that matter, anywhere. Perhaps these factors stem from the way in which poemcards have been distributed. Libraries have never developed efficient means of acquiring small press publications consistently; this can largely be attributed to the primitive, often idiosyncratic, distribution methods employed by the presses. Unless libraries have been fortunate enough to maintain subscriptions, or standing orders, for a poemcard series, they typically acquire them from bookdealers specializing in contemporary poetry. Such dealers usually sell poemcards as individual broadsides, regardless of whether they were originally issued in series.[2]

Another possible factor contributing to the dearth of complete collections of poemcard series in library collections might stem from the fact that poetry postcards were often distributed to individuals who actually used them as postcards. One certainly encounters poemcards among the correspondence series in literary papers where, in such contexts, the curatorial emphasis is usually placed upon the correspondence, rather than on the printed poemcard which thus becomes hidden in the literary archive. Most libraries also tend to focus their collecting upon specific authors and it is not uncommon for a collection to acquire only the work of authors exactly within its collecting scope, even if it means collecting bits and pieces of a poemcard series. Finally, poemcards, like other ephemeral materials, are seldom regarded as a cataloging priority by librarians faced with an ever-increasing backlog of materials to process. I suspect that a number of libraries, particularly those which aspire towards comprehensiveness in twentieth century poetry, may hold uncataloged collections of poemcards in their backlogs.

I would hardly pretend to characterize my survey as being in any way comprehensive. I have been able to examine sufficient examples of individual poetry poemcards, and poemcard series, published by a wide variety of presses. I believe my report can demonstrate that the poetry postcard has been a significant part of the small and fine press poetry publishing scene of the last thirty years and, as such, merits greater attention from research libraries. Although numerous presses have experimented with the poetry postcard format, only a very few have made this genre an integral part of their printing program. Three American presses in particular–Burning Deck Press, the Unicorn Press, and The Alternative Press–represent the apex of poetry postcard publishing. All three presses began as small presses in the 1960s and have published a broad range of chapbooks, broadsides, and literary ephemera. They have also produced the most innovative series of poetry postcards to date. Although the three presses share similar characteristics, they have all explored their own unique concerns. A closer look at each will demonstrate the potential of the poemcard as a literary genre.

Burning Deck Press was originally launched as a little magazine in 1961 in Ann Arbor, Michigan, by Keith and Rosmarie Waldrop, University of Michigan graduate students whose interest in poetry and printing led to the acquisition of a letterpress.[3] The Waldrops ended the magazine *Burning Deck* after only four issues and shifted their efforts towards the publication of poetry chapbooks, fiction, broadsides, and poemcards.

From the outset, Burning Deck Press has been characterized by the eclecticism of its poetry and its commitment to the craft of printing. Over the last thirty years Keith and Rosmarie Waldrop have published the work of an astonishing array of contemporary authors in beautifully-produced letterpress editions. The Burning Deck "poem postcards," as the press officially terms them, were issued in four separate series between 1974 and 1978, with several out-of-series poemcards produced earlier between 1970 and 1972, for a total of forty-four individual poemcards. The Burning Deck poemcards were handset in various typefaces and printed on a variety of paper stocks. They were then issued as sets of ten cards in envelopes in editions of between 100-150 copies. The Burning Deck "poem postcards" are characterized by fine letterpress printing on quality paper with interesting design and typography. The poemcards usually approximate the traditional size and shape of an actual postcard and, in all cases, include a verso which bears the printed imprint of Burning Deck and a space for an address and postage. The envelopes in which the poemcards are issued are themselves an integral part of the series and are printed with unique designs and illustrations. They also contain important bibliographic information. The poems printed in the series are usually first appearances and commissioned by the publishers either for the poemcard series or for other Burning Deck publications. The Burning Deck poemcards printed the work of a number of prominent poets, notably William Bronk, Thomas Disch, Larry Eigner, Mark Strand, John Taggart, and Diane Wakoski.

The Burning Deck "poem postcard" series exemplifies the heights to which the humble poemcard can ascend. They are printed imaginatively and with great skill; they contain unique graphic designs and illustrations; and they print original work by significant contemporary poets. The Burning Deck "poem postcard" series also helped the press become one of the pre-eminent literary small presses of its time, and it continues today, based in Providence, Rhode Island, to produce an eclectic mix of poetry and fiction in letterpress publications.

The Unicorn Press was founded in the late-1960s in Santa Barbara, California, by Alan Brilliant, an artist, printer, and book designer, and his wife, the poet and translator Teo Savory.[4] Brilliant had worked as a printer for Black Sparrow Press, one of the most successful independent American literary publishers, during its initial years in the early 1960s. When he and Savory founded the Unicorn Press, their focus was on contemporary poetry. They began with the publication of poetry chapbooks and broadsides in attractive limited editions, and developed a specialty for printing poetry in translation. With the Vietnam War at its height during the late 1960s and early-1970s, the Unicorn Press also printed a good deal of political poetry, as well as English translations of Vietnamese poetry.

The Unicorn Press quickly developed an important list of poets which included Robert Bly, Kenneth Rexroth, Diane di Prima, Jerome Rothenberg, Louis Zukofsky, Thomas Merton, W. S. Merwin, and James Tate. Unicorn usually accepted work from such authors to use in a chapbook or anthology, but would often select one or more poems for their broadside and poetry postcard series which were published concurrently. The Unicorn Press Poetry Postcard series was particularly popular and ran to three separate series published between 1968 and 1972. More than twenty poemcards, by the above poets and others, were printed. Curiously, almost to reinforce the fact that this seemingly-ephemeral format could take on a more lasting character, the Unicorn Press Poetry Postcards series were also printed in special signed editions usually limited to between thirty and fifty signed and numbered copies. During the late 1970s, Unicorn Press moved to Greensboro, North Carolina and although its poetry postcard series ceased with the third series, Unicorn Press continues to publish a diverse list of poetry and translations.

The Alternative Press was founded in Detroit, in the late 1960s, by the poet Ken Mikolowski and his wife, the artist Ann Mikolowski.[5] The Mikolowskis acquired a letterpress, which was formerly the property of the Detroit Artists Workshop, one of the legendary small presses of the 1960s, and set the press up in the basement of their home. They began printing broadsides, postcards, bookmarks, bumperstickers, and an occasional chapbook. Originally these publications were distributed free, in the best small press tradition. By the early 1970s, with printing costs rising, the Mikolowskis began charging a small subscription fee for annual packets of their Alternative Press ephemera. The Alternative Press has since moved, first to Grindstone City, Michigan, and later to Ann Arbor. The Mikolowskis continue to print the work of some of the most interesting contemporary poets and artists. Although The Alternative Press continues to publish chapbooks, they are probably best-known for the annual packets of ephemera, each of which always contains several poetry postcards.

The Alternative Press poetry postcards are published in two distinct series. The more traditional series is similar to the poemcards of Burning Deck. They are printed letterpress on quality paper and are often illustrated with an understated drawing by Ann Mikolowski. Authors who have had their poems printed in The Alternative Press poetry postcards series include Amiri Baraka, Charles Bukowski, Allen Ginsberg, Clayton Eshleman, Robert Creeley, Tom Clark, Diane di Prima, Gary Snyder, Anne Waldman, Robert Bly, and a host of other prominent poets. Much of the poetry the Mikolowskis publish as poemcards represents first published appearances so the poems are bibliographically significant as first separate publications.

The second poemcard series produced by The Alternative Press consists of unique contributions from poets and authors in what have been described as "multiple originals."[6] Individual poets and artists are each sent five hundred blank postcards on which are printed only The Alternative Press imprint and perhaps a device representing a space for postage. The recipients then have the opportunity to write, or draw, or paint, or do basically whatever they want with the postcards. The result has been the production of thousands of original, hand-written poems and artwork. Some poets and artists have opted to treat the cards as five hundred unique creations. Others have approached these projects as larger, thematically-linked works; however, upon completion, the final thematic whole remains unrecognized to all but the poet/artist, because the Mikolowskis disperse the individual cards to The Alternative Press subscribers, each of whom receives a postcard as part of the annual packet.[7] A number of poets and artists have turned these projects into unique collaborative efforts with other poets and/or artists.

The two poetry postcard series produced by The Alternative Press are probably the most successful and innovative of those of any press. Like the Burning Deck and Unicorn series, The Alternative Press has taken the poemcard to new creative heights. In the process, The Alternative Press also presents a host of challenges to librarians, scholars, and bibliographers who seek to document the poetry of the latter half of the twentieth century.

Although the Burning Deck Press, Unicorn Press, and The Alternative press poemcard series are perhaps the most important poemcard series, there are a number of other poemcard series which also merit attention. The Cold Mountain Press of Austin, Texas, produced an interesting poemcard series during its years of operation between 1973 and 1983.[8] Cold Mountain Press was run by a triumvirate of editors, Ryan Petty, an Austin poet who actually founded the press, the well-known poet Joseph Bruchac, and Michael Hogan, a poet who was an inmate at the Arizona State Penitentiary. During its ten-year existence, Cold Mountain Press printed a variety of publications, but is best remembered today for its poetry broadside and poemcard series. The Cold Mountain Press poetry postcards appear to have been issued in two main series of ten cards each. They were usually printed letterpress with striking graphics and illustration in editions of one thousand copies. Like the Unicorn press poemcard series, Cold Mountain also issued special editions limited to fifty copies all of which were signed by the poets. The Cold Mountain series printed work by an interesting mix of poets, including Robert Bly, Diane Wakoski, Allen Ginsberg, Denise Levertov, Wendell Berry, William Stafford, Donald Hall, Peter Wild, and all three of the press's editors.

The White Pine Press based in Buffalo, New York, and edited by the poet Dennis Maloney, has established itself as a significant literary small press which publishes poetry, fiction, translations, and other works by an interesting mix of regional and nationally-known authors. White Pine Press has issued several poemcard collections as part of its Pinecone series which has included books and chapbooks, as well as poetry postcards. Among the poemcard series published within the Pinecone series have been *At the Carrying Place: Poems from the 1978 Artpark Poetry Festival* (Pinecone 3), a collection of original poetry postcards by twenty-three different poets, and a "poemcard of the month" series (Pinecone 7). White Pine has also produced several other unique collections of poemcards.

In the late 1970s, the New York-based poet Jeff Wright launched an interesting poemcard series that featured the poetry of Anselm Hollo, Jayne Ann Phillips, Amiri Baraka, Anne Waldman, Allen Ginsberg, and others. Having encountered Hard Press poetry postcards only infrequently over the years, I suspected that it was somewhat short-lived; however, during my research for this survey I discovered that although Wright has branched out into book publishing, the postcard series was up to seventy-six different postcards by the early 1990s, though some of these are comprised entirely of original artwork with no accompanying text. Wright's Hard Press poemcards vary quite a bit in quality of printing and design; yet he has managed to put together an imaginative series of original poetry in the postcard format.

Robert L. Barth, a Kentucky-based poet, bookseller, and small press poetry publisher since the early-1980s, has produced several interesting groups of poemcards. In his initial two series, which began in the late-1980s, Barth printed previously unpublished poems by a variety of poets. In 1990, he started a little magazine, *The Epigrammatist,* and in a short-lived experiment issued several poemcards printing work from the magazine as special supplements. Barth remains committed to the genre and continues to print poemcards which he then issues, somewhat serendipitously, in conjunction with his poetry chapbooks. To date, nearly forty poemcards have been issued under the Robert L. Barth imprint, including work by such prominent authors as Turner Cassity, Thom Gunn, Janet Lewis, Donald Hall, and Robert Mezey.

The Jargon Society, which was founded in the 1950s by the poet Jonathan Williams, is one of the most important independent literary publishers of the twentieth century. Williams has printed poetry, prose, artwork, and photographs, in virtually every format imaginable, by many of the twentieth century's most significant literary figures. In the mid-1970s he launched the Jargon Society Postcard Series. The series currently numbers over twenty poemcards.

Two very interesting British poemcard series which first appeared in the 1970s are the Mencards series published by the Menard Press (London) and the Daedalus Pin-Up Poems printed by Daedalus Press (Stoke Ferry, Norfolk). Both presses maintained distinguished lists of poetry and their poemcard series featured original work by some of the most significant British, Irish, and Scottish poets writing during the late-1960s and 1970s. By including the Daedalus Pin-up Poems in this survey, I may in fact be stretching the boundaries of my definition of poetry postcard. They are, however, identical in size and shape to traditional poetry postcards and are often described as such in dealer and library catalogs. One poem in the second series, by the poet Edward Lucie-Smith, is actually titled "postcard." The Daedalus Pin-up Poems were issued in at least two separate series during the late 1960s; although they bear no copyright or other information which might establish the exact dates of publication. They are of uniform dimensions, but strikingly dissimilar in terms of color, design, and poetry. Poets whose work appears in the series include Kathleen Abbott, Alan Bold, Richard Burns, Kevin Crossley-Holland, and a host of other contemporary poets, as well as several poets from the past.

The Mencard poemcards were originally issued in the early 1970s. The first two series consisted of packets containing twelve to fifteen poemcards featuring translations from various languages into English. The Menard Press found its Mencards series to be quite popular and has continued to publish the poems. There are currently over one hundred separate poemcards in the Mencards Series. In terms of numbers and longevity, the Menard Press represents one of the most successful poetry postcard series.

I mentioned earlier that poetry postcards have also taken the form of magazines. Perhaps the best-known such example is that of *Fishpaste*. *Fishpaste* was the creation of three Leicester, England, artists and poets: Rigby Graham, Peter Hoy, and Toni Savage. *Fishpaste One* appeared in February 1967 and immediately set the tone for the issues which followed. The recto featured a striking linocut illustration by Rigby Graham, the verso contained a short translation from the verse of René Char. The illustration and poem were printed on an actual blank postcard leaving no room whatsoever for a message or an address, should anyone have actually wanted to send it through the mail. Most subsequent issues of *Fishpaste* were also printed over both sides of actual postcards. *Fishpaste* ran to twenty-two numbers, with several out of series issues as well, with the last number appearing in August 1968. In addition to Graham's artwork, *Fishpaste* featured poetry by a variety of authors, as well as occasional issues made up entirely of letters to the editor or announcements. Following its demise, the editors of *Fishpaste* packaged together the remaining issues– or perhaps printed new ones–and sold them as complete sets. The final issue of *Fishpaste*, in fact, takes the form of a colophon describing the bibliographical history of the magazine. With its whimsical tone, striking design and artwork, and original poetry *Fishpaste* demonstrates the creativity that talented poets, printers, and artists can bring to the poetry postcard format.

The Canadian little magazine *Cross Country* issued a special postcard issue in 1979. *Cross Country* No. 12 consists of twenty poemcards featuring original work by Canadian and American poets, including Margaret Atwood, George Bowering, William Bronk, Tom Clark, Anselm Hollo, and others. The poemcards are all the same size; however, each contains unique artwork or graphics to complement the poems. Unlike *Fishpaste*, the postcards of *Cross Country* print poetry and artwork on one side, leaving the versos free for messages and addresses. Still, this special postcard issue of *Cross Country* does aspire to be a magazine to be kept and read. It was issued in a special wrap-around card cover in an edition limited to seven hundred fifty copies.

J Stone Press Weekly was published irregularly during the mid-1970s in various locales throughout the United States. *J Stone Press Weekly* appears to have printed nearly one hundred issues over the space of a few years, each of which consisted of a poetry postcard by an individual poet. Such prominent poets as Allen Ginsberg, Ed Dorn, Andrei Codrescu, and Robert Creeley had poems printed as *J Stone Press* poetry postcards. Curiously, though *J Stone Press Weekly* should by all rights be the most prolific poetry postcard series in history, I discovered very few surviving examples of the magazine among cataloged library collections.

There have been a number of short-lived poetry postcard efforts which are worth noting. Several of these are from presses I have never encountered before or since and know only from their poemcards. Victoria Press (Gravesend, Kent, England), issued at least one series in 1979 and printed postcard poems by Vernon Scannell, Richard Burns, Thom Gunn, and several others. The press of C. M. Rumpus (Swansea, England), also produced a rather interesting single series in the late-1960s that featured two poemcards each by Alison Bielski, Tony Curtis, and Christopher Morgan. Croupier Press (Denver, CO) printed a series of six poetry postcards, between 1969-1971, the best-known poet in which is Diane di Prima. I also encountered hundreds of additional poetry postcards which appear to have been issued, or at least have only managed to survive, in single or few examples. Some of these were produced by established presses, others by unknown printers, and there are also a good many privately-printed poemcards. Most of the poemcards in this category featured work by relative unknowns; but there are odd little poemcards which print work by poets of some note. The fact that there has been such widespread, miscellaneous poetry postcard publishing adds to their status as a format of some significance.

All poetry publishing houses send out advance printings of poetry from forthcoming collections. The poetry postcard is a unique means by which to advertise a new collection. Since these advance printings often constitute the first separate publications of poems, they assume bibliographical significance. Black Sparrow Press (Santa Barbara, CA) has long been renowned for producing unique ephemeral publications, including poetry postcards, in advance of or even accompanying its publications. Wake Forest University Press, which maintains one of the most ambitious Irish poetry lists, produced an entire poetry postcard series in 1979 to announce forthcoming collections by the Irish poets Thomas Kinsella, John Montague, and Paul Muldoon. The series was sent to bookstores accompanied by an envelope containing ordering information. Poetry postcards produced for promotional purposes are represented inconsistently in research library collections, simply because they are rarely retained by their recipients.

Most of the presses I have covered in this survey have their roots clearly in the small and fine press traditions. Although these presses certainly hope to generate income from the sale of their publications, including poetry postcards, they seldom aspire towards commercial gain. One fairly recent effort which might be the lone exception to this rule is a rather garish publication titled *The Zoland Books Poetry Postcard Collection*, edited by Roland Pease (New York: Zoland Books, 1989). This sixteen-page booklet features seventeen glossy-printed poetry postcards, of varying sizes, by contemporary poets, including Donald Hall, Marge Piercy, May Sarton, and John Updike. The poemcards are all equipped with perforated edges, ready for the buyer to rip out and mail. A cover note also informs the prospective buyer that "These poets have been heard on Phone-A-Poem, 617-492-POEM."

This survey demonstrates that poetry postcards represent an important area of collecting for research libraries building collections of contemporary poetry. Certainly the sheer number of presses and poemcard series indicate that the poemcard format is widespread. Many poemcard series print original poetry by contemporary authors. Such publications are important to bibliographers seeking to document the first appearances by poets. Although the ephemeral nature of poetry postcards may diminish their worth to librarians and scholars, bibliographers documenting the poetry of the last thirty years have discovered that they cannot ignore the idiosyncratic, ephemeral efforts of small and fine press poetry publishers. Many of our most important contemporary poets have had the vast majority of their work published by small and fine presses in little magazines, chapbooks, as broadsides, and in ephemeral publications such as poetry postcards. Such prominent poets as Robert Creeley, Diane Wakoski, Allen Ginsberg, Robert Bly, Charles Bukowski, and Denise Levertov, for example, have been regular contributors to poemcard series. Research libraries must confront the ephemeral in contemporary literature and begin to give it the attention it merits, not only by collecting it, but also by giving it an appropriate level of cataloging.

NOTES

1. The Poetry/Rare Book Collection of the State University of New York at Buffalo houses what is probably the largest collection of poetry postcards in the United States. I did the bulk of my research in this collection. The collections of Washington University Libraries and the University of Delaware also proved useful. In addition, the availability of individual library holdings, such as the extensive broadside collection at Brown University, via the Internet and OCLC also proved useful to identify examples of poemcards and collections.

2. During the course of my research for this article I examined extensive collections of catalogs from dealers, past and present, who have specialized in contemporary poetry, notably the following: Am Here Books, Ampersand, Anacapa Books, Asphodel, Chloe's, Gotham Book Mart, Phoenix Bookstore, and Sand Dollar Books.

3. A useful historical account of Burning Deck Press can be found in *A Century in Two Decades: A Burning Deck Anthology, 1961-1981* (Providence: Burning Deck, 1982). A checklist of Burning Deck publications is also included.

4. Historical and bibliographical information on the Unicorn Press can be found in the following two articles: "A Checklist of Unicorn Press Publications, 1966-1986" *Books at Brown*, 3 (1986); "Teo Savory and Unicorn Press," *Translation Review* 2 (Fall 1978).

5. The best source of historical and bibliographical information on The Alternative Press is the catalogue for an exhibition of the Press's work held at the Detroit Institute of Arts: *Art Poetry Melodrama: 20 Years of The Alternative Press* (Detroit: The Detroit Institute of Arts, 1990).

6. *Art Poetry Melodrama: 20 Years of The Alternative Press*, p. 6.

7. An interesting account of one such "multiple original" assignment can be found in Ted Berrigan, *A Certain Slant of Sunlight* ([Oakland, Calif] O Books [1988]). Berrigan, a prolific poet who was printed regularly by The Alternative Press, completed his five hundred "multiple originals," many of which are collaborations with other poets and artists, just prior to his death in 1982. His widow, the poet Alice Notley recounts Berrigan's approach to the assignment and published a large selection of the "multiple originals" in this collection.

8. Historical information concerning Cold Mountain Press is drawn from the unpublished finding aid to the Archives of the Cold Mountain Press which are held at the Harry Ransom Humanities Research Center, The University of Texas at Austin.

ORGANIZATIONAL ISSUES

George Watson Cole:
A Man, His Postcards,
and the American Antiquarian Society

Jennifer Henderson

Every writer as he passes along the highway of life selects some object, picks it up, and casts it as his contribution on the cairn within which knowledge universal lies buried. The bibliographer passes that way, rearranges the heterogeneous mass, reduces it to order and symmetry, and by so doing erects to her a worthy and fitting monument.

George Watson Cole[1]

George Watson Cole (1850-1939) was a bibliographer extraordinaire as well as a teacher, lawyer, librarian (he graduated in the first class of Melvil Dewey), writer, and collector. He compiled bibliographies of the periodical literature of Bermuda and of Elihu D. Church's book collection (the most renowned U.S. collection of rare books ever assembled at the time). In a bibliographical study, he determined the correct arrangement of

---

[Haworth co-indexing entry note]: "George Watson Cole: A Man, His Postcards, and the American Antiquarian Society." Henderson, Jennifer. Co-published simultaneously in *Popular Culture in Libraries* (The Haworth Press, Inc.) Vol. 3, No. 2, 1995, pp. 173-186; and: *Postcards in the Library: Invaluable Visual Resources* (ed: Norman D. Stevens) The Haworth Press, Inc., 1995, pp. 173-186. Single or multiple copies of this article are available from The Haworth Document Delivery Service [1-800-342-9678, 9:00 a.m. - 5:00 a.m. (EST)].

173

Shakespeare's First Folio. Undaunted by huge tasks, he and his staff cataloged the vast holdings of Henry E. Huntington. This collection grew to 80,000 books and manuscripts before it was moved from New York to the new Huntington Library in San Marino, California, during the summer of 1920. Cole also served as the Huntington's first librarian until he retired in 1924.[2]

The scholarship and detail apparent in his bibliographies enhanced Cole's reputation. He was a life member of the Bibliographic Society of America, serving as its president from 1916 to 1921; the American Library Association, where he was the treasurer from 1893 to 1896; and the American Historical Association.

In conjunction with his library and bibliographic endeavors, Cole wrote several articles, many of which he privately published as preprints and reprints in short runs of 150 to 400 copies. These he distributed to colleagues and libraries of choice. Our purpose here is to concentrate on Cole's penultimate book, a brief 1935 edition entitled *Postcards, the World in Miniature: A Plan for Their Systematic Arrangement with an Index.*

During his travels in the United States, Bermuda, and Europe, Cole assembled a large and varied collection of picture postcards.[3] He advised: "The wise traveller on reaching a stopping-place will, therefore, do well to make his first visit a postcard shop, and there look over its views of the place he is in, from which he can select such objects as he may desire to see. Then and then only can he intelligently start out to behold its showplaces and feel assured that in the end he will have seen all that are really worth his inspection." Previewing postcards prior to touring continues to be a sensible approach, whether one visits capital cities, French castles, roadside attractions, or suburban libraries. A tourist may "now obtain view postcards not only of every important feature of the city or town he is visiting, but even of the contents of its museums and art galleries, nearly all of which provide fine examples of their most treasured exhibits." Because landmarks, special features, and local events have been portrayed on souvenirs since mass production allowed for them, postcards remain one of the most handy and economical choices ever devised. Cole knew this as he wrote, "nothing in print is more universal than the postcard."[4]

Since Cole spent much of his life compiling lists of other collections and bringing order to a country's or an individual's assemblage of printed works, he approached postcards as an identical challenge: "Whoever makes a collection of postcards is often puzzled how to make it most available and how to so arrange it that he can put his hand upon any particular card at a moment's notice. Having had considerable experience with a collection of several thousand cards, collected here and abroad, I have solved this difficult problem to my own satisfaction." He did not like sticking them in albums that restrict handling and studying both sides, so he "finally settled upon the card-catalogue plan."[5]

Cole valued this plan, yet some questions about it persist and will be addressed herein. Did his book actually document the way his collection was arranged, as the reader might at first think, or was it a simplified outline to encourage and assist a collector or librarian in organizing the assorted topics that may be found in one or more boxes of postcards?

As a bibliographer who needed to put everything in order and strive for standardized patterns, Cole was extremely concerned with uniformity. In the late 1880s he devised a measuring card, called the Cole Size Card, which conformed to the American Library Association's size rules for measuring books. He believed others should adopt the ALA rules and his card would "make their application more uniform and accurate."[6]

Aspiring to an overall standard may perhaps explain why he liked postcards. Beyond their pictorial and historic appeal, postcards were all the same size, a characteristic Cole found appealing. When writing about the card-catalogue plan for his postcards, he believed "this is quite feasible, owing to the uniform size in which they are generally printed."[7]

The introduction and proliferation of continental-sized cards (those that measure 4 inches by 6 inches and have become the industry norm) as well as the forever-difficult-to-store oversized cards that can grow to file-folder dimensions (which many collectors refuse to save) would have caused Cole much stress. Modern cards often defy order.

Postcards, the World in Miniature addresses Cole's primary fascination. In their tiny, tidy way, postcards depict what did or still does exist. These paperboard gems record how the world looks for an instant, since structures and natural features are forever changing. Even something as fundamental as trees are in constant flux by growing taller and broader, being pruned, or cut down from disease, disaster, and progress. By focusing on what is pictured rather than how, Cole declines to cover such basics as artists, publishers, and types of cards, whether chromolithographs, hand-tinted sepias, or signed illustrations. He did, however, get involved with photographs and photographers when writing about California mission postcards, which he collected with zeal. Mission cards will be discussed in detail later.

Within the book's 27 pages, Cole offers a 61-point outline for arranging postcards. Some of the headings include: "3a Portraits of Rulers and their Families: kings, emperors, presidents, sovereigns"; "9c Inland steamers, tugboats, fireboats, other vessels"; "14a Street views: avenues, boulevards (not parked)"; "21b Parked driveways, boulevards, esplanades, etc."; and "43a Salons of Modern Art." Of particular interest might be the category "41 Libraries: endowed, public and private" under which are "41a Outside views" and "41b Interiors and furnishings." It is difficult to follow the logic behind portions of his scheme. Why, for example, do the watery categories "28a Fountains: artificial cascades and waterfalls" through "28c Mineral springs" interrupt sections on buildings, e.g., "27a Historic Buildings: (real or fictitious)" and "29a Government Buildings: capitols, legislative?" Far more helpful is the painstakingly detailed 7-page index.

He devotes considerable space to architectural creations: museums, skyscrapers, opera houses, bridges, and religious institutions. Cathedral cards are classified extensively as to exterior and interior details (rose windows and organs), structural components like doorways and spires, and monuments beneath which shrines and crypts are placed. Under "48b Campaniles and baptisteries" are cloisters, chapter houses, Scala-Santas (holy stairs), libraries, and Episcopal residences.

Cole was the consummate organizer; what else could explain separate index headings for towers (as architecture), towers (monumental), towers (of city walls), and towers (water works)? He also inserted some unusual subjects like abattoirs, beguinages, cromlechs, dreadnoughts, menhirs, and strands.

When I discovered an autographed copy of *Postcards, the World in Miniature* in Chicago's Newberry Library, I was charged with curiosity. What became of Cole's postcard collection? Was it broken up and sold at auction, lot by lot to other collectors? This seemed unimaginable due to Cole's devotion to libraries and saving printed works for the public good. Could it be housed in one of the libraries where he had worked? From 1888-1890 he assisted Newberry Director William F. Poole, but though 61 entries in the Newberry card catalog refer to Cole's writings, not one mentioned a collection of postcards. Nor were the postcards located at the Huntington Library.

Thanks to Donald C. Dickinson, Cole's biographer, I learned that Cole had donated his personal papers to the American Antiquarian Society in Worcester, Massachusetts. A letter from Thomas Knoles, Curator of Manuscripts, informed me that yes, Cole had given them approximately 35,000 postcards.

As Cole points out, the *OED*'s earliest reference to postcards is 1870, but their first period of extensive popularity, roughly 1900-1917, occurs after the AAS collection's cut-off date of 1876. Due to their relatively late date, postcards are not an acquisition priority or research interest at the American Antiquarian Society, at least not until now. It takes a curious deltiologist from Chicago to enter these hallowed halls, blow the dust off boxes of cards, and dig in to learn about Cole's collection.

If you are planning a trip to Worcester and the Society, try to be there on Wednesday afternoon. Their weekly 90-minute behind-the-scenes tour not only introduces the researcher to AAS collecting parameters but also includes visits to the stacks and various departments where you will be shown printed items rescued from time and disinterest. The tour really personalizes the place. Staff members warm up after welcoming you into their offices and answering questions in their areas of expertise. Initial fears of aloofness faded as research needs were anticipated and service remained friendly and courteous.

The American Antiquarian Society was founded in 1812 by Isaiah Thomas, the printer whose Whig newspaper, *The Massachusetts Spy*, regularly taunted the British. He and his printing press fled Boston only three nights before the Battle of Lexington and Concord. Reestablished in Worcester, Thomas–and the famous press which is on display at AAS–became the major printer in the new United States after the Revolutionary War. He started the Society following the purchase of files from several colonial newspapers with the belief that printed works from this fledgling nation needed to be sought out, preserved, and studied. As a result of his campaign, AAS houses two-thirds of all known documents printed in this country from 1640 to 1821. Because Cole was a member of the Society, elected in 1918, his papers and postcards were accepted.

Two years prior to publishing his postcard book, Cole started corresponding with AAS regarding the donation of all his written materials. "I am now in my 83rd year," he noted, "and have recently been looking over my possessions with a view to their final resting place after I shall have ceased to care for them." As a meticulous saver, Cole offered files of correspondence going back to 1851, diaries, cash journals, newspaper clippings, manuscripts, printed works, and postcards. In January 1933, he wrote AAS Director Clarence S. Brigham and stated, "I have a collection of some 25,000 or more postcards; collected mainly during my travels in Europe and in this country. These are in boxes arranged like a card catalogue with numerous index cards."[8]

Robert Vail, AAS Librarian, wrote back that he was delighted at Cole's offer and acknowledged the value of his papers. "I believe that there is no library in the country where the results of your manifold labors could be more properly preserved. For over one hundred years this Society has devoted itself largely to American bibliography."

He was a bit more cautious about Cole's postcards: "Of the material listed in your letter, we should be most anxious to acquire everything that it mentions, with the single exception of the European post cards. In restricting our collecting to North and South America, we have steadfastly turned our faces against the material published by the rest of the world. As it happens, we have a very large collection of over 30,000 American post-cards, arranged geographically." He told Cole that they would take the entire collection but only "If you yourself thought it proper . . ."[9]

After he prepared the donation's groundwork, nothing further transpired until after *Postcards, the World in Miniature* was issued. Cole self-published his postcard book in a limited edition of 250 copies. On his "List of those to whom *Postcard Pamphlet* has been sent" were names of the 248 recipients. These included university and public libraries from across the United States and in Europe, Canada, and Bermuda, associations and clubs with which he was affiliated, individuals with whom he was acquainted, and the *New York Times Book Review.*[10]

Many of these colleagues and friends sent responses which were placed chronologically in his 1935 file of correspondence. Samuel Leask of Santa Cruz, California, wrote, "I must confess to a feeling of envy at the facility with which you can reduce a mass of unrelated material to perfect system and order."[11] Joseph Quincy Adams, director of the Folger Shakespeare Library in Washington, D.C., wrote, "I have often wondered why the collecting instinct expended so much energy on stamps, and so little on the far more interesting postcard. Your study of how to form and arrange such a collection should do much to stimulate collecting. The idea of using the card-catalogue scheme to classify and preserve the material furnishes a perfect solution of the problem."[12]

Vail commented that the manual would be helpful to AAS catalogers as the "first attempt to treat postcards in an orderly arrangement."[13] Brigham, after praising Cole's effort, explained the Society's collection: ". . . we collect only post cards for the two Americas. It all started from a collection of about 12,000 cards which was offered to us as a gift some five years ago." Thus informing Cole that their collection was started in 1930 and reconfirming the desire to limit acquisitions to the "two Americas." Brigham continued, "We have taken what has come in since and now have about 20,000 cards. Most of them are of places and are arranged geographically by States and towns, rather than by subject like canals, bridges, churches, &c. Those which do not admit of a geographic arrangement, we arrange by subject such as portraits, naval craft, flowers, sports, humor, &c. Your subject arrangement for a public library would be especially useful, particularly when accompanied by your excellent index."[14]

In 1936 following a long illness Cole again wrote Brigham to inform him that accompanying the 14 cases of manuscripts he was sending were about 25 boxes of "domestic postcards which I accumulated during the past quarter of a century."[15] He thus heeded both men's recommendations and refrained from sending his foreign cards.

These he donated to Trinity College, where he had received an honorary L.H.D. in 1920. Peter J. Knapp, Trinity College Archivist, confirmed that "the gift consisted of 22 boxes containing an estimated total of 10,000 postcards" and appear to be primarily viewcards from Great Britain and the European continent.[16] My trip east could not extend to Trinity, so I leave the door open for others to investigate. Trinity houses no other postcards. This fortuitous situation means that his cards were not interfiled with an established collection. They may, then, be in the order Cole intended them: "I have found it most convenient to arrange large divisions by countries, states, counties, and cities or towns." Remembering, of course, "some cards have a national significance, such as a nation's coat-of-arms, its flags, coins, postage-stamps, portraits of its rulers, etc. These naturally precede those of a local character."[17]

Cole also noted in his last letter to Brigham that he was sending a vast array–more than 2,500–of California mission postcards and photographs.

He was fascinated with the pictorial representations of the old Spanish missions in California, the chain of 21 Franciscan outposts started in 1769 by Father Junípero Serra. During the time he sought mission cards, the hobby of collecting postcards was extremely popular. Cole found that the most common way to view missions was by buying and studying postcards. "Though of all degrees of merit, these cards are for the most part reasonably good," he wrote. "They are ephemeral in their nature and there seem to be fashions in them as in clothes or books. To-day certain cards may be as numerous as autumn leaves and in a few months they will be equally hard to find. This we have learned from actual experience while searching for some particular mission card seen in a rival collection, for it has been our aim to secure as many different postcards of the missions as possible."[18]

In 1908 after finishing the E. D. Church catalog, he and his wife visited Cole's sister near Santa Cruz, California. On the agenda for this trip was library research in Berkeley. While there he became absorbed with the missions and tried to obtain a complete set of them on postcards. "As my interest in them continued to grow, I decided to go to San Diego, which I did. After exhausting all the opportunities of acquiring pictures of that mission, I went to San Luis Rey, and from there continued going north from mission to mission until I reached Los Angeles."[19]

Cole was methodical in gathering these cards. I found more than two boxes filled with California mission postcards at AAS. These boxes are

titled, California: Los to Missions (General); California: Missions (C) to
Missions (San J); and California: Missions (San L) to Mount Lowe.

Yet nowhere in *Postcards, the World in Miniature* are missions suggested. The fact that Cole omitted missions as a category is stunning,
especially considering the effort and enthusiasm he invested in these rustic
stucco structures.

Cole's interest in missions is evident by his 1910 published article
entitled, "Missions and Mission Pictures: A Contribution towards an Iconography of the Franciscan Missions of California." This treatise discusses various mission depictions on paper such as sketches, etchings,
lithographs, paintings, photographs, and postcards. His long-term examination of these renderings continued in 1935 with an unpublished
update of the mission article that is filed with his other papers at AAS.
Cole concluded that "the old missions are certainly the most characteristic
works of man to be found in California. The early history of the State
while under Spanish domination is so intimately associated with them that
no more appropriate and artistic decorations can be placed on the walls of
its educational institutions, libraries, public buildings, and homes than the
beautiful views of them."[20]

As a passionate collector, Cole attempted to locate any and all California mission cards. In so doing he became acquainted with various photographers and publishers and the number of cards each issued. Some include
Paul C. Koeber, Arthur Clark Vroman, Edward H. Mitchell, Adolph Sei-
lige, Pacific Novelty, the Newman Postcard Company, and the Detroit
Publishing Company. Although Cole enjoyed collecting as many mission
cards as he could find, he did express disappointment that complete sets of
the 21 missions were not sold by one vendor.

In 1897 A. C. Vroman spent his vacation traveling to and photographing all the California missions. He took about 250 photos that Cole had a
chance to view. From these original shots, Vroman issued 36 sepia postcards, available only as a complete set. Each set contained 18 of the
missions along with a map postcard of the mission region. Cole praised the
map, although "this extremely useful feature seems, strangely enough, to
have been overlooked by every other publisher."[21]

"As they can be procured at a small cost," he wrote of postcards,
"there is every temptation to purchase them in considerable numbers."[22]
Cole bought at least 13 of these sets so that he could pull out the map card.
He then underlined the name of a specific mission and filed it with cards of
that name. These underlined map postcards were found for San Juan
Capistrano, San Antonio, San Luis Obispo, San Jose, San Miguel, San
Diego, San Fernando, San Rafael, San Juan Bautista, San Francisco de

Solano, and San Luis Rey, and two without underlining were discovered with booklets of mission cards. Perhaps Cole mailed the extra cards from the Vroman sets to friends, maybe even sending some with his 248 books, since three recipients thanked him for the mission card that had been received. Or perhaps he traded some since he sought out other collectors with whom he competed for cards.

Even without an interest in missions, I found this group of postcards intriguing. The cards capture a portion of California history with mission exteriors, chapel interiors, close-ups of bells, and candid real photos of farmers taking a smoke outside San Fernando mission. From San Luis Rey, a dozen different cards portray one Father O'Keefe dressed in his brown cassock. In the postcard scenes, he moves about the mission pausing on stairs, standing in arched doorways, and posing beside stone pillars, sometimes with his hand grasping the rope belt around his middle.

Some real photos were shot by Harold A. Taylor, N. H. Reed, and M. Ruggles Baird. In one of Cole's mission files I ran across a mimeographed sheet from Harold A. Taylor of Coronado, California, of numbered negatives that correspond to some of Cole's real photo mission cards. Taylor's list concludes with a brief statement that he would gladly share information learned about the missions he had photographed. Cole surely took advantage of this offer.

Thomas Knoles, who so thoughtfully assisted my research, believes that AAS "never actively sought postcards but accumulated them when they came in." He directed me to the archive of Society correspondence that was maintained until the 1970s. A 3-inch by 5-inch index card titled "Post Cards" lists 13 headings, dating from 1933 to 1956, which may provide a paper trail for most of the donations that comprise their postcard collection, although Cole and the Worcester Public Library, which donated some cards, are missing. References to J. R. Burdick and W. Bourcy-Beckley are significant. Both Burdick and Bourcy-Beckley authored books on postcards; Burdick's *Pioneer Postcards*, originally issued in 1957, remains the primary source on mailing cards up to 1898 while Bourcy-Beckley distributed the first postcard price guide in 1954.[23] Also cited are the Post Card Collectors Club and the Post-Card Shop.

The published count of picture postcards in the AAS collection is approximately 115,000.[24] Deep in the stacks are 130 long black boxes that house them. These cardboard boxes, each identified as "Macy Transfer Case 46B" by a label on one end, measure approximately 16 inches by 7 inches and hold anywhere from 700 to 1,000 cards. Most date from before 1915 but a few later cards are mixed in. The latest, postmarked in the early

1960s, are a miscellaneous assortment of chromes from Las Vegas and Washington, D.C.

To organize his cards Cole explained that "index-cards, inserted at convenient intervals are necessary, if a given card is to be located with the greatest ease."[25] He also mentioned index cards (no hyphen) in a letter quoted earlier to AAS Director Brigham.

By "index-cards," Cole probably meant cardstock dividers somewhat larger than the postcards themselves. Many dividers were used. These usually had identifying numbers and descriptive phrases such as "122 Puente Cabrillo," "225 Various Arches," and "384 Site and Pear Orchard" written on them. Cards were then filed behind the appropriate divider.

Many of the dividers that Cole donated with his cards have been turned over and recycled for a different use–"151 Statuary Architectural" was flipped to the clean side and became "Los Angeles Streets A-Z"–as his cards were interfiled with the AAS core collection. By matching Cole's handwriting in his correspondence with the numeric codes on these original dividers, I hoped to uncover some clue to link them with his book.

This proved difficult. One of the California boxes holds a divider titled "Pasadena–A-Hos," but on the other side is printed in black ink in Cole's hand, "130 Churches, Courts, Colonnade, etc." Consulting the book index, I found churches (as cathedrals) coded as "48a-f."

Postcards filed behind Cole's divider titled "Los Angeles 27 Hotels A-Z" start with a view of the Hotel Alexandria. Written on the reverse side in black ink is his code "11d" (on the left) and "27-1" (on the right). Next in the box comes the Angelus Hotel with "11d" and "27-2"; then the Baltimore Hotel: "11d" and "27-3"; Gates Hotel: "11d" and "27-4"; Hotel Hayward: "11d" and "27-5"; and Hotel Lankershim: "11d" and "27-6." These appear in alphabetical order from 27-1 through 27-6. But the numbers might also indicate that these hotel cards were obtained at the same time.

What could "11d" mean? It does not designate hotels, which are numbered "33d," as classified under "Transportation and Hotels" in Cole's book, and it does not refer to a geographic location, a code perhaps exclusively reserved for Los Angeles or California. Much to my surprise, "11d" was also found on a black-and-white view of the Manufacturers and Liberal Arts Building at the World's Columbian Exposition.[26] Actually, "11d" refers to "bridges: viaducts," (but not "bridges: railroad" which is "17b" or "bridges: highway, foot," found at "18b").

Even though a mission category is glaringly absent from *Postcards, the World in Miniature*, Cole's enigmatic codes and categories appear on some of the recycled dividers and can be linked to mission postcards. In an Ohio box, the divider for "Dayton to Portsmouth" was recycled from one originally for "294 Mission and Grounds"; which mission and what "294" means are unknown. The peach-colored "Kansas" divider once read "390 Mission Play"; "279 Missions" became "Newark, New Jersey"; and in a miscellaneous foreign box, the divider for "Nevis" was recycled from Cole's "307 Interior of Mission." Who knows what morsels of information may be found from further study of these dividers?

Cole was 85 and in failing health when he issued his postcard book. Yet as one friend who received a copy noted, "You seem to have many devices to keep from going old!"[27] Nonetheless, there still remains the question about what his book shows, whether it served as a master catalog to his collection or a formula to sort out, systematize and settle cards into an order that served collectors and library patrons quickly and efficiently. Looking at both sides of many cards and comparing them with the "systematic arrangement" in his book leads one to speculation since no logical explanation presents itself.

Maybe Cole cross-numbered his cards based on a private, uncirculated list that supplied an alternative plan for arranging his cards into the levels of minutiae he desired. Cole was such a saver that it was puzzling to find almost nothing in the book to match what was written on the postcards and dividers. Maybe he started renumbering and never changed his previously numbered cards. Since he wrote in black ink, altering numbers would be difficult. Maybe clues to solve this mystery are hidden in his foreign cards housed in Trinity College.

Even after an intense 2-1/2 days of research into AAS materials, during which time I checked 30 of the 130 boxes of postcards, mine was not an exhaustive study. I poured over his correspondence, clippings, and cards for clues, yet never located the key to Cole's collection. Throughout my research, there had been the expectation that the working list indicating how Cole organized his cards would materialize. In the book he wrote, "The system of arrangement here set forth, I have found to work well in practice. It does not profess to be scientific in character, but will, I believe, be found a good practical working basis for the arrangement of a somewhat numerous collection."[28] If it did "work well in practice," what he published does not appear to be the layout for his own collection. Perhaps he realized that what he actually used, with its obscure categories and codings, was too complicated for other collectors and instead he presented an abbreviated version, a streamlined form, a prototype from which others could begin to use and modify his plan.

Although all the postcards are stored together at AAS, nobody on the

staff knows very much about them. And few think to use them. As touched
on earlier, postcards became most popular after the turn of the century
while the Society seeks printed materials that date up through 1876. Seldom do researchers, when delving into the history of a community, request
a box of postcards from Massachusetts (there are 26), New York (there are
13), or any other state.[29]

These cards could add historical, architectural, and even personal dimension to whatever city and state an individual or family may hail from.
Messages written on cards offer a flavor of the times, as in spellings and
phrases that describe current events like births, elections, or floods. In
Postcards, the World in Miniature Cole wrote, "Postcards represent the
changes that are constantly taking place in every town." He believed that
libraries should strive to acquire those of local interest whenever possible.
By saving these pictures of the past, libraries could preserve "accurate
representations of old buildings or historic sites, monuments, historic
characters and scenes, views of the daily appearance of its streets or
principal thoroughfares and the busy crowds that traverse them."[30]

Above all else, George Watson Cole was a bibliographer. Striving to
create order from chaotic piles of printed paper, he cataloged libraries,
privately held book collections, and his own postcards. That he concluded
his publishing career with a book intended to organize postcards is a fitting
tribute to a man driven to make sense from clutter. And it is a worthy end
to his printed works that they came to rest at AAS. As he wrote, "experience has thus proved that those libraries are the most useful which are the
largest, oldest, and have long been the resort of scholars."[31]

Since few libraries maintain postcard collections, it is crucial to support
those that do. Thomas Knoles mentioned that I was the first person he
knew of who ever arrived specifically to look at the AAS postcard collection. Next time your travel plans include Boston, remember that the American Antiquarian Society is only about an hour's drive away. Try to schedule a visit. This treasure chest of early American history houses postcards
that could use some more dusting off.

NOTES

1. George Watson Cole, *Bibliographical Problems with Few Solutions*. Preprinted for private distribution from *Papers of the Bibliographical Society of
America* 10, no. 3 (1916): 119.

2. To learn more about Cole's varied career, refer to Donald C. Dickinson,
George Watson Cole 1850-1939 (The Great Bibliographers Series, no. 8, Metu-
chen, N.J.: Scarecrow Press, 1990) and also by Dickinson, "George Watson Cole

(6 September 1850-10 October 1939)" in the *Dictionary of Literary Biography*, vol. 140 (Detroit: Gale, 1994), pp. 40-48.

3. Is it *postcard, post card,* or *post-card*? Postcard, now accepted as the norm, has been used throughout except in quoted material, where the original spelling–with a space or hyphen–has been retained.

4. George Watson Cole, *Postcards, the World in Miniature: A Plan for Their Systematic Arrangement With An Index* (Pasadena, Calif.: The author, 1935), p. 3.

5. Cole, *Postcards*, p. 5.

6. *Directions for Using Cole Size Card* was typeset on a separate sheet from the actual "Cataloguer's Size Card" (Boston: Library Bureau, 1889).

7. Cole, *Postcards*, p. 5.

8. Letter from Cole to Clarence S. Brigham, AAS Director, January 29, 1933. American Antiquarian Society correspondence files.

9. Letter from Robert Vail, AAS Librarian, to Cole, February 8, 1933. AAS correspondence files.

10. Cole's typescript "List of those to whom *Postcard Pamphlet* has been sent" included 248 names. American Antiquarian Society, George Watson Cole Papers, Red Box 29, folder 4.

11. Letter from Samuel Leask, Santa Cruz, California, to Cole, May 9, 1935. AAS Cole Papers, Box 11, folder 2.

12. Letter from Joseph Quincy Adams, director of the Folger Shakespeare Library in Washington, D.C., to Cole, April 26, 1935. AAS Cole Papers, Box 11, folder 2.

13. Letter from Robert Vail to Cole, April 15, 1935. AAS Cole Papers, Box 11, folder 2.

14. Letter from Clarence Brigham to Cole, April 15, 1935. AAS correspondence files.

15. Letter from Cole to Clarence Brigham, August 27, 1936. AAS correspondence files.

16. Letter to the author, December 21, 1994. The Cole Collection is housed in the Trinity College Archives.

17. Cole, *Postcards, the World in Miniature*, p. 6.

18. George Watson Cole, "Missions and Mission Pictures: A Contribution towards an Iconography of the Franciscan Missions of California," in the *Handbook and Proceedings of the Annual Meeting 1910* (California Library Association), reprinted from *News Notes of California Libraries* 5, no. 3 (July 1910): 62.

19. George Watson Cole, "How I Chanced to Become a Bibliographer." Undated manuscript in "Sixty Busy Years in Law, Libraries, and Bibliography," Autobiographical Notes, AAS Cole Papers, Red Box 9, folder 1.

20. Cole, "Missions and Mission Pictures," p. 66.

21. Cole, "Missions and Mission Pictures," p. 63.

22. Cole, *Postcards*, p. 3.

23. Background on 1940-1950s postcard publications was found in Lewis Baer, "Postcards Experience Collectibility Upswing," *Postcard Collector Annu-*

al, 3rd ed., 1993, pp. 36-37; and Roy and Marilyn Nuhn, "Price Guides & Their Writers, *American Postcard Journal*, 3 (September-October 1977): 35.

24. Nancy H. Burkett and John B. Hench, ed., *Under Its Generous Dome: The Collections and Programs of the American Antiquarian Society* (Worcester: American Antiquarian Society, 1992), p. 118.

25. Cole, *Postcards*, p. 5.

26. The card named, published by Girsch & Roehsler of New York and copyrighted Nov. 1, 1892, was part of a 12-card World's Columbian Exposition set. "This is believed to be the first American set of pictorial postcards," according to Frederick and Mary Megson in *American Exposition Postcards (1870-1920)* (Martinsville, N.J.: The Postcard Lovers, 1992), p. 28.

27. Letter from William Stetson Merrill, Oconomowoc, Wisconsin to Cole, May 13, 1935. AAS Cole Papers, Box 11, folder 2.

28. Cole, *Postcards*, p. 6.

29. To encourage future research, here's a state-by-state breakdown of the 130 AAS postcard boxes:

AL/AZ/AK–1	ME– 5	OK/OR– 1
CA– 13	MD– 1	PA– 4
CO– 1	MA– 26	RI– 2
CT– 5	MI– 3	SC/SD– 1
CT/DE– 1	MN/MS– 1	TN/TX– 1
DC– 2	MO– 1	UT/VT– 1
FL– 4	MT/NE/NV/NM–1 VT– 3	
GA/HI– 1	NH– 6	VA– 4
ID/IL– 1	NJ– 3	WA/WV– 1
IN– 1	NY– 13 (inc. NYC–3)	WI– 1
IA/KS– 1	NC/ND– 1	WI/WY– 1
KY/LA– 1	OH– 2	

+ 15 boxes misc. foreign, unsorted U.S., general holidays and folders

30. Cole, *Postcards*, p. 4.

31. George Watson Cole, *The Ideally Perfect Library*, reprinted in William Warner Bishop and Andrew Keogh, ed., *Essays Offered to Herbert Putman* (New Haven, Conn.: Yale University Press, 1929), p. 123.

The Automation
of the Frances Louise Day
Postcard Collection
of the Howard County Historical Society
(Ellicott City, MD)

Mary K. Mannix

In the second half of 1993 the Library of the Howard County Historical Society (Ellicott City, Maryland) inherited from one of its dues paying, but not active, members a collection that it did not know it would be receiving. This collection was the largest the Society, Museum or Library, had ever acquired. It substantially increased the Library's holdings. The donor, Frances Louise Day, had assembled a collection of scrapbooks, photo albums, slides, books, and government publications, dealing with a variety of subjects, most pertaining to Maryland and/or Howard County. Her collection also included approximately 2,000 postcards of Maryland scenes.

The Howard County Historical Society (HCHS), founded in 1957, is the oldest agency collecting historical materials in its county. The Society's Library is open two days a week for a total of 13 hours. During those hours the staff services approximately 800 researchers a year. The Library's growing holdings include approximately 1,500 books, 1,200 cataloged photographs, significant collections of governmental records, 200 volumes in a "record and account book" collection, ten drawers of vertical file material, and several dozen partially or unprocessed manuscript collections. The Society is also the repository for the archives of the Howard County Home Extension/4-H, the Howard County Garden Club,

[Haworth co-indexing entry note]: "The Automation of the Frances Louise Day Postcard Collection of the Howard County Historical Society (Ellicott City, MD)." Mannix, Mary K. Co-published simultaneously in *Popular Culture in Libraries* (The Haworth Press, Inc.) Vol. 3, No. 2, 1995, pp. 187-197; and: *Postcards in the Library: Invaluable Visual Resources* (ed: Norman D. Stevens) The Haworth Press, Inc., 1995, pp. 187-197. Single or multiple copies of this article are available from The Haworth Document Delivery Service [1-800-342-9678, 9:00 a.m. - 5:00 p.m. (EST)].

the county chapter of the Daughters of the American Revolution, and the Library of the Howard County Genealogical Society.

The postcards were chosen as the first element of the Day collection to be cataloged and it was determined from the start of the project that the cataloging would be automated. It is possible, although slightly awkward, to obtain access to many of the collection's other materials in their original state. Day labeled the scrapbooks, photo albums, and slide carousels with dates and topics. The postcards, however, were not as well marked. It was also much easier, with the other materials, to weed out items irrelevant to the Society's collecting focus, for example, scrapbooks exclusively dealing with the Kennedy family or Pope John Paul II. They were identified and usually self-contained. In order to locate Maryland postcards, all the postcards in the bequest, circa 7,000, had to be culled.

The initial survey of the Maryland postcards in Day's collection resulted in a count of 2,157. The tally, after six months of processing and the elimination of duplicates, dropped to 1,850. The staff of the Library saw the addition of this postcard collection as an opportunity to open up the Society to a new group of patrons: individuals whose interest was broader than just Howard County history and culture, who could make use of the postcards.

Postcards have research potential to a wide variety of researchers. Geographers, architectural historians, individuals renovating historic houses, and community planners are examples of possible research groups. These groups are all also common patrons in local history institutions. Postcards are also becoming increasingly popular with genealogists, the life blood of most historical societies, as they may supply the only images of ancestors' homes and related institutions.[1]

Postcards can also be exceedingly useful to the small institution. Besides interesting to a wide spectrum of researchers, they can also fulfill a variety of image needs. For example, they can be used in exhibits to illustrate ideas and topics unrelated to their main subject. Postcards are also often easy to collect, there are many out there. It has been "estimated that 140 billion postcards were mailed worldwide between 1894-1919."[2] Also, due to the extrinsic nature of their medium, many of them have survived. "Millions of postcards have survived because of their popularity as souvenirs and because the 'penny postcard' was the most convenient and economical form of communication for many years."[3]

Also, unlike other forms of photographs, many small communities were documented in postcards. Communities that otherwise would have been ignored by professional photographers were visited by traveling postcard photographers. In a publication co-authored by Enid T. Thompson and

Charles J. Semowich, "Post Card Collections in the Local Historical Society," the authors aptly explain that postcards "were created to provide a glimpse of contemporary life so that people who could not be part of the sender's immediate surroundings could share in that life. This helps to explain why many scenes exist only on postcards and not on any other photographic medium."[4]

Thompson in her 1978 resource *Local History Collections: A Manual for Librarians*, published by the American Association for State and Local History, stated that "photographs are usually the easiest of local history materials to collect";[5] this is not always true. There are communities which did not have active professional photographers and where the photographs taken for, or of, the local families are still in family hands. Her statement that "every town had its professional photographer, or one who visited on schedule" is also not true. For example, the *Directory of Maryland Photographers 1839-1900* lists only one photographer working in Howard County, Maryland during that time period. He had an office in Ellicott City, the county seat, for the brief period 1894-1895.[6] It would be reasonable to assume that this lack of working photographers in Howard limited the number of images taken of the area.

Postcards, however, often filled the documentary void created by a lack of active professional photographers. Private individuals could also produce postcards on commercially available postcard paper. Although these images are not always of the highest aesthetic quality–unposed, fuzzy people, poorly cropped–they are often all that remains to document some communities during the turn of the century. Such images are very authentic. Also, many small businesses commissioned postcards, even if only in small runs. "Of more importance to local history, however, is the fact that there were hundreds of small, local publishers of post cards, such as photographers, newspapers, drugstores, and dry goods stores."[7]

Although the Library's collection of 1,850 postcards is a small number in comparison to major postcard collections and the holdings of many collectors, it is a significant size for an institution like the Howard County Historical Society. It also appears to be a significant collection for an institution in the Baltimore region. The Howard County Historical Society collection now almost equals, in count, the collection of postcards at the *Maryland Historical Society* (MHS), located in Baltimore.[8] Although Lynn Cox and Helena Zinkham state, in a 1981 issue of Maryland Historical Magazine, that the MHS has "about 3,000" postcards[9] the present curator administering the collection states that they have approximately 2,000 postcards.

There are very few articles that discuss individual postcard collections.

The few which are cited in other articles and appear in bibliographies are usually for very large collections. Also, little attention is usually given to postcards in published descriptions of institutional holdings. Only one article has been identified dealing with a collection in Maryland,[10] Cox and Zinkham's before mentioned *Maryland Historical Magazine* article, "Picture Research at the Maryland Historical Society: A Guide to the Sources." There is, therefore, little documentation available on institutional postcard collections in the state.

In Cox and Zinkham, the Maryland Historical Society's postcard collection, which is located in its Prints and Photographs Division, is discussed in a brief paragraph giving the scope, quantity, inclusive dates, and description of the finding aids. Mention is made that postcards can also be found in the department in "lots" or collections "catalogued together because of a strong association with an individual, family, or organization."[11] The Manuscripts Division can also be a source for postcards. Cox and Zinkham, however, warn that "picture researchers should expect to examine quantities of non-pictorial material in order to locate images in the Manuscripts Division."[12] They elaborate that "card catalogues and description sheets make only general reference to pictures by medium; illustrations on individual items are rarely noted . . . picture researchers can use finding aids to track down collections of potential interest, and sift through boxes of documents to locate images, paying particular attention to folders labeled 'Miscellaneous.'"[13] These cautions and search strategies can be applied to almost any institution where postcards are interfiled among personal papers, vertical files, printed ephemera collections, photo collections, etc., which is probably every collecting agency.

A 1989 Maryland publication of institutional descriptions, *Baltimore's Past: A Directory of Historical Sources*,[14] compiled by the Baltimore History Network, a group of library and archival professionals, does not even use postcards as a term in its index. The index consists of an assortment of subject headings, personal names, key words, and genre types. Examples of medium terms which are listed include advertising posters, architectural drawings, atlases, city directories, and photographs. Only three institutions within the directory include postcards in their institutional descriptions–the Peale Museum of the Baltimore City Life Museums, the Maryland Department of Baltimore's Enoch Pratt Free Library, and the Prints and Photographs Division of the Maryland Historical Society. None of the three describes their collections in any detail. For example, none mention the scope or the size.

The Peale and the Maryland Department merely included postcards as one element in a listing of printed ephemera material they hold. Many institutions group their postcards with printed ephemera, a catch-all phrase which can stand for a wide variety of artifact types. Walter S. Dunn, Jr. in his AASLH Technical Leaflet "Cataloging Ephemera: A Procedure for Small Libraries" states that "Ephemera is all printed matter, other than books, complete series of periodicals, newspapers, and pictorial material."[15] This definition is not, however, universal. It is unfortunate when postcards are included in these collections, because printed ephemera tends to receive minimum cataloging, thus limiting even more the relevance of postcards as research material in many institutions' holdings.

Maryland postcards compilations have been identified, by searching the databases of both RLIN and OCLC, for Washington County, Cecil County, Garrett County, Allegany County, and the Chesapeake Bay. Both the Allegany and Garrett County publications have been revised and reprinted. It is interesting to note that these publications have largely been the product of collectors, and not institutions or professional historians.

Before the addition of the Day collection, any postcards owned by Howard County were interfiled in its photograph collection, a common practice. In *Local History Collections*, Thompson states that "in small collections, all graphic material is handled in the same way." [16] Thompson and Semowich declared that "in an institution that is gathering a collection of photographs, post cards that are photographic in nature and lithographic cards should be handled with the photographs."[17] Elizabeth K. Freyschlag in her 1981 article "Picture Postcards: Organizing a Collection" took the opposing view that "designed to serve a particular purpose, these cards possess certain characteristics of production which keep them, at times, from combining well with other properties such as photographs, pictures, and drawings."[18] Although later in the article she points out that "if, on the other hand, there are only a few loose postcards, the unmounted cards may most easily be integrated into the general picture collection."[19]

Thompson continued in *Local History Collections* "no one is surprised to find photographic clippings or postcards in a photo file, and scrapbooks or photo albums are gradually incorporated by making copy negatives and prints."[20] One may not be surprised by this method, but it overlooks the fact, argued by Jackie Dooley and Helena Zinkham in their chapter of *Beyond the Book: Extending MARC for Subject Access*, "The Object as 'Subject': Access to Genres, Forms of Material, and Physical Characteristics," that "many features of special materials other than creator, title, and subject play important roles in research."[21] For example, in Freyschlag's article she stated that "U.S. picture postcards of the period before 1918 are illustrations of former printing and color reproduction techniques and methods . . . These techniques make certain cards items of study for their superior craftsmanship by those interested in photography and the history of graphic arts."[22] Unless there is a way to retrieve postcards, or any other medium, placed in a mixed filing system, a portion of the item's research potential is being ignored. Interfiling without a way to retrieve by medium also makes it impossible to have a detailed survey of the institution's collections.

Although small institutions are usually advised to ignore that level of detail, it can be debated that in small agencies, even with the restrictions usually placed on such organizations by limited staff and work hours, that it is possible, and perhaps even easier, to record such detail. The museum consulting group, Museum Research Associates, also argues this point in their 1992 paper "Fundamentals of Computerized Information Management for Entry-Level and Prospective Computer Users in Small Museums." "Interestingly enough, small museums have a much greater opportunity to improve their information management systems and processes–to do it completely, and to get it right–than large museums, simply because the number of objects and records in a small museum is small."[23]

Before the start of this project, if a researcher requested postcards at the Howard County Historical Society, every folder, theoretically, in its photograph collection would have to be searched. This, of course, left the collection vulnerable to damage, theft, or simply misfiling. A lack of a method to recall postcards by their medium reduced their usefulness. Another article co-authored by Zinkham stresses "access to archival collections often depends on the identification of material by its form, genre, or physical characteristics."[24] After the cataloging of the Day collection, the other postcards within the Library, and all future accessions, will be cataloged in the same manner, although they will not be boxed with the Day collection to maintain its integrity.

Automating the cataloging of this collection would allow the Library to process the collection in more detail, as well as produce finding aids based on, for example, locale, building type, or creator. To perform this same level of cataloging manually would be very time consuming and labor intensive. It would be much too involved for the Library's staff of two part-time professionals and fifteen volunteers to tackle in their two-day work week. Automating the procedure would, however, make it possible to give these items a more detailed treatment and thus increase the research value of the material by making it accessible. Glen Gildemeister points out in his 1988 article "Automation, Reference, and the Small Repository, 1967-1997" that by "using the word-processing and data base interface, the small shop with limited staff and resources can produce specialized checklists, guides, calendars, and indices that it could not even have attempted ten years ago."[25] The Society, which had begun the slow process of automating selected aspects of its Library collection over five years ago, saw the postcard collection as an opportunity to implement such a procedure from the start of a collection's processing.

After evaluating the research possibilities of the Day postcard collection, and consulting with other institutions, a processing worksheet was developed and a database with corresponding fields designed. The cataloging process was divided into two stages. The first was the completion of a worksheet on every postcard not a duplicate. Over a period of six months eight staff members, all working part-time on the project, finished the first stage.

The worksheet includes sixteen fields. Not all of which are to be used for every postcard. The first field is the control number. It allows for the exact identification of every postcard and also allows for a running count of the size of the collection. The second and third fields–county and jurisdiction fields–place the image within the state of Maryland, probably the most often searched fields. It is believed that location will be most researchers' primary concern–images of a particular place. The staff's feeling in this matter is supported by Freyschlag. "While a postcard collection's users may be interested in political history, advertising literature, graphic arts, or anything associated with former times, the most frequent users will probably be those concerned with local history."[26]

There are six major subject fields. The software program the worksheet was originally designed for, AppleWorks, did not allow for the print-out of an integrated list of all subject headings used. Therefore, the subject headings determined to be the most used were broken into four main types–structural, people, animals, and geographic. It is believed that most postcards will be portraying one of these four types of subjects. In most situations, only one major subject heading was chosen for each postcard. Two minor subject fields were also established, subject headings considered possibly useful for illustrative purposes but not seen as overwhelmingly important to the interests of most researchers.

A field was established to record the title of the postcard. Most cards have descriptive titles which provide a great deal more information than "Wish You Were Here." These titles, sometimes located on the front, at other times on the verso, would serve almost as a main entry. If a report were formulated to print the title, without printing any subject headings, one would have a summary of the topic of the majority of the images. Of course, there was also a date field.

There are four fields relating to the creators of the image. These include the photographer, the publisher, the publication location, and the publication number, all important to certain types of researchers. They are also very useful in identifying, on paper, an exact postcard.

Two fields were also set up to document the condition of the postcard. Was it used, unused, or damaged? How exactly is it damaged? This allows the institution to keep informed on the preservation needs of the collection, as well as, of the quality of certain images.

A number of thesauri or authority files were chosen to guide the catalogers. Also called "vocabulary lists" by some sources, these serve as "tools used to guide people among terms and to make them aware of the range of vocabulary available in a particular catalog. Such lists contribute to consistent and predictable indexes."[27] For the county and the jurisdiction field the 1941 *Gazetteer of Maryland*, published by the Maryland State Planning Commission and the Department of Geology, Mines, and Water Resources, was chosen. Although over fifty years old, this is the most complete of Maryland's Gazetteers. Its major use in this project is to determine the county of entry for those communities which cut across county lines. For example, the town of Sykesville is in both Howard County and its neighboring county of Carroll–the *Gazetteer* places it in Carroll County. Laurel is in both Howard and Prince Georges County–the *Gazetteer* places it in Prince Georges. The age of this publication, however, requires that another source also be used. Hamill Kenny's *The Place-names of Maryland, Their Origin and Meaning* provides historical background on name changes. The "Key to County Abbreviations," on page x. of Kenny, was used for the one or two letter code entered in the county field.

The Library of Congress Thesaurus for Graphic Materials was chosen to act as the vocabulary list for all the subject fields, both major and minor. The HCHS Library staff has been using this thesaurus for over two years to catalog photograph collections. Thus, at least three staff members were already familiar with its lay-out and terminology. Also, due to the fact that postcards are easier to catalog than most other graphic images, the use of this thesaurus for cataloging the postcards can serve as an introduction to staff members and orient them to using the thesaurus for re-cataloging the Society's photograph collection, a project which has been in the planning stages for two years.

Appendix A, "Guidelines for recording probable and uncertain dates," from Elizabeth W. Betz's work *Graphic Materials: Rules for Describing Original Items and Historical Collections*, the visual world's version of

AACR2 or APPM, was used to guide the standardization of the entering of the postcard dates.

Postcards are easier to catalog than other graphic materials for a variety of reasons. Barbara Orbach stated in her 1990 article "So That Others May see: Tools for Cataloging Still Images" that "photos are not self-identifying"[28] however, most postcards are self-identifying. They are captioned, which assists a great deal in their cataloging. Unlike photographs, where "generally, it is not possible to determine confidently from the visual data presented what the photographer's purpose was in making the image of the circumstances under which it was made,"[29] most postcards, at least most picture photographs, are not that intricate. This again simplifies their cataloging. Cataloging postcards is a good starting point for training a staff member in cataloging photographs.

The second stage of the project is the entering of the information into the database. This stage has not yet taken place, due to a change in the Library's computer system. At the time the project was begun the HCHS's only computer was an AppleIIGS. Although a useful system it has many limitations. It does not have a hard drive, thus limiting storage capability. A number of the Library's other databases have to be placed on multiple floppy disks, thus greatly diminishing the effectiveness and speed of searching. The AppleWorks database is also very limited in the complexity of its searching capabilities. The decision was made to not begin data entry until the Library received the new computer system it knew it would be able to purchase at the end of 1994. The Library now has a Macintosh, with a hard drive and a more powerful database. Data entry will begin in the near future.

Although the Day collection is not yet generally open to the public, the cataloging project itself has had a positive effect on the Library. Many Library regulars have inquired into the project. One patron who is working on a history of golf in Maryland expressed a very strong interest in making use of the collection. She actively uses postcards in her research. A postcard collector in the community became aware of the project and volunteered for a day of cataloging. It was the first time he had ever been in either of the Society's buildings, although his office is located directly across the street, a very narrow street, from the Society. This individual also offered to loan items from his own collection for a future exhibit of Howard County postcards. Also in response to awareness of the project one small gift of postcards has already been made to the Library from one donor and there is the possibility of another larger gift from another donor. The cataloging project also prompted an article in the newsletter of the

Howard County Genealogical Society on using postcards in genealogical research.

It is hoped that the cataloging of the Frances Louise Day postcard collection will accomplish a number of different tasks at the Howard County Historical Society. First the level of detail possible through the automated system will allow the collection to be accessible to a wide variety of possible researchers, not customary users of the HCHS. It is thus hoped that this collection will increase the visibility of the Society state-wide. This will, of course, depend on the way in which the Society makes the collection known to the research community.

The cataloging of the Day collection will also assist the Society in the reorganization of its holdings. Cataloging the Day collection is introducing the staff to professional concepts largely ignored at the institution until this point–such as standardization and authority files.

NOTES

1. See Miriam Weiner, "Postcards: A Window on the Past." *Heritage Quest* (March 01, 1991): 35.

2. Rodney F. Allen and Laurie E.S. Molina, "People and Places on Picture Postcards: A High-Interest Source for Geographic Education." *Journal of Geography* 91(May/June 1992): 107.

3. Judith Ann Schiff, "Nonmanuscript Sources," In *Researcher's Guide to Archives and Regional History Sources*, Edited by John C. Larson. Hamden, CT: Library Professional Publications. 1988, p. 89.

4. Charles J. Semowich and Enid T. Thompson, "Post Card Collections in the Local Historical Society," American Association for State and Local History, Technical Leaflet No. 116 (1979): 1.

5. Enid T. Thompson, *Local History Collections: A Manual for Librarians*, Nashville, TN: American Association for State and Local History, 1978, p. 23.

6. Ross J. Kelbaugh, *Directory of Maryland Photographers 1839-1900*, Baltimore, MD: Historic Graphics, 1988, p. 66.

7. Semowich and Thompson, 2.

8. At this time, the Maryland Historical Society was the only institution in the state queried for information on its postcard collection. Knowledge of the status of postcards in Maryland's other county historical societies will be needed to truly compare the Howard County Historical Society's collection with its sister agencies.

9. Lynn Cox and Helena Zinkham, "Picture Research at the Maryland Historical Society: A Guide to the Sources," *Maryland Historical Magazine* 76 (Spring 1981): 12.

10. It should be kept in mind that articles may have appeared in the newsletters and bulletins of Maryland's county historical societies. These publications, unfor-

tunately, do not always appear in published bibliographies and never in electronic databases.

11. Cox and Zinkham, 9-10.

12. Ibid, 13.

13. Ibid, 13.

14. A new edition of this directory is presently in production.

15. Walter S. Dunn, Jr. "Cataloging Ephemera: A Procedure for Small Libraries," American Association for State and Local History Technical Leaflet 58, *History News* 27:1(January 1972): 1.

16. Thompson, *Local History Collections*, p. 23.

17. Semowich and Thompson, 3-4.

18. Elizabeth K. Freyschlag, "Picture Postcards Organizing a Collection." *Special Libraries* 71, 5/6(May/June 1980): 259.

19. Freyschlag, 261.

20. Thompson, *Local History Collections*, p. 23.

21. Jackie M. Dooley and Helena Zinkham, "The Object as 'Subject': Providing Access to Genres, Forms of Material, and Physical Characteristics." In *Beyond the Book: Extending MARC for Subject Access*. Edited by Toni Peterson and Pat Molholt. Boston, Massachusetts: G.K. Hall & Co., 1990, p. 43.

22. Freyschlag, 259.

23. Museum Research Associates, "Fundamentals of Computerized Information Management for Entry-Level and Prospective Computer Users in Small Museums," p. 54.

24. Helena Zinkham, Patricia Cloud, and Hope Mayo, "Providing Access by Form of Material, Genre, and Physical Characteristics: Benefits and Techniques," *American Archivist* 52 (Summer 1989): 301.

25. Glen A. Gildemeister, "Automation, Reference, and the Small Repository, 1967-1997." *Midwestern Archivist*. XVIII (1988): 8.

26. Freyschlag, 260.

27. Zinkham, Cloud, and Mayo, 305.

28. Barbara Orbach, "So That Others May See: Tools for Cataloging Still Images," *Cataloging & Classification Quarterly* 11(3/4): 164.

29. Orbach, 164.

Postcards:
Navigating the Preservation Options

Jan Merrill-Oldham

The preservation of collections of postcards is at once a simple and a complicated topic of discussion. While a prescription for ideal collections management is easy to write, determining the extent to which the achievement of that ideal is appropriate, given the nature, long-term value, and anticipated use of a given collection, can be challenging. To complicate matters, the cost implications of various preservation strategies vary significantly. Reviewed here are the issues, ideals, and compromises associated with the care of paper-based materials. Choosing from among the options is the business of collectors, curators, and scholars.

THE HAZARDS

Mechanical Deterioration

Postcards, if put to their intended use, are subjected to considerable handling. Typically, after manufacture they are packaged, shipped, unwrapped, put on display at a retail store (often in metal racks), and shuffled mercilessly by buyers as selections are made. Once purchased, postcards are likely to be stored carelessly (why not?) and are later written on–often with water-soluble inks. (In the past, writers sometimes chose water-soluble inks for fountain pens; today, many felt-tip pens carry inks that are fugitive in water. To test a pen for the permanence of its ink, simply write on paper, allow the ink to dry thoroughly, and spray or splash lightly with

[Haworth co-indexing entry note]: "Postcards: Navigating the Preservation Options." Merrill-Oldham, Jan. Co-published simultaneously in *Popular Culture in Libraries* (The Haworth Press, Inc.) Vol. 3, No. 2, 1995, pp. 199-213; and: *Postcards in the Library: Invaluable Visual Resources* (ed: Norman D. Stevens) The Haworth Press, Inc., 1995, pp. 199-213. Single or multiple copies of this article are available from The Haworth Document Delivery Service [1-800-342-9678, 9:00 a.m. - 5:00 p.m. (EST)].

199

water. The results are sometimes startling, and are fair warning to collectors to keep their holdings well protected from moisture.)

After stamps are stuck onto corners, postcards are slipped into mailboxes where they are often crumpled under the weight of the day's accumulation. Next they are loaded into bags, transported to post offices and dumped on counters behind the scenes, fed through automated cancellation machines (or, rarely these days, hand-canceled), sorted, rebagged, shipped, sorted again, delivered to a postbox, and retrieved by the addressee. From there, it's anyone's guess what happens to a postcard between the time it fulfills its intended mission and the time it is recognized as having sentimental, informational, and/or aesthetic value, and is *collected*. At this juncture, handling can either decrease because of perceived heightened value, or it can increase because it has become part of a heavily consulted reference tool.

The consequences of handling are familiar to all who are interested in paper-based information resources–soil, oil, stains, edge tears, rounded and split corners, and creases. Among the collector's curatorial challenges is to halt mechanical deterioration to the greatest extent possible, recognizing that unless he or she is either wealthy, a conservator, or both, the damage that is already done will never be reversed. Rather, it will remain as a record of past use, and to some extent, an interesting part of each item's history. Strategies for reducing wear and tear, and for minimal treatment of damage, are discussed later in this article.

Chemical Deterioration Resulting from Inherent Properties

Most postcard collectors have probably come across a discussion of the role of inherent acidity in promoting the deterioration of paper, and have handled brittle, crumbly specimens. Acid in paper catalyzes hydrolytic degradation, causing breaks in the long chains of glucose molecules that make up molecules of cellulose. These scissions cause paper to lose strength, which is often measured in terms of its ability to endure repeated folding without breaking (that is, its "fold endurance").[1] Paper may be acidic for one or more of the following three reasons. First, the source of the cellulose from which the paper is manufactured may not have been fully processed to remove the acids inherent in natural plant material. Cotton requires minimal processing; wood requires extensive processing.[2] Second, even if the raw plant material has been cooked and bleached to remove acids and other impurities, acid may have been reintroduced through such processes as sizing to create an effective printing surface, and/or dying to produce color.[3] Third, acids may have been transferred to the paper during handling, or as a result of storage in an acidic environment (an acidic box, for example).

Since the appearance of the postcard on the communications scene post-dates the introduction of acidic papermaking processes, the overwhelming majority of all specimens is acidic. Deterioration is inevitable but can be slowed drastically. Several deacidification processes have been developed to neutralize acids and impregnate paper with an alkaline reserve. Alkalinity, on the opposite end of the pH scale from acidity, extends the life of paper. The presence of an alkaline reserve inhibits re-acidification over time, and is referred to as a "buffer" (thus the term "alkaline/buffered paper"). While deacidification is possible, it is rarely practical. Treatment must be carried out professionally to ensure that appropriate decisions are made regarding which papers can be deacidified uniformly and without damage (some cannot), and whether a change in pH is likely to initiate color changes. Even in the best of hands there are risks associated with deacidification. Its place is in the conservation lab.[4] It is far better to invest in the creation of a hospitable storage environment for a postcard collection than to attempt to alter its chemistry. The curatorial role is one of stabilization and care–not of treatment.

With every passing year more alkaline/buffered papers are produced for printing, largely because it has become more economical to retool a papermaking plant and convert from acidic to alkaline processing systems than to continue to make acidic products. Whether the postcards produced in years to come will be made from long-lived card stock remains to be seen. (Few of the relatively new cards tested by the author using a pH indicator pen, available through archival supply houses, were alkaline.) New technical capabilities, environmental issues, and market forces will surely alter papermaking practices in the foreseeable future, and trends are uncertain.[5]

Deterioration Caused by Heat and Moisture

There is no greater threat to the survival of collections of postcards than environmental conditions that heighten rather than diminish the effects of inherent acidity. Heat and moisture accelerate both the hydrolytic and oxidative processes that degrade paper. For many years, the preservation literature promoted the following guidelines for climate control in library stacks: 50% relative humidity (RH), and 68°F (the low end of the human comfort zone). Thanks to the work of Donald Sebera, we have a much clearer understanding of these matters today. Sebera points out that the potential useful life of a paper at one combination of temperature and relative humidity can also be achieved at a higher temperature if the humidity is reduced, or at higher humidity if the temperature is reduced.

The two factors work together to influence environmental quality.[6] In "Isoperms: An Environmental Management Tool," Sebera cites examples to illustrate the usefulness of isoperm charts on which temperature, RH, and the expected life of a particular type of paper can be plotted. In one scenario he shows that where low-grade papers such as newsprint might have a useful life of 45 years under storage conditions of 68°F and 50% RH, at 95°F and 80% RH (conditions common to attics on humid midsummer days), the estimated life is reduced to 16 months.[7]

Research done in recent years has confirmed earlier beliefs that the lower the storage temperature the longer paper lasts. Recent relative humidity studies, however, suggest that for unbound paper, RH levels ranging as low as 30% (but no lower) are desirable because of the strong relationship between moisture content and the rate that paper deteriorates through hydrolysis. Clearly, there is no easier way to destroy a collection than to allow it to bake in the attic or to languish in a damp basement. What can and should be accomplished within these two extremes is dependent on many factors. Strategies for improving environmental conditions are discussed later in this article.

A *stable* climate for paper storage is also critical. In controlled studies conducted recently by the Library of Congress Preservation Research and Testing Office,[8] papers were aged in a programmable oven. The temperature was held throughout at 90°C ± 0.2°C, and the effects of four different RH levels were compared. Paper aged at 40% RH ± 2% degraded most slowly (as measured by folding endurance, pH, and brightness levels), followed by paper aged at 50% RH ± 2%. Papers that were subjected to a steady RH of 40% for 11 hours, followed by a one-hour transition to 60% RH, maintenance at 60% RH for 11 hours, followed by a one-hour transition back down to 40%, and the 24-hour begun again, aged almost as rapidly–and in some cases *more* rapidly–than did paper aged at a steady 60% RH. Researchers suggest several possible reasons why RH cycling speeds up degradation, but theories are not yet proven. The important thing to note is these laboratory test conditions are mild compared to the extreme variations in temperature and RH that can take place over short periods of time in a building that is not air conditioned.

Deterioration Caused by Fungi, Insects, and Small Animals

The effects of mold are well-known to anyone who has spent time poring over paper artifacts. Mold causes disfiguring stains both in its active and inactive stages (foxing, for example, probably results from the presence of inactive fungi). If allowed to flourish, mold draws nourishment from cellulose, weakening and ultimately eroding it. Damage is usually irreversible. Mold growth is almost inevitable when RH is over 70% for sustained periods.[9] Temperature also plays a role. "Most microbial forms grow in temperatures ranging from 59° to 95°F, although there are forms which will grow at almost freezing and others which thrive at over 150°F."[10] Paper is most vulnerable to mold when it is actually damp or wet. Pipe breaks, leaking roofs, and storms have destroyed many private and public collections. While all but certain types of paper (coated stock, for example) are readily salvaged after becoming water-soaked, if mold is allowed to grow before action is taken, damage will be permanent. Once vigorous growth begins it can spread easily under certain conditions, infecting large quantities of material. Mold is a potential threat not only to paper, but to human health.[11]

Like mold, insects and rodents also appreciate a good cellulose-based meal. Cockroaches, silverfish, and booklice are common pests, leaving in their wake paper marred by holes, trails, and major losses. Mice and rats, if given the opportunity, make even quicker work of destroying paper.

Deterioration Caused by Light

As paper absorbs light energy, it becomes subject to photochemical deterioration. Photochemical processes are complex, but the effects of light that is too bright, too sustained, and/or that has a high ultraviolet (UV) component are easily discerned: discoloration, fading, and embrittlement. Certain media, water colors for example, are extremely light sensitive, while others take longer to react. The popular literature tends to focus on ultraviolet radiation as the chief concern of the curator. (The only type of radiation in wavelengths shorter than ultraviolet is x-ray. The shorter the wavelength, the more energetic the light and the greater its potential for inducing photochemical deterioration.[12]) Sunlight has a high UV component, as does light from many types of fluorescent bulbs. It is important to know, however, that *all* light, regardless of its nature and source, has the potential to degrade paper; and that in addition to filtering out UV, the intensity and duration of all light are factors that must also be controlled. If an appropriate storage system is designed for postcards, light should present problems only when a collection is exhibited.

Deterioration Caused by Air Pollutants

Among the gaseous pollutants known to be damaging to cellulosic materials are sulphur dioxide, nitrogen oxides, and ozone. Sulphur dioxide, for example, readily converts to sulphuric acid under certain conditions, causing paper to darken and become brittle. Most pollutants pass from the outside in, through air handling systems and open windows. Some pollutants are generated from within buildings. Although surface finishes such as paint and wallpaper, and materials such as fire retardant fabric and particle board, off-gas most intensely immediately after application or manufacture, emissions can persist for a long time thereafter.[13] Particulate matter, such as air-borne dirt (a particular problem in rural areas), sand, mold, and concrete dust, are also problematic. Some particulates are capable of causing chemical damage. Even the most benign dust is damaging. It settles on materials and readily absorbs and holds moisture, creating a humid blanket that stimulates degradative activity.

APPROPRIATE RESPONSES

Housing Systems–The First Line of Defense

Proper storage of postcard collections is an essential first step in their care, and may in fact be one of the few actions that the collector can take. Companies that supply a wide range of archivally sound storage products simplify decision making, in that they carry only merchandise that is widely regarded as appropriate for use.[14] Initial decisions hinge on whether a collection will be consulted frequently. At the very least, postcards should be stored in alkaline/buffered boxes of appropriate size. This system is vastly improved when the cards are placed in individual alkaline paper envelopes and then in boxes. Paper envelopes protect postcards from wear during sorting and searching; shield them from light; and are porous, so allow the escape of harmful byproducts given off as the postcards degrade. Best, they create an alkaline microenvironment that retards deterioration. A combination of envelopes and boxes provides some protection from water damage, and seems to buffer rapid changes in temperature and RH. Envelopes should have a pH of at least 7.5 and an alkaline buffer of at least 2%, and should be constructed using an adhesive that is not acidic. Whether the envelopes have a flap over the opening is a matter of choice, but there should be no thumb cut, which encourages repeated handling at the same spot each time a card is removed from its envelope.

If paper envelopes are to be marked, this should be done before postcards are inserted. Use a pencil, permanent ink (advertised as such in archival supply catalogs), a typewriter, or laser printer. Postcards can be stored on their edges for easy browsing. Boxes should have metal reinforced edges for sturdiness.[15] They should neither be filled so full that postcards are difficult to remove, nor so empty that postcards are lean and curl. To support cards in partially filled boxes, purchase alkaline-buffered corrugated board (available through archival supply catalogs), and cut spacers using a utility knife and heavy metal yardstick. These can be removed gradually as postcards are added. A low-cost alternative is to support the cards using crumpled alkaline paper.

Keep in mind that unless a box is advertised as being alkaline and buffered it is probably very acidic. Several types of alkaline box boards are available through archival supply catalogs. It is important that the board be alkaline throughout. Avoid those that are made up of an acidic core surfaced with alkaline paper. The core will off-gas harmful byproducts. Some boards are advertised as "lignin free." These are usually (but not always) tan colored. "Lignin is often called the cement that glues the fibers together in [a] shrub or tree and gives it the structural strength to stand straight and grow tall. [Unlike cellulose] Lignin is a three-dimensional polymer, it is amorphous, and it has no ordered structure. It is not fibrous."[16] It makes up 1% of cotton fiber, 30% of a typical softwood, and 20% of a typical hardwood.[17]

Lignin is the component in newsprint that causes the paper to darken quickly when exposed to light. It has been widely regarded as a damaging impurity, and various means have been developed to remove it from pulp. Box boards that are advertised as "alkaline/buffered and lignin-free" probably have no more than trace levels of lignin. Those advertised as "alkaline/buffered" usually have an alkaline/buffered (but not "lignin-free") core, with lignin-free paper laminated to its surfaces. At present, whether lignin lowers the quality of board and paper is the subject of fierce debate, with many industry leaders asserting that lignin is not harmful.[18] It is anticipated that research into the relationship between lignin and paper permanence will begin in 1995. In the meantime, librarians, archivists, and collectors are buying a bit blind. If money is not a determining factor, curators typically store less valuable materials in boxes made from alkaline/buffered board, and more valuable materials in alkaline/buffered board that is lignin-free. For a small collection, there is little reason not to choose lignin-free board.

Small metal file drawers are acceptable alternatives to boxes. Newly purchased metal furniture should have a powder coat rather than a baked enamel finish. Baked enamel off-gases, while studies to date suggest that powder coatings do not. These are sprayed onto metal in powder form (not liquid), and are fused using heat. Wood cabinets should probably be avoided if one has a choice. Wood furniture can off-gas harmful substances for years after its manufacture.

A system comprised of paper envelopes and boxes has a single disadvantage. A postcard has to be pulled out of its envelope each time it is consulted. This introduces the potential for damage (abrasion, edge tears, the transfer of dirt and oil from fingertips). In short, the system doesn't yield a readily browsable collection. Plastic sleeves are an alternative. Polyester is the preferred plastic (*Mylar Type D* and *ICI Melinex 516* are two frequently recommended brands). Uncoated polyester is extremely stable, strong, and clear; it lies flat (so does not promote curling); and is rigid enough to provide good support. Some forms of polyethylene are also stable and safe to use, but selection is difficult. Low-density types can contain anti-block and slip agents that cause the plastic to adhere readily to the surfaces of photographs (and thus, perhaps, to certain kinds of postcards). High-density types are naturally slippery, so do not require anti-block or slip agents, and thus have less tendency to stick. If one were to ask a vendor whether a particular polyethylene product were additive free, however, it's likely that he or she would be unable to answer the question. Buy from a reliable dealer (again, see footnote 14). Polyethylene is translucent rather than clear, soft (so less supportive), and scratches easily. It provides protection from handling, however, which is a primary objective.

Avoid polyvinyl chloride (PVC). Says Henry Wilhelm, writing about the storage of photographs, "To make PVC flexible, plasticizers, usually organic compounds, are added in large amounts (40 to 100 parts plasticizer per 100 parts PVC) . . . Particularly when stored in high-humidity conditions, the plasticizers can gradually exude from the PVC, depositing sticky droplets or gooey coatings . . . [furthermore,] PVC plasticizers can support fungus growth in humid conditions . . ."[19] Many of the sleeves and album pages available in retail stores are made from PVC plastic. Unsuspecting buyers, thinking they are investing in the protection of their collections, may instead damage them unintentionally. Purchase storage supplies from reliable source that specializes in "archival quality" products.

In addition to the main advantages that plastic sleeves have over paper (browsability), plastic provides more protection from water damage. One disadvantage is cost. (Polyester sleeves are the most expensive type available.) Another disadvantage is that because plastic is less porous than paper, the sleeves can trap both moisture and the damaging byproducts that are produced as acidic paper deteriorates. This problem has been noted increasingly in recent research. Acetate film rolled and stored in reel boxes, for example, deteriorates much more rapidly in an accelerated aging oven than do strips hung from the roof of the oven. Gases emitting from the free-hung strips are allowed to escape into the surrounding atmosphere, whereas they inflict damage to film in reel boxes. This phenomenon has caused one researcher to go so far as to speculate that perhaps we should be storing preservation microfilm in perforated boxes.

In summary, comparing the attributes of alkaline envelopes and plastic sleeves illustrates the point that there are no perfect solutions. Leaving price aside, one has to decide which is more important for a given postcard collection: browsability, or optimum long-term protection. The answer will depend on both the artifactual value of the collection and how it will be used.

Albums are an alternative to envelopes and boxes for postcard storage. They can take many forms, and afford maximum browsability. If cards are to be mounted on paper pages, the paper, of course, must be alkaline/buffered, and the mounting technique must be non-damaging. It goes without saying that the cards should *not* be glued directly to pages. Polyester and alkaline paper mounting corners, available through archival supply catalogs, are an appropriate alternative. Such a system is impractical, however, if the back sides of the postcards are to be consulted often. Furthermore, repeated flexing of pages can abrade the surfaces of the cards. To reduce the potential for damage, pages should be turned one-by-one or a few at a time. To protect paper and other types of albums from dust and light, store them in metal-edged alkaline/buffered boxes.

Paper album pages are available with both polypropylene and polyester cover sheets. The plastic provides added protection from handling and greater security for mounted items. Polyester sheets are non-damaging. The polypropylene used in such applications is surface treated, however, and has been known to adhere to the surfaces of photographs.[20] A disadvantage is that cover sheets make access to the reverse sides of postcards even more difficult than if they were simply mounted on paper.

Album pages made from sheets of polyethylene, polypropylene, or polyester, welded to create pockets into which paper objects can be slipped, are also available. Again, polyester is a good choice. Both sides of the postcards are readily accessible provided they are not put back-to-back in pockets. As with polyester sleeves, these pages have the drawback of trapping moisture and the byproducts of paper deterioration—considerations that must be weighed against access.

There is also a type of pocket-style album page that is mounted on the same kind of metal strip as is used for hanging file folders. This makes it possible to store pages in standard file cabinets. Cabinets offer protection from light and dust, and are a tidy solution to storage. Unlike albums and three-ring binders, file cabinets do not allow for casual browsing. On the positive side, however, this system eliminates the abrasion that can result from repeated turning of pages.

Postcards with materials adhered to their surfaces (glitter or buttons, for example), and cards with vulnerable surfaces present special problems. An example of the latter would be a painted card–a miniature work of art. Handling glitter-covered cards, whether in envelopes, sleeves, or on album pages, will probably cause the decoration to shed; as will storage in plastic enclosures, which generate static electricity. This may or may not be a concern. A card that carries a unique image, however, might well be worthy of first-class treatment.

An optimum storage solution is to mat the cards in alkaline/buffered rag board as if they were small prints. The services of a conservator ensure that appropriate materials, adhesives, and techniques are used. A postcard should "float" inside the window of its mat (that is, the window should be larger than the card so the edges of the card can be seen). Small paper objects often look best when mats are at least somewhat oversized. If a card has been properly hinged onto the back board of the mat, one should be able to lift the card (using a stiff piece of paper) to view its verso. Another option is to make the window double-sided so that the verso of a card can be viewed by flipping over the mat. The value of this approach is that the mat, because of its thickness, protects the surface of the postcard from contact with other materials. Collections of matted postcards can be stored in metal-edged alkaline/buffered boxes. To minimize movement of materials in a box, mats should be like-sized even if the size of the post-cards varies. This is common practice in libraries.

Postcards made from materials other than paper also require special attention. Consideration should be given to storing wooden cards in paper rather than plastic, because of their acidity. Metal postcards, while they appear to be comparatively rugged, are subject to scratching; and damage from the corrosive oils, salts, and urea-derivatives present in fingerprints. Like paper cards, they should be protected from excessive handling. Leather postcards are sometimes soft and pliable, and are prone to wrinkling. For safe storage, cut a piece of alkaline paper twice the height of the storage envelope that will be used, and just slightly narrower than the envelope. This paper will become a sleeve. Fold it in half across its height. Now the postcard can be placed in the sleeve, the sleeve folded, and the sandwich inserted into the envelope, folded edge first. The sleeve protects the postcard from wrinkling, abrasion, and handling as it is removed from and replaced in its envelope. Cards with moving parts (flaps that open and close, for example) will also benefit from a sleeve-and-envelope housing.

Cleaning

Unless a postcard is very dirty, it is best left alone. Cleaning can result in damage that is a great deal more defacing than the problem it was meant to correct. In general, there is no need to refurbish postcards unless they have been stored in an extraordinarily dirty environment or have been through (and survived) a fire. Where cleaning is felt to be absolutely necessary, use a vinyl eraser ("Magic Rub" is one reliable brand) and a soft dusting brush (available at art supply stores and through archival supply catalogs). Work on a clean surface and proceed slowly and carefully. Every stroke of the eraser should begin away from the edge of the card and work outward. Alternating backward and forward strokes, beginning from the outer edge of the card and working inward, or working hastily, is sure to result in damage. Brush eraser crumbs from the work surface at frequent intervals, and brush both surfaces of the postcard very thoroughly before storing it.

What to Do About Repair

To repair paper properly and with minimal risk requires appropriate tools, materials, and skills, and an ability to anticipate the ways in which various kinds of paper react to various kinds of treatment. (Conservators employ numerous techniques for repairing paper, making decisions based on multiple factors.) There are better ways to handle an edge tear than to repair it inexpertly. Simply store damaged postcards in polyester sleeves, even if the bulk of a collection has been housed in paper sleeves. The polyester sleeve helps to prevent further damage and protects the postcard from direct handling. A sleeve is mistake-proof and leaves no doubt about the condition of the card. Regarding pinholes and similar problems, they should be ignored.

A possible exception to the "protect–don't treat" rule is removal of the residue that remains on the backs of cards that were once mounted in photo albums. Paper and adhesive residues are not only defacing (a tolerable situation), but are also damaging. Assuming that the adhesive is an older, water-soluble type and not modern plastic glue, proceed as follows: Purchase distilled water (often available in grocery stores for use in steam irons), cotton swabs, and a slim metal spatula (available through archival supply catalogs). Work on a clean surface under good light. Dip a swab into water, then depress it against the sides of the water bowl to remove excess moisture. Roll the swab along the surface of the offending paper and glue residue. After the residue has softened, gently scrape away as much as can be removed easily, wiping the spatula clean whenever necessary. Redampen the remaining residue, again ensuring that the swab is not saturated and that the postcard does not become wet. Return to the card at intervals, gradually working away the paper and glue. When most of the residue has been removed, blot corners with white paper toweling and allow the postcard to air dry.

There are pitfalls associated with this practice. Patience is paramount. Residue needs to be worked off a little at a time. If a card is written on with water-soluble ink and the ink is allowed to become wet, it will run, and both the verso and the image side of the card may be damaged. Water can leave rings behind if applied immoderately, and applying too much pressure to the spatula can abrade the surface of the postcard. These problems are pointed out because treatment is generally risky business, and sometimes comes to no good end.

Climate Control

The development of an environment that is truly ideal for promoting the longevity of paper is extraordinarily expensive. Building features include top quality roofing, vapor barriers, and insulation; high-end fire suppression systems; surface finishes that don't off-gas (as many wall and floor coverings and finishes do); lights that emit minimal UV radiation; and an air handling system that filters out gaseous and particulate pollutants and is sophisticated enough to maintain low, stable RH levels regardless of conditions outside. Few major libraries, archives, or museums have been able to construct such buildings to date–let alone home owners. One's goal, then, is to understand the threats to collections of paper-based materials, and to make adjustments that are practical and affordable.

Basic strategies for improving a storage environment are obvious. Important collections of paper materials should be kept in the part of a building (be it house, library, or historical society) that is most likely to be consistently cool and dry. That may translate into nothing more than moving materials from a cabinet on the sun porch to a first-floor den. Rooms where fireplaces or wood stoves are used are inhospitable. The temperature, and consequently RH, will fluctuate wildly, and the air will inevitably carry higher levels of damaging gases and particulates than will other parts of the building. If there is a choice between an air conditioned room and a room where open windows suffice for summer relief, one should choose the former. (To some extent, air conditioners filter out particulates and prevent dust and dirt from blowing in on breezy days.) In spaces where humidity is a potential problem, a monitoring device of some kind is useful.[21] A household dehumidifier can be turned on when RH rises above

50%, and a fan can be used to circulate air. (Mold grows best where air is stagnant.)

Work on collections can be done in spaces where overhead and task lighting is incandescent rather than fluorescent, and collections can be shielded from direct sunlight at outdoor displays. If there are fluorescent lights in an area where a collection will be exhibited, bulbs can be fitted with sleeves that filter out most UV radiation (filters are available through archival supply catalogs). Where exhibit cases have interior fluorescent or incandescent lights (which transform them into accelerated aging ovens), consideration might be given to declining an opportunity to display a collection. Plants can be removed from rooms where collections are stored (soil sometimes carries fungi that have potential for infecting collections), and rooms can be kept clean and food-free. (Food, of course, attracts insects and rodents.) The principles of integrated pest management can be applied, through actions such as caulking cracks in foundations, screening ducts, sealing pipe traces, repairing screens, removing debris from garages and basements, eliminating sources of standing water, and ensuring that trash is removed from the premises regularly.[22] The general principles of emergency management can also be applied. Librarians, archivists, and collectors alike should know how to prepare for, reduce the possibility of, and respond to the various kinds of emergencies that threaten or affect collections.[23]

Preservation of Library and Archival Materials, edited by Sherelyn Ogden and published by the Northeast Document Center with support from the Institute of Museum Services,[24] explores environmental issues in practical terms. Connecticut State Librarian Richard Akeroyd once described this manual of technical leaflets as "out-of-the-gate information" (that is, it begins at the beginning). While the text is written for non-specialists and offers basic information regarding environmental control, storage, handling, conservation, and other key areas of concern, it draws from a rich body of scientific and technical literature, and benefits from the regular communication that takes place between researchers in the field and NEDCC staff. Brief bibliographies point the reader toward core literature. Because the target audience is librarians and archivists, some information is out of scope for the private collector. Nonetheless the manual is recommended to anyone who wants to understand and respond better to preservation issues.

The care of historical collections of any kind–be they public or private, large or small, of international value or of modest local interest–demands that the caretaker be well informed, thoughtful in decision making, attentive to detail, and patient when preservation plans must be implemented incrementally. The basic ingredient in a successful approach to collections management is a commitment to ensure that the yield of a collector's efforts will be passed on through succeeding generations. The actions one takes follow naturally from that commitment.

NOTES

1. Chandru J. Shahani and William K. Wilson, "Preservation of Libraries and Archives," *American Scientist* 75 (May-June), 240-51.

2. For an understandable explanation of the differences between cotton and wood as sources of cellulose for papermaking, see Roy P. Whitney, "Chemistry of Paper," in *Paper–Art & Technology: The History and Methods of Fine Papermaking with a Gallery of Contemporary Paper Art* (San Francisco: World Print Council, 1979), 36-44.

3. A landmark overview of the history of papermaking, which focuses on decreasing quality over several centuries and the development of modern "acidfree" paper, is presented by Verner W. Clapp in "The Story of Permanent/Durable Book Paper, 1115-1970," *Scholarly Publishing* 2 (Jan., Apr., July 1971), 107-24, 229-45, 353-67.

4. The SAIC Conservation Referral Group helps people locate and select professional conservation services, providing a computer-generated list of conservators who can meet a client's specific needs. Additional information is available from the SAIC office, 1717 K Street, N.W., Suite 301, Washington, D.C. 20006; telephone 202-452-9545.

5. Trends and issues related to paper permanence are followed closely in the *Alkaline Paper Advocate* (Abbey Publications, 7105 Geneva Drive, Austin TX, 78723), a newsletter published six times annually.

6. Donald K. Sebera, "A Graphical Representation of the Relationships of Environmental Conditions to the Permanence of Hygroscopic Materials and Composites," in *Proceedings of Conservation in Archives* (Ottawa: National Archives of Canada, 1989), 51-75.

7. Donald K. Sebera, *Isoperms: An Environmental Management Tool* (Washington, D.C.: Commission on Preservation and Access, June 1994), 7.

8. Chandru J. Shahani, Frank H. Hengemihle, and Norman Weberg, "The Effect of Variations in Relative Humidity on the Accelerated Aging of Paper," in *Historic Textile and Paper Materials II: Conservation and Characterization*, ed. S. Haig Zeronian and Howard L. Needles (Washington, D.C.: American Chemical Society, 1989), 63-80.

9. Sandra Nyberg, "The Invasion of the Giant Spore," *SOLINET Preservation Program Leaflet Number 5* (Atlanta: Southeastern Library Network, 1987).

10. Mary Wood Lee, *Prevention and Treatment of Mold in Library Collections with an Emphasis on Tropical Climates: A RAMP Study* (Paris: UNESCO, June 1988), 12.

11. "Mold as a Threat to Human Health," *The Abbey Newsletter* 18, no. 6 (Oct. 1994), 65.

12. The properties of light are explained well by J. Macleod in "Museum Lighting," *Technical Bulletin 2* (Ottawa: Canadian Conservation Institute, April 1975).

13. Norbert S. Baer and Paul N. Banks, "Indoor Air Pollution: Effects on Cultural and Historic Materials," *The International Journal of Museum Management and Curatorship* 4 (1985), 9-20.

14. Companies that carry a broad range of preservation-related supplies include: University Products (517 Main Street, P.O. Box 101, Holyoke, MA 01041-0101; telephone 1-800-762-1165); Gaylord Brothers (P.O. Box 4901, Syracuse, NY 13221-4901; telephone 1-800-634-6307); and Light Impressions (439 Monroe Avenue, P.O. Box 940, Rochester, NY 14603-0940; telephone 1-800-828-6216). Companies that carry a narrower range of (mostly storage) supplies include Archival Products (2134 E. Grand Ave., Des Moines, IA 50317; telephone 1-800-526-5640); Conservation Resources International; (8000-H Forbes Place, Springfield, VA 22151; telephone 1-800-634-6932); Hollinger Corporation (9401 Northeast Drive, P.O. Box 8360, Fredericksburg, VA 22404; telephone 1-800-634-0491); and Conservation Materials (1275 Keppy Lane #10, P.O. Box 2884, Sparks, NV 89431; telephone 702-331-0582).

15. Good line drawings and discussions of this and other systems appear in *Gaylord Preservation Pathfinder No. 2: Archival Storage of Paper* (Syracuse, NY: Gaylord Bros, 1993). Available free from Gaylord, telephone 1-800-634-6307.

16. Whitney, "Chemistry," 38.

17. Whitney, "Chemistry," 38.

18. Ellen McCrady, "Lignin on Trial: A Report of the ISR Workshop July 6-8 at ASTM Headquarters," *The Abbey Newsletter* 18, no. 3 (July 1994).

19. Henry Wilhelm, *The Permanence and Care of Color Photographs: Traditional and Digital Color Prints, Color Negatives, Slides, and Motion Pictures* (Grinnell, IA: Preservation Publishing Company, 1993), 499. (Chapter 14 of this book, "Envelopes and Sleeves for Films and Prints," 485-506, is a thorough exploration of the characteristics of various protective enclosures. Most of the information is pertinent to paper storage.)

20. Wilhelm, *The Permanence and Care of Color Photographs*, 495.

21. Monitoring Temperature and Relative Humidity," in *Preservation of Library Materials: A Manual, revised and expanded*, ed. Sherelyn Ogden (Andover, MA: Northeast Document Conservation Center, 1994), unpaginated.

22. For an excellent discussion of integrated pest management that includes a good overview of preventive measures, see James D. Harmon, *Integrated Pest Management in Museum, Library and Archival Facilities: a Step by Step Approach for the Design, Development, Implementation and Maintenance of an Integrated Pest Management Program* (Indianapolis: James D. Harmon, 1993).

23. "Emergency Management" in *Preservation of Library Materials*, unpaginated.

24. *Preservation of Library & Archival Materials*, available for $40.00 including postage (Northeast Document Conservation Center, 100 Brickstone Square, Andover, MA 01810-1494).

BIBLIOGRAPHIES

Reference Works on Postcards
and Postcard Collecting:
A Selective Bibliography

Chris Wolff

The works listed here have been found by experience to be most useful to the postcard collector and researcher. The listing is admittedly slanted towards American themes and topics, as those are mostly collected in this country. General works of utility have been selected; a few specialized works and monographs also are listed.

Postcard collecting as a modern hobby began in the late 1940s. The earliest collectors of picture postcards were stamp collectors who became fascinated with the numbers and variety of the picture postcards they encountered. Borrowing from the stamp world, they formed collectors' clubs, and much of the earliest research on picture postcards is found in the pages of club journals and in hobby magazines of the period. These collectors did primary research with the cards at hand. Most works on picture postcards are still written by dedicated collectors, often self-published in small editions, and difficult to find. Luckily a number of the better works were issued by trade publishers, but many of these are out-of-print. Current in-print and out-of-print status is noted in the entries. Items

[Haworth co-indexing entry note]: "Reference Works on Postcards and Postcard Collecting: A Selective Bibliography." Wolff, Chris. Co-published simultaneously in *Popular Culture in Libraries* (The Haworth Press, Inc.) Vol. 3, No. 2, 1995, pp. 215-219; and: *Postcards in the Library: Invaluable Visual Resources* (ed: Norman D. Stevens) The Haworth Press, Inc., 1995, pp. 215-219. Single or multiple copies of this article are available from The Haworth Document Delivery Service [1-800-342-9678, 9:00 a.m. - 5:00 p.m. (EST)].

of particular research value are marked with an asterisk. A few groups of annual publications of value and one magazine are also included.

I am indebted to Virginia Faulkner and Lois Densky-Wolff for comments and suggestions.

Burdick, J.R. *Pioneer Postcards: The Story of Mailing Cards to 1898 with an Illustrated Checklist of Publishers and Titles.* N.Y., Nostalgia Press, 1967. 144p. In-print.

> Burdick's text is the only thorough work on the earliest U.S. Postcards. He was the first collector to write systematically on American cards and his primary research has not been supplanted. The 1967 edition brings together the original 1956 edition and the extensive supplement.

Byatt, Anthony. *Picture Postcards and Their Publishers: An Illustrated Account Identifying Britain's Major Postcard Publishers 1894 to 1939 and the Great Variety of Cards They Issued.* Malvern, England, Golden Age Postcard Books, 1978, 391p. In-print.

> A thorough reference to every significant British postcard publisher, this guide, which is organized by company, includes notes as to the types of cards produced.

Corson, Walter. *Publisher's Trademarks Identified.* Newton Square, Pa., Deltiologists of America, 1979, 44p. In-print.

> While difficult to use, this is an irreplaceable guide to identifying U.S. and foreign publisher from their logos and back styles.

Fanelli, Giovanni & Ezio Godoli. *Art Nouveau Postcards.* N.Y., Rizzoli, 1987, 375p. In print.

> This is a well illustrated and extensive work covering over 500 artists, with an excellent biographical directory. The directory also includes notes on each artist's postcard production.

Greenhouse, Bernard L. *Political Postcards 1900-1980: A Price Guide.* Postcard Press, 1984, 109p. Out-of-print.

> This book covers only U.S. presidential election postcards. Within this framework, Greenhouse discusses each election with notes on the postcards produced, and their scarcity.

*Holt, Tonie & Valmai Holt. *Picture Postcards of the Golden Age: A Collectors Guide.* Folsom, Pa., Deltiologists of America, 1971, 214p. Out-of-print.

> The Holts have produced the best and most comprehensive general survey of British postcards to date.

Masburn, J.L. *The Postcard Price Guide: A Comprehensive Listing* (2d ed.). Enka, N.C., Colonial House, 1994, 464p. In-print.

> The improved second edition is listed here because it is the best currently available price guide to U.S. postcards. *However*, nothing presently available is very satisfactory as a guide to current prices. As a general rule, one should always read the preface of any price guide before using it.

Morgan, Hal and Andreas Brown. *Prairie Fires and Paper Moons: The American Photographic Postcard 1900-1920*. Boston, Mass., David R. Godine, 1981, 191p. Out-of-print.

> A pictorial survey, with commentary, this book presents some of the real-photo postcards. The appendix on dating photographic postcards is particularly valuable.

Megson, Frederic and Mary Megson. *American Advertising Postcards: Sets and Series 1890-1920*. Martinsville, N.J., The Postcard Lovers, 1985, 335p. In-print.

> This exceedingly thorough checklist, with prices, also contains a very useful section on identifying publishers.

Megson, Frederic and Mary Megson. *American Exposition Postcards 1870-1920*. Martinsville, N.J., The Postcard Lovers, 1992, 287p. In-print.

> In addition to a comprehensive checklist, with prices, of the postcards of international, national, and interstate expositions held in the U.S. before 1920, this encyclopedic text provides an extensive history of each exposition.

*Miller, George and Dorothy Miller. *Picture Postcards in the United States 1893-1918*. N.Y., Clarkson Potter, 1976, 280p. Out-of-print.

> Indispensable to the serious researcher and collector, this is the best and most thorough survey of American postcards to date.

Neudin, Joelle and Gerard Neudin. *l'Officiel International des Cartes Postales Des Collection*. Paris, Éditions de l'Amateur, 1974- . In-print.

> Each volume of this annual price guide to French postcards contains an extensive special section on one subject, not repeated in later years. The text is in French and prices are given in francs. This is the basic price guide to French postcards.

Postcard Collector. Dubuque, IA, Antique Trader Publications. Back issues available.

> Issued monthly, the leading U.S. postcard periodical covers news of current events and publications, but also includes research articles on many facets of postcard collecting.

Postcard Collector Annual. Dubuque, IA, Antique Trader Publications, 1991- . In-print.

> These annuals contain basic articles on postcards and postcard collecting, as well as extensive club listings and a dealer directory. The annual club directory is an especially useful feature.

Saleh, Nouad A. *Guide to Artists' Signatures and Monograms on Postcards*. Boca Raton, Fla., Minerva Press, 1993, 375p. In-print.

> Covering over 4500 artists, this guide shows facsimiles of signatures used on postcards, with notes as to the type of work each artist produced.

Smith, J.H. D. *IPM Catalogue of Picture Postcards and Yearbooks*, Truro, England, IPM Publications, 1975-. In-print.

> This is the annual price guide to British postcards. The 1995 edition has been completely revised with much added material.

Smith, Jack H. *Military Postcards 1870 to 1945*. Greensboro, N.C., Wallace Homestead, 1988, 241p. Out-of-print.

> Smith's coverage of postcards issued in wars, from the Franco-Prussian War to World War II includes a short history and chronology of each. The notes on the postcards produced by the combatants, as well as a rarity scale are very useful.

*Staff, Frank H. *The Picture Postcard and Its Origins*. N.Y., Frederick A. Praeger, 1966, 96p. Out-of-print.

> This is the best work on the early history of the picture postcard. Written by an expert in postal history, the work covers nineteenth century antecedents to the postcard as well.

Ward, Robert. *Investment Guide to North American Real Photo Postcards*. Bellevue, WA, Antique Paper Guild, 1991, 208p. In-print.

> The title of this work does not reflect the solid experience and research that went into it. The author divides photographic postcards into topical groups, and illustrates several hundred of them. The commentary on the desirable and undesirable features of each card, along with the price it realized at auction are illuminating. The foreword and subject commentaries are extremely useful.

Ward, Robert. *Real Photo Postcards: The Life-Size Edition*. Bellevue, WA, Antique Paper Guild, 1994, 204p. In-print.

> The author illustrates at full size and describes over 400 cards that have passed through his auction gallery. The commentary is very useful as is the introduction.

SOURCES

The following are sources for most of the books mentioned in the article.

Antique Paper Guild
Box 5742
Bellevue, Washington 98006

Antique Trader Publications
100 Bryant Street
Dubuque, Iowa 52004

Colonial House
Box 609
Enka, North Carolina 28728

Deltiologists of America
Box 8
Norwood, Pennsylvania 19074

Gotham Book Mart
41 West 47th Street
New York, New York 10036

Greater Chicago Productions
Box 595
Lisle, Illinois 60532

IPM
6 Barons Walk
Lewes, Sussex BN7 1EX
ENGLAND

Minerva Press
Box 696
Boca Raton, Florida 33429

Neudin
35 rue G, St. Hilaire
75005, Paris
FRANCE

The Postcard Lovers
Box 482
Martinsville, New Jersey 08836

Reflections of a Bygone Age
Brian and Mary Lund
15 Debdale Lane
Keyworth, Nottingham NG12 5HT
ENGLAND

Postcard Based Research:
A Representative Bibliography

Norman D. Stevens

When the archaeologists of the thirtieth century begin to excavate the ruins of London, they will fasten upon the Picture Postcard as the best guide to the spirit of the Edwardian era. They will collect and collate thousands of these pieces of pasteboard and they will reconstruct our age from the strange hieroglyphs and pictures that time has spared. For the Picture Postcard is a candid revelation of our pursuits and pastime, our customs and costumes, our morals and manners.

James Douglas (English Journalist) 1907 (Cited in Eric J. Evans and Jeffrey Richards *A Social History of Britain in Postcards* 1870-1930. (1980) p. 4)

INTRODUCTION

Postcards, as the essays in this volume demonstrate, constitute an important body of visual information that can support major scholarly research. Most of the books and articles about postcards, to date, have dealt primarily with either the history of postcards or with postcards as postcards (i.e., with the content of a group of postcards by a particular artist, photographer, or publisher, and/or a particular theme such as depictions of Santa Claus). Most of the books and articles about postcards, to date, have been written by postcard collectors and enthusiasts for other postcard

[Haworth co-indexing entry note]: "Postcard Based Research: A Representative Bibliography." Stevens, Norman D. Co-published simultaneously in *Popular Culture in Libraries* (The Haworth Press, Inc.) Vol. 3, No. 2, 1995, pp. 221-233; and: *Postcards in the Library: Invaluable Visual Resources* (ed: Norman D. Stevens) The Haworth Press, Inc., 1995, pp. 221-233. Single or multiple copies of this article are available from The Haworth Document Delivery Service [1-800-342-9678, 9:00 a.m. - 5:00 p.m. (EST)].

collectors and enthusiasts, or by amateur historians. Most of that material has not been published by scholarly publishers or appeared in scholarly journals. Some of it is very good. Some of it is very bad. The best of it constitutes a solid base of research that is essential for serious scholarly research based on postcards.

In fact, the growing body of postcard based research that is being done by scholars in a variety of disciplines would not be possible without the pioneering efforts of those who have explored the history of postcards and written so much about postcards as postcards. In the past two decades, a small, but extremely important, new body of research has emerged that relies on the information contained on, and conveyed by, postcards. Those scholars undertaking that research have utilized postcards in imaginative ways. They have set new standards for serious postcard based research. Most of their work has a strong subject orientation for which postcards provide an essential body of information. In many cases, those scholars have also sought to place the information derived from postcards into a broader perspective by relating it to other work in the field, testing their ideas against existing theories, and otherwise establishing an intellectual context for their use of postcards. They have also generally sought to establish a rigorous methodology for analyzing the information found in, and on, postcards and to scrutinize the validity of that information with the same care with which scholars examine other information.

The capability to search, from one physical location, the online public access catalogs of a large number of research libraries, and a wide range of electronic indexing and abstracting services covering a variety of disciplines, was invaluable in the assembly of this bibliography. It would not have been possible to discover such a wide range and variety of postcard based research without that capability. In particular, the capability to conduct keyword searching for books and articles using the term postcard(s) was essential to the identification of much of this material. As is generally the case, keyword searching also turned up a considerable number of false drops (i.e., an extensive body of research in which participants in a study are asked to return a postcard) as well as a considerable body of popular articles about postcards and postcard collections. All of that material was carefully screened and most of it was eliminated.

Even with those capabilities, much of the information about this kind of postcard based research is elusive. It would not have been possible to compile this bibliography without the considerable assistance of a number of other people including many of the contributors to this volume. Many other friends and acquaintances to whom I mentioned my efforts to identify such research provided me with important new references.

The resulting bibliography lists and describes a representative sample of the best postcard based research that I have been able to identify. It is by no means complete and additional references are welcome. The annotations for each of the items in this bibliography focus on the way(s) in which the author(s) used postcards as a key resource in the investigation of a particular subject and/or the methodology that was applied to the examination of postcards. This bibliography is a starting point. I hope that it will demonstrate to other scholars the important contributions that postcards can make to their research. I hope that it will demonstrate to librarians the need for libraries to continue to build strong postcard collections and, especially, the need to call those collections to the attention of researchers who may not realize the contribution they can make to their work.

Above all, I hope that this bibliography will encourage others to track, identify, and record in published form postcard based research on an ongoing basis. This bibliography, along with the other articles in this volume, also suggests the very real need for a major article, if not a book, that reviews all of the work that has been done to date on the methodology and techniques of postcard based research. Such a research guide would go a long way to enhancing the use of existing postcard collections, encouraging libraries to build new collections, and promoting the use of such collections by scholars.

Albers, Patricia C. and William R. James. "The Dominance of Plains Indian Imagery on the Picture Postcard," in George P. Horse Capture and Gene Ball, eds. *Fifth Annual Plains Indian Seminar in Honor of Dr. John Ewers, 1981.* Buffalo Bill Historical Center, 1984. p. 73-97.

Albers, Patricia and William R. James. "Illusion and Illumination: Visual Images of American Indian Women in the West," in Susan Armitage and Elizabeth Jameson, eds. *The Women's West.* University of Oklahoma Press, 1987. p. 35-50.

Albers, Patricia C. and William R. James. "Images and Reality: Postcards of Minnesota's Ojibway People 1900-1980," *Minnesota History,* 49:229-40, 1985.

This is a representative example of the several important postcard based research projects by these authors, who have been pioneers in the use of postcards, that are listed here. In this article they analyze the relationships between the images depicted on postcards and the reality of Ojibway life in Minnesota. They also show how image and reality has changed over time (e.g., over 90% of the postcards from

1920-1950 that they examined show Ojibways wearing war bonnets that were never part of their native costume).

Albers, Patricia C. and William R. James. "Tourism and the Changing Image of the Great Lakes Indian." *Annals of Tourism Research*, 10:128-48, 1983 (#1).

Albers, Patricia C. and William R. James "Travel Photography: A Methodological Approach." *Annals of Tourism Research*, 15:134-58, 1988.

> Based on a random sample of 40,000 ethnographic postcards, this landmark article examines the importance of photographic media in representing ethnicity in tourism, the ethnic pictures and messages that travel photographs convey, several methodological approaches, and photographs in the context of tourist ideology. It emphasizes the "rediscovery of meanings [of such postcards] appropriate to the time and place in which they were used and to the public who made and viewed them" (p. 139). Their discussion of metanymic and metaphoric conventions, content and semiotic analysis, and motifs as key methodological approaches is especially valuable. This article is the culmination of their extensive body of research that uses postcards to examine the image of Native Americans.

Albers, Patricia C. and William R. James. "Utah's Indians and Popular Photography in the American West: A View from the Picture Postcard." *Utah Historical Quarterly.* 52:72-91, 1984 (#1).

Allen, Rodney F. and Laurie E. S. Molina. "People and Places on Postcards: A High-Interest Source for Geographic Education," *The Journal of Geography,* 91:106-11, 1992.

> This article, which is aimed at elementary and secondary school teachers, describes a number of ways, not all of which seem realistic, in which "the picture postcard may serve as a catalyst to enhance students' motivation to learn about other places" (p. 107).

Alloula, Malek. *The Colonial Harem.* University of Minnesota Press, 1986. 135 p.

> Alloula's bitter philosophical attack on the way in which France's colonial presence in Algeria during the first three decades of the twentieth century distorted Algerian society, and deformed Algeria's social order, is based on the arrangement and annotation of a selection of picture postcards of Algerian women. His critique suggests that an "intense preoccupation with the veiled female body" (p. x) produced

an unparalleled set of stereotyped photographs of women designed to be distributed to public view.

Baldwin, Brooke. "On the Verso: Postcard Messages as a Key to Popular Prejudices," *Journal of Popular Culture*, 22:15-28, 1988 (#3).

That the messages on postcards offer a fertile base for research is amply demonstrated in this examination of a large number of the messages found on early twentieth century American postcards depicting Blacks. Using an anecdotal, rather than a statistical approach, Baldwin examines not just the messages but other information (e.g., names, addresses, postmarks, etc.) found on an undefined body of postcards. She uses her analysis as the basis for a discussion of the role of those messages in socializing white children into a racist society, reinforcing stereotypes, and validating common beliefs.

Beard, Mary. "Souvenirs of Culture: Deciphering (in) the Museum," *Art History*, 15:505-32, 1992.

In an unusual use of postcards, Beard discusses the significance of museum postcard sales in terms of the nature of visitors' preferences in souvenirs, why some postcards are popular and others aren't, and how that reflects on the 'museum experience.' Using raw data about the roughly 750,000 copies of 300 different postcards sold each year from 1988 to 1991 at the British Museum, she provides fascinating insights as to why, for example, the postcard of the Rosetta Stone is always the best seller!

Brown, Donald R., Robert A. Heilman, and Henry C. Westenberger, comp. & ed. "Lebanon County: A Postcard History," *Lebanon County Historical Society*, 1992. 204 p.

This is one of the best examples of how postcards, especially real-photograph postcards, can be used to present local history. Each of the 26 townships in Lebanon County is represented by an array of postcards depicting major buildings, scenes, and people. Each of the cards is accompanied by a brief annotation containing detailed information about the image on the card.

Chapman, Anthony and Nicholas J. Gadfield. "Is Sexual Humor Sexist?" *Journal of Communication*, 26:141-53, 1976 (#3).

Fifteen English "seaside postcards," which were carefully selected and categorized from a batch of 320 cards, were shown to men and women in an effort to analyze their sex-role attitudes, including the rating of women participants on the Women's Liberation Ideology

Scale, based on their reactions to the postcards. This article contributes an understanding of postcard based research by emphasizing the importance of establishing categories that relate to the purpose for which the information on postcards is to be used. It is related to the earlier research of Wilson et al. listed below.

Cohen, Erik. "Who Are the Chao Khao? 'Hill Tribe' Postcards from Northern Thailand," *International Journal of the Sociology of Language,* 98:101-25, 1992.

Based in large measure on the work of Albers and James (see above), this article examines what can be learned about the "hill tribes" of Northern Thailand from the names and identifications that they are given in the English captions of 576 contemporary postcards acquired in 1988-1989. Cohen uses the information on those postcards to examine unresolved issues pertaining to the ethic, cultural, and linguistic classification of those tribes, as well as their place in Thai society and their uncertain political future.

Cohen, Erik. "The Study of Touristic Images of Native People: Mitigating the Stereotype of a Stereotype," in Douglas G. Pearce and Richard W. Butler, *Tourism Research: Critiques and Challenges,* Routledge, 1993. p. 36-69.

Cohen analyzes touristic images of the West Coast Indians of Canada, the "hill tribe" people of northern Thailand, and the Arabs of the occupied territories of Israel as represented in postcards and other items (e.g., dolls and figurines). This article is especially important for its discussion of the methodology of analyzing such images that challenges some of the conclusions of Albers and James in their landmark article in the *Annals of Tourism Research* (see above).

Corbey, Raymond. "Alterity: The Colonial Nude," *Critique of Anthropology,* 8:75-92, 1989 (#3).

Corbey, who regards Alloula's *The Colonial Harem* (see above) as "perceptive, but somewhat pathetic and querulous" (p. 91), discusses on an item-by-item basis thirteen postcards of nude African women from an album assembled by a French colonist from 1900 to the 1930s. He examines those cards from the perspective of "the history of Europe's interpretations of its others, [and] of its authoritative representations and protocols for dealing with the alien" (p. 75). A more detailed analysis of that album can be found in his *Wildheid: en beschaving: De Europese verbeelidng van Afrika* (1989) for which an English translation is reported to be in preparation.

David, Philippe. "La Carte Postale Africaine (1900-1960)," *Revue Juridique et Politique Indépendence et Cooperation*, 40:166-77, 1986.

In this article, and the two that follow, David analyzes postcards from colonial Africa as "objects of cultural consumption produced in colonial societies for the needs of expatriate communities" (p. 173).

David, Phillipe. "La Carte Postale Senegalese de 1900 a 1960," *Notes Africaines*, 157:3-12, 1978.

David, Philippe. "De Fernande à Berthe, ou le Temps des Cartes Postales (1903-1904)," *Notes Africaines*, 153:11-2, 1977.

Dubin, Steven C. "Symbolic Slavery: Black Representations in Popular Culture," *Social Problems*, 34:122-40, 1987.

This article is a broad examination of popular culture items, including postcards, produced from 1890 to the 1950s that represent "Blacks in degrading, stereotyped ways, and objectify former sets of work roles and social relations" (p. 122). In addition to examining particular kinds of materials, Dubin discusses their relationship in white society to social control mechanisms, status anxiety, social solidarity, and feelings of superiority.

Evans, Eric J. and Jeffrey Richards. *A Social History of Britain in Postcards 1870-1930*. Longman, 1980. 151 p.

This is a major study of the depiction of industrial England as captured in the world of the picture postcard as it presented and represented: urban life; work; food, shops, and marketing; travel and transport; leisure and recreation; and seaside resorts.

Goings, Kenneth W. *Mammy and Uncle Mose: Black Collectibles and American Stereotyping*. Indiana University Press, 1994. 123 p.

Goings approaches Black collectibles, including postcards, as "texts" that he uses to illuminate and illustrate his discussion of their contribution to the stereotyping of Afro-Americans. Each chapter begins with a description of the social setting of the period he is discussing that precedes his discussion of how Black collectibles or memorabilia relate to that period. By weaving postcards, and other collectibles, into his narrative, and especially by using carefully selected black and white and color illustrations of many postcards, he presents a more sophisticated way of using postcards as an aid to scholarly research.

Killen, John. *John Bull's Famous Circus: Ulster History Through the Postcard 1905-1985*. O'Brien Press, 1985. 160 p.

Using a minimum of text, Killen presents a range of political post-cards that were used as propaganda in the ongoing battle over the governance of Ireland and the structure of Irish society.

Lofgren, Orvar. "Wish You Were Here! Holiday Images and Picture Post-cards," *Ethnologica Scandinavica*, 223L 90-107, 1985.

Lofgren offers some valuable insights into the class distinctions in holiday leisure pursuits as reflected in, on the one hand, tasteful scenic postcards and, on the other hand, tasteless comic holiday cards. He builds on, but adds significantly to, Orwell's essay (see below).

McDonald, Ian. "Postcards and Politics," *History Today,* 44:5-9, 1994 (January).

This brief article looks at how Joseph Chamberlain, and his allies and opponents, used postcards as a key element in the campaign for tariff reform in Great Britain in 1902-1904 and how their effective role in that campaign set the pattern for similar cards in the elections of 1910 and 1911. McDonald has also written two books, *The Boer War in Postcards* (1990) and *Vindication: A Postcard History of the Women's Movement* (1989), that take the same approach.

Mamiya, Christin J. "Greetings from Paradise: the Representation of Ha-waiian Culture in Postcards," *Journal of Communication Inquiry,* 16:86-101, 1992.

Mamiya uses the model advanced by Edward Said in *Orientalism* (1978) as the basis for his analysis of how Hawaiian culture is represented in contemporary postcards. He describes the role of postcards as one element of a marketing strategy designed to sell paradise that selectively presents, and distorts, native Hawaiian cul-ture.

Marsh, John. "Postcard Landscapes: An Exploration in Method," *Cana-dian Geographer,* 29:265-7, 1985.

Marsh's brief article, which is based on an analysis of his own postcard collection of Glacier National park in British Columbia, considers such issues as the sites shown, those not shown, and the ratio of natural as opposed to cultural features. He offers some spec-ulative thoughts based on his interpretation of that analysis and suggests some of the additional issues critical to the effective analy-sis and interpretation of postcards.

Marsicano, Edward Farrell. *The 'Femme Fatale' Myth: Sources and Manifestations in Selected Visual Media* 1880-1920. Emory University, 1983. 287 p. (AAC 8405574)

> In his doctoral dissertation, Marsicano studies the image of the beautiful but dangerous female as presented in 550 visual representations including postcards. He integrates his study of postcards with that of other visual images. He also uses ideas from various scholarly disciplines (art history, literary history, psychology, and social history) to show how art is affected by society as well as how art, and the myths created by art, affects society.

Mellinger, Wayne Martin and Rodney J. Beaulieu. *Pictures of American Apartheid: Images of African Americans in Popular Media Culture: 1900-1950* [in press].

> This is an extended scholarly analysis of the racist images of African Americans found on American postcards from 1893 to World War II. Mellinger and Beaulieu provide a thorough discussion of the representations of racism, racism and social theory, cultural studies and representations of race, the other-as-beast, the other-as-child, photos of the Old South, white fantasies and black bodies, postcard sender's messages, and Black resistance to these negative images. This is a major contribution, which builds on Mellinger's articles that follow, to the field of postcard based research that critically analyzes racist representations in postcards.

Mellinger, Wayne Martin. "Postcards from the Edge of the Color Line: Images of African Americans in Popular Culture, 1893-1917," *Symbolic Interaction,* 15:413-33, 1992.

Mellinger, Wayne Martin. "Toward a Critical Analysis of Tourism Representation," *Annals of Tourism Research,* 21:756-79. 1994.

Miller, George. *A Pennsylvania Album: Picture Postcards, 1900-1930.* Pennsylvania State University Press. 1979. 160 p.

> One of the first books to use postcards to represent the history of a locality in a meaningful way, this album uses both real photograph and commercial postcards to depict Pennsylvania views, transportation, advertising and business, agriculture and industry, education, religion, amusements, signs of the time, and celebrations.

Moors, Annelies and Steven Machlin. "Postcards of Palestine: Interpreting Images," *Critique of Anthropology,* 7:61-77, 1987 (#2).

This is a card-by-card interpretative commentary on 16 postcards issued from 1890 to 1948 as they depict various aspects of Palestine.

Orwell, George. "The Art of Donald McGill" in his *Critical Essays,* Secker & Warburg, 1960. p. 99-111.

Originally published in 1941, this is perhaps the earliest, and perhaps still the best, social commentary on picture postcards. In it Orwell examines the art of Donald McGill as represented in the comic illustrated postcard genre often associated with British seaside resorts. As these kind of cards, many bearing McGill's signature, are still widely distributed, this essay remains especially valuable. He provides, among other things a delightful analysis of the subject matter of "these ill-drawn post cards leading a barely legal existence in cheap stationers' windows" that he "should be sorry to see . . . vanish" (p. 111).

Peterson, Nicolas. "The Popular Image" in Ian Donaldson and Tamsin Donaldson, ed. *Seeing the First Australians.* Allen & Unwin, 1985. p. 164-80.

Peterson examines the way in which photography, through its widespread popular use in postcards, contributed significantly to the popular image of the Aborigines in the first two decades of the twentieth century. He bases his analysis on three ideological frameworks (romanticism, realism, and documentary) first proposed by Rochelle Kolodny in a 1978 thesis. Over 80% of the 291 postcards that he analyzed fit into the realistic framework. The assignment of a low status to the Aborigines in those photographs and postcards, Peterson suggests, eased social concern over the apparent dying out of the group and fit into the strong White Australia policy of the time. This is the first part of a more general analysis of the social significance of photographs of the Aborigines that Peterson is working on.

Prochaska, David. "Fantasia of the Phototheque: French Postcard Views of Colonial Senegal," *African Arts,* 24:40-7, 98, 1991 (October).

As a collector of old postcards from colonial Africa, Prochaska tended not to take them seriously until he realized that "they might say something about the market for such things, about the people who bought and sold them, and about their mentalité" (p. 40). In this article he analyzes 900 postcards from the Archives Nationale du Sénégal in Dakar dating from 1900 to 1960 by assigning them to such categories as ethic and racial types, views of places, women, the world of work, social life, and political or historical events. He concludes that in producing those postcards Edmond Fortier, who was the largest and most important postcard publisher in colonial West Africa, and others were applying photographic conventions developed in France and Europe in a colonial situation and weren't operating in a cultural or historical vacuum.

Samponaro, Frank N. and Paul J. Vanderwood. *War Scare on the Rio Grande: Robert Runyon's Photographs of the Border Conflict, 1913-1916.* Texas State Historical Association, 1992. 135 p.

The Robert Runyon Photograph Collection, in the Eugene C. Barker Texas History Center at the University of Texas at Austin, contains nearly 14,000 images of his photographs that are also now available on microfiche. As a major postcard publisher, Runyon produced and sold both his own real photograph cards and printed cards that he had made of those images he could sell in larger quantities. Samporano and Vanderwood use his work, which is an important source for the study of the lower Rio Grande valley and northeastern Mexico in the 1910s and 1920s, to present the story of the Mexican-American border conflict of 1913 to 1916 in a way that makes it come to life.

Schor, Naomi. "Cartes Postales: Representing Paris 1900," *Critical Inquiry,* 18:188-244, 1992.

Schor, Naomi. "Collecting Paris" in John Elsner and Roger Cardinal, eds. *The Cultures of Collecting.* Harvard University Press, 1994 p. 252-74, 299-302 (references).

In her lengthy article, and the more abbreviated version of it in Elsner and Cardinal, Schor describes how through postcards "Paris produced an iconography that was abundant, systematic and cheap, and that offered its citizens (and proffered to the world) a representation of itself that served to legitimate in a euphoric world its nationalistic and imperialistic ambitions" ("Collecting Paris" p. 252). In both contributions she begins with an examination of the ideological analysis of photography, and of the psychology of collecting, as a means of placing her subsequent discussion of the history of postcards and of the "postcarding of Paris" into context. Her thoughtful discussion of the postcards of Paris as cultural artifacts is especially valuable because it offers another important methodology for analyzing the significance of postcards.

Shields, Rob. "The 'System of Pleasure': Liminality and the Carnivalesque at Brighton," *Theory, Culture & Society,* 7:39-72, 1990 (#1).

> This sociological analysis of "the cultural positioning of Brighton as a seaside resort and . . . its position as a place" (p. 39) uses postcards as one of several popular indicators of the nature and meaning of that resort. Shields' discussion in the section "Postcards: the Body on the Beach" (p. 55-59), which reviews the universalized stereotypes of fat bathers, holidaying dandies, and buxom ladies as portrayed on those cards, is reminiscent of Orwell's earlier commentary on Donald McGill and his seaside postcards (see above).

Street, Brian. "British Popular Anthropology: Exhibiting and Photographing the Other" in Elizabeth Edwards, ed. *Anthropology and Photography 1860-1920.* Royal Anthropological Institute and Yale University Press, 1992. p. 122-31.

> Postcards, along with photographs and exhibits, were an important means by which the general British public at the turn of the century were offered images of other societies in the context of evolution, race, and hierarchy. In this essay, which builds on the methodology developed by Kolodny as utilized by Peterson (see above), Street examines how, as "primitive" peoples, the Ainu from northern Japan and the Batwa from the Ituri forest region of the Congo were represented as an exotic and colorful contrast to the real world of scientific and commercial progress. He points out the extent to which those images offered older views of race and evolution even as anthropologists were moving away from those views.

Vanderwood, Paul and Frank N. Samponaro. *Border Fury: A Picture Postcard Record of Mexico's Revolution and U.S. War Preparedness 1910-1917.* University of New Mexico Press, 1988. 293 p.

> As one of the first major scholarly studies based on real photograph postcards, this examination of another aspect of Mexican American relations in the 1910s amply illustrates the fact that postcards can provide information that may not be available from other sources. It does so by using the information contained in the photographs and messages on such postcards, mainly those published by Walter H. Horne, that: (1) yield more precise information on the equipment and weapons used by both sides than any other available source; (2) reveal the importance of that border experience in allowing the U.S. military to experiment with new equipment and to modernize, and train for, new military techniques; and (3) dramatize the jingoistic

patriotism of so many U.S. soldiers who disdained the Mexicans as human beings. Vanderwood and Samporano also suggest that the widespread dissemination of those postcards played an important role not just in forming U.S. public opinion about Mexicans and the Mexican revolution but in stimulating the patriotism that was to sweep the U. S. into World War I.

Wilkinson, Billy R. "American Library Postcards," *College & Research Libraries News*, 49:646-51, 1988; 50:363-71, 1989.

Wilkinson, Billy R. "Library Postcards–The Messages" in Norman D. Stevens *A Guide to Collecting Librariana*. Scarecrow Press, 1986. p. 68-73.

In his two pieces in *C&RL News* Wilkinson provides a description, with some limited statistical analysis based on the cards in his own collection, of the exteriors and interiors of library buildings as depicted on postcards. In his article on the messages on library postcards, he categorizes such messages as being comments on architecture, comments on the book collection, chauvinistic comments, or the usual miscellany of remarks that one might expect. That article demonstrates the importance of establishing groupings appropriate to the images on postcards in studying the messages on postcards.

Wilson, Glenn D., David K. B. Niss, and Anthony H. Brazendale. "Vital Statistics, Perceived Sexual Attractiveness, and Response to Risque Humor," *The Journal of Social Psychology*, 95:201-5, 1975.

Wilson, Glenn D. and Anthony H. Brazendale. "Sexual Attractiveness, Social Attitudes, and Response to Risqué Humor," *European Journal of Social Psychology*, 3:95-6, 1973.

These articles set the pattern for later more structured work, such as that of Chapman and Gadfield (see above), that uses seaside postcards containing risqué sexual humor as a tool for relating responses to such humor to other characteristics.

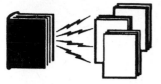

Haworth
DOCUMENT DELIVERY
SERVICE

This valuable service provides a single-article order form for any article from a Haworth journal.

- *Time Saving:* No running around from library to library to find a specific article.
- *Cost Effective:* All costs are kept down to a minimum.
- *Fast Delivery:* Choose from several options, including same-day FAX.
- *No Copyright Hassles:* You will be supplied by the original publisher.
- *Easy Payment:* Choose from several easy payment methods.

Open Accounts Welcome for . . .
- Library Interlibrary Loan Departments
- Library Network/Consortia Wishing to Provide Single-Article Services
- Indexing/Abstracting Services with Single Article Provision Services
- Document Provision Brokers and Freelance Information Service Providers

---

MAIL or *FAX* THIS ENTIRE ORDER FORM TO:

Haworth Document Delivery Service
The Haworth Press, Inc.
10 Alice Street
Binghamton, NY 13904-1580

or FAX: 1-800-895-0582
or CALL: 1-800-342-9678
9am-5pm EST

PLEASE SEND ME PHOTOCOPIES OF THE FOLLOWING SINGLE ARTICLES:

1) Journal Title: _____

    Vol/Issue/Year: _____ Starting & Ending Pages: _____

Article Title: _____

2) Journal Title: _____

    Vol/Issue/Year: _____ Starting & Ending Pages: _____

Article Title: _____

3) Journal Title: _____

    Vol/Issue/Year: _____ Starting & Ending Pages: _____

Article Title: _____

4) Journal Title: _____

    Vol/Issue/Year: _____ Starting & Ending Pages: _____

Article Title: _____

(See other side for Costs and Payment Information)

COSTS: Please figure your cost to order quality copies of an article.

1. Set-up charge per article: $8.00
   ($8.00 × number of separate articles) _____

2. Photocopying charge for each article:

   1-10 pages: $1.00 _____

   11-19 pages: $3.00 _____

   20-29 pages: $5.00 _____

   30+ pages: $2.00/10 pages _____

3. Flexicover (optional): $2.00/article _____

4. Postage & Handling: US: $1.00 for the first article/
   $.50 each additional article _____

   Federal Express: $25.00 _____

   Outside US: $2.00 for first article/
   $.50 each additional article _____

5. Same-day FAX service: $.35 per page _____

GRAND TOTAL: _____

METHOD OF PAYMENT: (please check one)

❏ Check enclosed ❏ Please ship and bill. PO # _____
(sorry we can ship and bill to bookstores only! All others must pre-pay)

❏ Charge to my credit card: ❏ Visa; ❏ MasterCard; ❏ Discover;
❏ American Express;

Account Number: _____ Expiration date: _____

Signature: *X*_____

Name: _____ Institution: _____

Address: _____

_____

City: _____ State: _____ Zip: _____

Phone Number: _____ FAX Number: _____

MAIL or *FAX* THIS ENTIRE ORDER FORM TO:

Haworth Document Delivery Service
The Haworth Press, Inc.
10 Alice Street
Binghamton, NY 13904-1580

or FAX: 1-800-895-0582
or CALL: 1-800-342-9678
9am-5pm EST)